Who's Who in Non-Classical Mythology

Who's Who in Non-Classical Mythology

EGERTON SYKES
Revised by Alan Kendall

DISCARD

OXFORD UNIVERSITY PRESS
New York 1993

Copyright © 1952 by Egerton Sykes
Revised material copyright © 1993 by Alan Kendall

First published in the United States by Oxford University
Press, Inc
200 Madison Avenue, New York, New York 10016

Oxford is a registered trademark of Oxford University
Press

First published by J M Dent 1952
Revised 1961
This edition 1993

Library of Congress Cataloguing-in-publication Data
Sykes. Egerton.
Who's who in non-classical mythology / Egerton Sykes:
revised by Alan Kendall.
p.   cm.
Rev. ed. of: Everyman's dictionary of non-classical
mythology.
ISBN: 0 460 86136 0
1. Mythology—Dictionaries.   I. Kendall, Alan, 1939–
II. Sykes, Egerton. Everyman's dictionary of non-classical
mythology.   III. Title.
BL303.S9   1993
291.1′3—dc20

Printed in England by Clays Ltd, St Ives plc

J M Dent Ltd
The Orion Publishing Group
Orion House
5 Upper St Martin's Lane
London WC2H 9EA

Printing (last digit)2 4 6 8 10 9 7 5 3 1

Contents

Introduction

For centuries, in the Western world, mythology almost always implied Classical mythology, that is, the mythology of ancient Greece and Rome, and the fact that the word myth (μῦθος or *muthos*) is Greek has tended to reinforce this impression. Undoubtedly the legacy of Classical mythology is a rich and prolific one, and it has permeated Western literature deeply for centuries. Small wonder, then, that it has tended to exclude almost all other mythologies to the point where they might not have existed. There is a very good explanation for this, in that mythology has always been intimately and inextricably bound up with the development of a particular culture or civilization, as human beings began to explore their environment and reflect on their origin.

At the outset, therefore, mythology was an individual matter, relevant only to a particular people. Inevitably, however, exploration, conquest and the expansion of trade routes brought awareness of the existence of other mythologies, beliefs and religions, with inevitable comparisons, syncretism, adaptation and adoption. It was the strength of the Classical tradition and the extent to which it became part of Western culture that excluded so much else – what we in fact now term non-Classical mythology – for so long.

Nowadays the words 'myth' and 'mythology' have regrettably taken on a pejorative connotation, and indeed amongst the ancient Greeks themselves we find that, by the time of the death of the poet Pindar (518–438 BC), *muthos* had become the equivalent of the Latin *fabula*, thus denoting something that was essentially fiction, as opposed to λόγος or *logos*, a true historical tale. In its primary sense, however, *muthos* was used of anything that was imparted orally, that is by word of mouth, and therefore at its most basic denoted speech in general. From this we may readily appreciate that far from being a sophisticated literary device, a myth as originally formulated was a response, an answer to a question, whether posed internally by the enquiring mind, or put directly, much as a child might ask, 'Where did I come from?'. Indeed, it is no coincidence that almost every culture that has a recorded mythology has at the heart of that mythology its creation myth.

If one considers the creation myth by way of example, it soon becomes apparent that not only does it seek to answer the question 'Where from?', but quickly, and almost unavoidably, it touches on the related questions of 'How?' and 'Why?'. Even today such questions have no simple, factual answers, though it is conceivable that in the fullness of time the 'Where?' and the 'How?' may be satisfactorily answered. The early myths may well have been formulated as an attempt at answering those basic questions, but the way in which the myths were subsequently cherished and handed down from generation to generation, and have survived as long as they have, indicates that for some reason, some intrinsic quality they possess, they have persisted in spite of the acquisition by the human race of more and more extensive information about the 'real' nature of the universe. Indeed, had myths only ever been taken at face value, they would have perished long ago, having long outlived their purpose or usefulness.

Clearly, then, myths rapidly moved out of the sphere of being quasi-factual tales that might be regarded ultimately as either true or false. The persistence, and indeed the very survival, of myths indicates that almost as soon as the human race had begun to formulate them, they began to fulfil a much deeper purpose. Seen in this context, the historical accuracy of the myth was never a criterion by which one measured one's reaction to it; the importance of the myth lay in what it conveyed to the believer, and the use of the term 'believer' indicates that myth was essentially a part of religion, whether it be among the seemingly endless ramifications of the Egyptian pantheon or the homely, almost naive doings of the gods of what are usually known as primitive peoples. However elaborate or primitive the religion when judged by the criteria of subsequent civilizations, the myths were developed within the context of that religion, and we ignore this fact at our peril when considering mythology in general. We may well approach the myths themselves with great sympathy and affection, and enjoy the richness and colourfulness of their expression, but without sensitivity to their deep underlying purpose we are almost inevitably destined to remain on the outside looking in, as one might read a work in translation from a language not our own. No matter how good the translation, there will be some sort of impediment to total comprehension of the original purpose of the author.

In religion, human beings seek to explain and extend their understanding of themselves, of their intrinsic nature, and of their environment. When we consider a myth, therefore, we are dealing with something which is an attempt to express in narrative form these reflections, which are deep concerns about the very nature of human existence. By this token, therefore, the creation myth is far more important to a people for its reflections on that existence, than as a potential rival theory to that propounded subsequently by Darwin or anyone else. A myth detailing how a saviour figure became immanent in the world is not important for its supposed historical accuracy – though this may well have been important to the earliest propagators of the myth itself – but for the extent to which it indicates the saviour's significance in the religion and beliefs of the people.

We may take this one stage further. Myths not only express the reflections of human beings on the fundamental meaning of life, they also constitute the rules by which human beings live, and provide the foundation for the organization of individual societies, because the way in which a society is organized derives its authority ultimately from the concepts enshrined in its mythology. From this it is a natural step to find the role of myth as that of guardian and propagator of a moral code, providing human beings with models on which they may base their own lives.

Myths quickly ceased to be merely narratives, or even symbolic accounts of how and why phenomena occurred. Myths recount the actual workings of the supernatural, and because they do so, whenever they are retold or re-enacted, they are deemed to release or set in operation that supernatural activity. For this very reason, in some societies, some of the names of the deities are too sacred to be uttered by certain of their members. Through the myth, the force or power that was active at the creation of the world may be made present now, and the continued existence of the sacred is thereby ensured.

Thus the function of myths may be said to give the members of a society the basis for its moral and religious conduct, to elaborate and systemize its beliefs, and provide a source of divine or supernatural energy. When we approach a myth, therefore, we are not dealing with a historical narrative which may or may not turn out to be true, nor are we simply looking at beautiful literature that has grown out of what was initially an oral tradition. We are being given access to the world view of a people, of its understanding of itself, its society and its god or gods.

It is because of the enormous significance of the role that it plays that myth has to be effective as a means of communication, and at the same time convey deep symbolic content. It must therefore use such language and terms that will touch the listener and reader. The language may well be very colourful and full of images, but the terms may well be arcane to a person outside that culture. It is not surprising, then, if the outsider is more arrested by what he or she sees as the more picturesque elements, and so misses the more profound matter that lies beneath the surface. We may become so fascinated by the expression of the myth that we fail to see the truth that it expresses. There is no implied adverse criticism here, however, merely a warning. Inevitably cultures differ, and it is not always possible to enter adequately, let alone fully, into another's world.

For those living in an industrialized, materialistic society, myths may well seem to be totally irrelevant. Indeed, over the last century or so one has seen in operation in Western civilization a deliberate process of 'demythologizing', applied consistently to almost every aspect of society, and of course one might well accept that such a process is a sign of intellectual and emotional maturity. Yet such an approach totally ignores the more far-reaching function of myth in underpinning society, in preserving the sense of the sacred. If a society has no use for the sacred it will probably have no use for myth either, except perhaps as a euphemistic term for indicating what it takes to be a lie.

In this context it must be said that, as they have come down to us, some myths, indeed whole mythologies, were recorded too late to ensure that they remained unaffected by external influences. One thinks especially in this context of the effect that incoming Europeans had on indigenous populations of America and the Pacific islands. Then, on the other hand, through the vicissitudes of fate almost entire mythologies have been lost to us, or even deliberately destroyed. What is clear, however, is that a large number of references of one sort or another, or even complete stories, remain where they have found their way into the literatures of other peoples, and the curious reader will always need to elucidate a point or identify a character. Sometimes, it must be admitted, it is not always possible to give a simple answer. Often several traditions, some of them conflicting, exist side by side, and later writers often chose the tradition that best suited their purposes, or altered details as they saw fit. Reference was made at the beginning of this introduction to Pindar, for example, who consciously 'moralized' some of the myths he reproduced in his writings. Small wonder, then, that a similar process was adopted by subsequent writers, for a great variety of ulterior motives. When the Western explorers came into contact with the islanders of the Pacific, they tended to equate the myths that they encountered with the myths they had been brought up with in their own cultures. In this way, for example, attempts were made to identify a supreme being, where in reality none existed.

In this present volume, as appropriate to a 'Who's Who', references have been restricted to persons and personifications, though with the major characters much is included in the entries that is supplementary to this basic process of identification, with extensive cross-referencing to assist the process of establishing the relationships between them. The field is enormous, covering as it does such a vast part of the globe, and within any one mythology there are often several names found for any one deity, or several different manifestations of the same deity. For this reason, suggestions for further reading are given in the bibliography, so that the reader may explore further any particular areas that are of interest. At the very least, mythology provides us with potentially illuminating and certainly strikingly different ways of regarding many of the phenomena that all too often we tend to take for granted.

A

God 'A' He is Hunhau† or Ahpuch†, the Maya god of death, who ruled over Mitnal. In the codices he is represented as a being with exposed vertebrae and a skull-like countenance. He may be taken to be the same as Mictlantecuhtli†, the Aztec god of the dead, with the difference that while the Aztec deity presided over the north or south his Mayan counterpart presided over the west. His symbol is that for the day Cimi, 'death', his hieroglyph is a corpse's head and a skull together with a flint sacrificial knife.

Aah-te-Huti Egyptian moon god, symbolically represented by an ibis head surmounted by a crescent and a disk. He was a manifestation of Thoth†.

Ab In Egyptian religion the will, the emotion and passion of the Egyptian, symbolized by the heart, which was brought up for judgment, in the Book of the Dead†.

Abac Irish spelling of Addanc†.

Abominable Snowman *See* Yeti†.

Abora The supreme being worshipped on the island of Palma in the Canary Islands. Seated in heaven, Abora caused the stars to move in their courses.

Abtu In Egyptian myth one of a pair of sacred fish which swam before the boat of Ra† to warn him of danger. It also announced the rise of the Nile. The other was Anet†.

Abuk The first woman, according to the Dinka of the Sudan. She and Garang†, the first man, were made of clay, and were initially very small and put into a pot. When the pot was opened, they grew and god gave them a grain of corn a day. Abuk, however, was greedy, and ground more grain than was necessary. She is the patron of women, gardens and grain used in brewing beer, which is the task assigned to women. Her emblem is a little snake.

Achomawi Indian Creation Legend This tribe of Californian Indians tell that the Creator originally emerged from a small cloud and that Coyote†, who assisted him, came from a land mist.

Acoran The supreme being worshipped on the island of Gran Canaria in the Canary Islands. His temples were built in the mountains and were consequently ideal for those seeking asylum.

Adad Babylonian god of wind and rain, storm and thunder. Originally a deity of the Amorites of northern Mesopotamia, Adad may be equated with Enlil†, the Sumerian storm god. He was known as Hadad† in Syria and Palestine, where he also took the title of Baal† ('the lord') as Baal-Hadad†, Hadad-Rimmon, or simply Rimmon† or Ramman†. He had a role also as a fertility god, and his cult animal was the bull. He is often depicted holding lightning bolts.

Adapa A sage of Eridu, was initiated into wisdom by Ea† although eternal life was withheld from him. Once, while fishing, the south wind capsized his boat, and in his fury he broke the wings of the wind, which ceased to blow. Anu† summoned him to appear for punishment, and Ea, out of jealousy, warned him not to accept anything to eat or drink. However, both Tammuz† and Gishzida† intervened on his behalf, explaining that Ea had revealed all wisdom to him and that if he but had eternal life he would be a god. Anu then offered him the bread and water of life but he refused, thus losing for ever immortality for men. Adapa was the mortal with pure hands who helped the bakers of Eridu to make bread and cleared the holy table of the temple there. Some later versions make Adapa the son of Ea.

Adar In Babylonian myth an alternative name for Ninib†, the god of the summer sun.

Adda A variant of Adad† or Hadad† found in letters written in Akkadian, from Palestine and Syria, at Tell el-Amarna in Egypt, dating from about 1400–1360 BC.

Addanc In Celtic myth a dwarf† or marine monster who dwelt by Lake Llyon Llion† and who caused a deluge. He was eventually disposed of by being hauled from his lair by the oxen of Hu Gadarn†, or alternatively, he was killed by Peredur†. His relationship to this deluge myth is similar to that of Haya-Griva† in Hindu legend. An alternative spelling is Avanc†, whilst in Ireland the word was Abac†. Some further details are given in Celtic† Creation Legend.

Aditi In Hindu myth the mother of the gods from whom all things sprang. A personification of the generative powers of nature. Daksha†, her son, was later considered as her father, while her husband Vishnu† also appeared as her son when he was incarnated as a dwarf. She was the mother of the Adityas†, and in this connection appears to have taken on the stature of a sun goddess.

Adityas The twelve Adityas, or gods of the months of the year, were: Ansa†, Aryaman†, Bhaga†, Daksha†, Dhatri†, Indra†, Mitra†, Ravi†, Savitri†, Surya†, Varuna†, and Yama†.

Adonis In Babylonian myth a title applied to Tammuz†, derived from Adon meaning lord. The classical use of this name probably arose from a misunderstanding of its meaning.

Adraste A war goddess in ancient Britain, to whom Boudicca prayed before going into battle. Andraste is found as a variant of the name, and Andarta among the Gauls.

Adro A god revered among the Lugbara people around Lake Albert in Africa. His presence is perceived in phenomena such as whirlwinds and fires, though he tends to inhabit rivers with his wives and children. A creator variant is known as Adroa, though he is now far removed from the material world.

Adsullata A river goddess of the continental Celts. The resemblance of the name to Sullat would indicate that she may have been a priestess of hot springs.

Adu Ogyinae He is remembered as leader of the first men, who emerged from the ground, among the Ashanti of Ghana.

Aegir The ocean god of the Norsemen; although accepted as an equal, he was not one of the Aesirt. He is encountered in three of the Eddas; in the Hymiskvida or Lay of Hymir, he entertained the Aesir at the feast of the autumnal equinox. His supply of drink being too little for Thort, the latter sets out with Tyrt to capture Odherir, the magic cauldron of the giants. Later in the Aegisdrekka, or Carousal of Aegir, the Aesir drink from the cauldron and are grossly insulted by Lokit who slays a servant and flees. This Eddic story is also known as the Lokasenna. It is to Aegir that Bragit tells the stories enumerated in the Bragiraedur. Aegir seems to be a pre-Nordic culture hero who was too firmly established to be absorbed or displaced by the Aesir. His wife was named Rant, by whom he had nine daughters.

Aër (a) In the Phoenician Creation Legendt of Damascius, son of Omiclet by Potost, representing purity without intelligence. He mated with his sister Aurat, and produced Otost, meaning reason. (b) In the Phoeniciant Creation Legend of Philo Byblos, Aër and Chaost were in the beginning, and produced Windt (Kolpiat) and Desiret (Potost). (c) In the Phoenician Creation Legendt of Mochus, Aër and Ethert engendered Oulomost.

Aesir In Nordic myth the group of lead-

ers forming the entourage of Odint. Originally there seems to have been a coven of a chief with a retinue of twelve and it may be assumed that, of the sixteen names listed below, never more than a dozen were included at any one time. Their feast day was the Yule festival.

The Aesir seem to have arrived in Scandinavia shortly after the Vanirt, with whom they at first fought and subsequently allied themselves. The stories of their wars against the giants may have related to their struggles with the Finna. The Eddas tell one side of the story, the Kalevala and the Hero of Estonia portions of the other.

Asgard, the fabled city of the Aesir, with its palaces and assembly halls, may be a memory of their actual capital city before they migrated to north-west Europe. It is possible that some of the names of the Aesir were hereditary titles, whilst others may have been the names of those who belonged to the Aesir at various times: Baldert, Baugit, Bragit, Forsetit, Freyrt, Heimdallt, Hodert, Hoenirt, Lokit, Mimirt, Odint, Thort, Tyrt, Ullrt, Valit, Vidart.

Other details are given under Asynjort, Nornst, Valkyriest.

Aesma (**Aeshma**) The Zoroastrian Daeva or evil spirit of wrath, to whom was applied the term 'with the terrible spear'. He was the inspirer of vengeance and of perseverance in evil; he was third in the hierarchy of demons, his good opponent being Sraoshat. In the Book of Tobit he was known as Asmodeust.

Af A form of Rat, the Egyptian sun god, as he nightly journeys through the underworld. An alternative spelling is Auf.

Afi God of rain and thunder amongst the Abkhaz in the western Caucasus. Women may not use his name, but refer to him as 'he who is above'.

Afikoman The Jewish ceremony of hiding the Passover cake may be equated with Hapi† Qementu (Hapi is found). In this case Hapi was equivalent to Osiris†, and the piece of Passover cake which is hidden in the ritual is Osiris, while the other two pieces, which are not lost, are Isis† and Nephthys†.

Aganju In Yoruba† myth he was the son of Oduduat† and brother and husband of Yemaja†, by whom he was the father of Orunjan† and of sixteen other gods, including Ogun†, Oko†, Olokun†, Shango†, Shankpanna†, the sun, the moon, and several of the river goddesses.

Agassou Panther fetish god of the former royal house of Benin†.

Agdistis In Phrygian mythology a bisexual monster which lost its male organs when Dionysus made it drunk and tied them to a tree. When Agdistis awoke the organs were torn off, and from the blood the first almond tree grew. One of the fruits impregnated the daughter of Sangarios†, the river god, and she gave birth to Attis†, with whom Agdistis fell in love. In the tragic sequel Attis went mad and castrated himself under a pine tree. Agdistis is clearly a manifestation of Kybele†.

Agni A fire god of the primitive Aryans and the divine fire of the Vedic religion. Fire was one of the eight Vasus†. With the development of Brahminism he was one of a triad of gods, the others being Indra†, ruler of the air, and Surya†, ruler of the sky, while he was the ruler of the earth. The numerous references to him in Vedic law show the great importance which was attached to fire by the Indo-Germanic tribes. Horses were sacrificed to him annually, presumably to provide new steeds for his chariot. Matarisvan†, the messenger of the gods, brought Agni to Bhrigut†, the Rishi. The word 'agni' comes from a Sanskrit word meaning 'fire', and as such has passed into the Slavonic languages.

Agrona Celtic goddess of slaughter, after whom the river Aeron in Wales is named.

Ahi In Hindu myth, an Indian serpent god slain by Trita†, later replaced by Indra†, the war god, of whom it is said: 'With his vast destroying thunderbolt, Indra struck the darkling mutilated Vritra†' (the alternative name for Ahi).

Ahpuch Maya god of death who ruled over Mitnal. He is usually referred to as God 'A'†.

Ahriman In Zoroastrian myth the leader of the powers of evil, who is in constant conflict with Ahura Mazda†, the leader of the powers of good. The Daevas†, or followers of Ahriman, may well have been the culture heroes and gods of the early Persians before their conquest by the Indo-Germans, and the process of Dualism may have been designed to offset their attractions for the masses by the increased value given to their opponents, the new gods. *See also* Angra Mainyu†.

Ahsonnutli Bisexual god of the Navajo† Indians, also known as 'the

Turquoise Hermaphrodite.' It is possible that he may have been a later development of the Turquoise Woman, who is frequently mentioned in Navajo myth. He is considered as the creator of heaven and earth and to have placed men at each of the cardinal points to uphold the sky.

Ahura In the early Aryan languages there were two general words for God: Asura† (Zend, Ahura) and Daiva (Sanskrit, Deva†, Zend, Daeva). In the Vedas† Deva meant a benign power and Asura an evil power. To the Zoroastrians Daeva meant an evil power and Ahura meant a benign one. In Buddhism† both words had largely lost their meaning.

Ahura Mazda In the Zoroastrian theogony the chief benign divinity as opposed to Angra Mainyu† or Ahriman†, leader of the powers of evil. The name, which means lord of knowledge, can be assimilated to the Vedic Asura†. One fifth-century Armenian historian tells us that Ohrmazd† or Hormazu† (or Ahura Mazda) and Ahriman† were the twin sons of Zurvan†, one of whom was to be the creator of the earth and of all things good. Just before their birth Zurvan said: 'He who first comes to me, will I make king.' Hearing this Ahriman immediately emerged from his mother's womb and claimed the throne. Zurvan, in order not to break his word, gave him the right to rule for 9,000 years, after which Hormazu† would become supreme ruler, as had been his father's original intention.

Ahy In Egyptian myth an alternative name for Herusmatauy†, or Ihy†, the son of Horus† and Hathor†.

Ailill In Celtic myth an early king of Connaught whose wife Medhbh† had formerly been the wife of Conchobar†. The name seems to be that of a dwarf or elf, which presumably means that he was not of Celtic stock. When Fergus† of Ulster had been defeated by Conchobar he sought refuge at the court of Ailill where he was well received.

Aimon Kondi In the Creation Legend of the Arawaks† of Guiana he scoured the world with fire from which Marerewana† and his followers sought refuge in underground caverns. Later there was a great flood from which the survivors escaped in canoes.

Aine Celtic fairy queen whose activities were centred on Cnoc Áine in County Limerick, Ireland.

Ainnle In Celtic mythology the brother of Ardán† and Naoise†, who accompanied the latter when he eloped with Deirdre†.

Aino Heroine of the Kalevala (the Finnish national epic), sister of Joukahainen†, who is pledged to Väinämöinen†.

Aion Child of Kolpia† and Baau† in the Phoenician† Creation Legend; with Protogonos†, the parent of Genos† and Genea; first to discover edible fruits. The word Aion means life.

Airavata In Hindu myth the Elephant of Indra†. An alternative spelling is Airabata. It was one of the objects produced by the churning of the ocean† in the Kurma† avatar.

Airgedlámh *See* Argetlam†.

Airmid In Celtic myth the daughter of Dian Cécht†, the god of healing and sister of Miach, whom she assisted in the healing of Nuadh†.

Aiwel Founder of the hereditary priesthood known as the Spear Masters by the Dinka people of the upper Nile. Aiwel's mother conceived him by allowing the waters of the river to enter her after her own husband had died. From early childhood Aiwel possessed the ability of a Spear Master to make his word come true, no matter what the consequences. In some versions of the myth he is known as Aiwel Longar, or simply Longar, a name taken from an ox that he acquired†.

Aizen-Myoo Japanese god of love.

Aka-Kanet A grain and fruit god of the Araucanian Indians. He presides over harvest festivals and appears to have originated as a culture hero. His evil counterpart and possibly twin brother was Guecubu†.

Akatauire In the Mangaia† Island myth he was the brother of Rangi†, the husband of Ruange†, and one of the co-rulers of the island.

Akongo A creator being, and supreme god of the Ngombe people of the Congo.

Akra In Persian myth alternative name for Sinurqh†, the bird of immortality. This word may be related to the Aka-rana of Zervan Akarana†, the Zoroastrian† Father Time.

Akua In Polynesian myth a generic name for the full gods of Hawaii.

Akupara In Vedic myth the tortoise on which the earth rests.

Ala Earth goddess of the Ibo people of eastern Nigeria. As well as being a fertility goddess, she is queen of the underworld.

Alaghom Naum Wife of Patol†, chief deity of the Tzental tribe of the Mayas†. She was known as 'the Mother of Mind' and was credited with the creation of mind and thought. She appears to have been a mother goddess whose position was too firm for her to be displaced by her husband. She was also known as Iztat Ix†.

Alalu Among the Hurrians in northern Syria he was king in heaven for a period of nine years before being defeated by Anu† and sent down to the underworld.

Alannus Also known as Alaunus, he was a Celtic version of the god Mercurius in parts of western Europe.

Alatuir The magic stone which in Slavonic† myth was to be found on the island of Bouyan†. From beneath it flowed a river whose waters healed all ailments. At some stage of Slavonic myth Alatuir became a stone at the cross-roads which warned heroes of impending danger, and later still it became the stone on which stood the Cross.

Alberich In the Nibelungenlied and the Ring Cycle the dwarf Andvari†, the guardian of the treasures, is known by this name. As he was also Aelf-Ric the elf king, this presupposes that the position of guardian was hereditary, and that Andvari may have been the family name.

Albiorix A name given on an inscription at Avignon to a Celtic war god, who may have been Tiwaz† or Teutates†.

Alcis A pair of twin gods mentioned by Tacitus as worshipped in northern Europe, especially in coastal areas. The etymology of the name is not clear, though they may be connected with elks or stags.

Aleion Baal In Ugarit myth the son of Baal†. He represented an intermediary stage between men and gods, in that in his father's age-long fight with Mot† both adversaries are killed, only to be resurrected to continue the fight. Aleion is god of the clouds, winds, and rain. He is accompanied by a troop of wild animals, including eight bears. He is god of spring, and possibly that of winter or air. On one occasion he joins with Koser-et-Hasis against his father and is defeated, for which deed he is reproached by Ashtar†. Further details are given under Phoenician Creation Legends.

Alfadir One of the epithets given to Odin†, meaning 'all-father' or 'father of all'.

Alfar In Nordic myth there were several groups of dwarfs†, and of these one was named the Alfar. From them comes the word elf (O.E. *ælf*) of popular story. A member of the Lovar†, another group of dwarfs, was named Alfr, which may indicate some relationship between these two groups.

Alfatin Moorish hero who with his horse, which is green, sleeps in a cave in the Sierra de Agner from whence he and his steed will emerge at the appointed time to avenge his people. Green as a colour is connected both with Islam and with fairyland. Other instances are given under Sleeping Princes†.

Alfheim The home of the elves† or dwarfs† in Nordic myth; the dwelling place of Freyr†.

Alfreiker A version of Aelf-Ric, applied to Alberich† as elf king.

Algonkian Indian Creation Legends One of the myths of this tribe of North American Indians tells how Manibozho†, their culture hero, took refuge on a mountain when a great lake overflowed and submerged the world. He sent out three messengers in succession, a raven, an otter, and finally a musk-rat, before he was satisfied that the flood had disappeared. Another legend tells how Gluskap† and his twin brother Maslum†, representing the good and evil creative powers, formed the solar system and the human race out of their mother's body. After defeating Maslum, Gluskap was involved in a series of combats with Kewawkqu†, Medecolin†, Pamola†, Wimpe†, over all of whom he was victorious.

A third creation legend of this tribe is given under Gros-Ventres† Indian Creation Legend.

Alisanos Celtic god of the rock. In Gaul there have been attempts to link his name with the mountain ash or rowan tree, and with the place name of Alesia.

Allah Islamic name for God. Is derived from Semitic El†, and denoted the creator of the earth and giver of water. Allat† is the female counterpart of Allah.

Allantide The apple-time, a Cornish name for Samhain†. The word is related to Avalon†.

Allat(u) Female counterpart of Allah† from the pre-Islamic pantheon condemned by the Koran: 'What think ye then of Al-Lat?' She is also Ereshkigal†, queen of the lower world, who ruled over Aralu, the Babylon Hades, and was the enemy of Ishtar†.

Almaqah A moon god venerated in southern Arabia, with a bull as his cult animal.

Alviss A dwarf† of Nordic myth who is mentioned in the Alvis Mal Edda† as having been promised the hand of a daughter of Thor† in marriage. When he went to fetch his bride Thor detained him by asking questions until the dawn came and Alviss was forced to depart alone. The story may relate to an early attempt at alliance between the dwarfs and the pre-Aesir†.

Amaethon Son of Dôn† in Celtic myth, his name means 'great or divine ploughman' and as such he was clearly a god of agriculture.

Amaite-Rangi In Mangaia† myth he was a sky demon who was defeated in battle by Ngaru†.

Amalivaca Culture hero of the Orinoco† River Indians who taught them to till the soil and instructed them in the arts of life.

Amaravati In Vedic myth the capital city of Swarga†, the heaven of Indra†, built by Visvakarma†, the architect of the gods. It is situated on the eastern spur of Mount Meru†.

Amasis In Babylonian myth a name given to Ararat as the landing place of the Ark. May possibly come from the grandson of Noah, who had that name. For further details *see* Babylonian† Creation Legend.

Amaterasu Japanese sun goddess, the child of Izanagi† and Izanami†, and sister of Susano†, the Japanese ocean god. From the marriage of these two sprang eight children, from one of whom the Japanese royal family claims descent. The story of her having shut herself up in the Cave of Heaven as a result of her brother's ill treatment appears to be an attempt to link the personality of the sun priestess with some great catastrophe of the past. She was the most prominent member of the Shinto pantheon and her exalted rank shows that she belongs to a period anterior to the adoption of Chinese anti-feminist ideas in Japan. She had a sacred bird, the Yatagarasu†, which may be identified with the Yangwu† of Chinese myth.

Amathaon *See* **Amaethon†**.

Amathaounta, or **Amathaon** Sea goddess of the Aegean. A part of the tribe of that name founded Hamath in Syria, and another went to Palestine, where it founded Amathus. The Amathites are mentioned both in Genesis and in Chronicles.

Ambika In Vedic myth an alternative name for Uma†, the wife of Siva†, or of Rudra†.

Ambisagrus A god of the continental Celts considered by the Romans to resemble Jupiter.

Amemait In Egyptian myth an animal monster, part crocodile, part lion, part hippo, which devoured the hearts of those who failed to pass the great balance, when weighed by Mayet or Maat† in the presence of Thoth†, as against the yellow feather (Maat) of virtue, as laid down in the Book of the Dead. Amemait was also an attendant of the Lord of Amenti, first region of the Place of Reeds, to whom were delivered for total destruction the souls and bodies of the unvirtuous.

Amen The famous cauldron of Ceridwen†, included in the treasures† of Britain.

Ament In Egyptian myth a mother goddess; consort of Amon†. She was originally the goddess of the Libyan province to the west of Lower Egypt. At Thebes she was equated with Mut†.

Amenti In Egyptian myth the Land of the Dead and first region of the Place of Reeds, where dwell souls who lived upon earth offerings. Ruled over by Menuqet†. The name is also given to the West or Other World, as the region of darkness to which souls must go on their way to the Elysian Fields. In the Tuat†, or What is in the Next World, reference is made to the Horn of Ament, the utmost boundary of the horizon of Amenti, as being one of the boundaries of the Elysian Fields. Other regions were Sekhet Aaru†, Sekhet Hetep†, Sekhet Tehant†. Also known as Pet†.

Ameretat One of the seven Immortal Holy Ones, the attendants of Ahura Mazda†. Ameretat represented immortality, and was the genius of trees and plants.

Amergin (**Amhairghin**) In Celtic myth one of the leaders of the Milesian† conquerors of Ireland and the first to land there after the murder of Ith by the three kings of the Tuatha Dé Danann†, who were subsequently defeated in battle by the invaders.

Ameshas In the Zoroastrian religion, the seven Immortal Holy Ones, the attendants of Ahura Mazda†, were thus named. They have been compared with the Seven Spirits before the throne of the Book of Revelation. They were Ameretat†, Armaiti†, Asha†, Haurvatat†, Kshathra†, Spenta Mainyu† Vohu Manah†. Collectively they were also known as the Amshaspands† or Amesha Spentas†.

Amhairghin *See* Amergin†.

Amida Japanese Buddhist deity, originally an abstract ideal of boundless light, who is supposed to dwell in the west in some distant retreat. The Daibutsu, some fifty feet high, known as the Great Buddha of Kamakura, is a representation of him.

Amma Creator god of the Dogon people of southwestern Sudan and Mali. According to one tradition, Amma was lonely, so approached female earth, first cutting down a termite hill in order to achieve union. Instead of twins being born, however, a jackal appeared.

Amon A pre-dynastic Egyptian god, so ancient that he is never found alone but always in association with some other god such as Ra†. As Amon-Ra he was 'king of the gods, creator of the universe, lord of Karnak, and father of the Pharaohs'. He was Great God of Thebes, and became Supreme Deity of Egypt during the eighteenth dynasty. His theophany was a ram. The Triad of Thebes was composed of Amon-Ra, his wife Mut†, and his son Khensu†. Originally he appears to have been a god of agriculture, and as such became associated with death. At Siwa he was worshipped under the name of Jupiter Ammon†.

Amor God of the Amorites; also known as Martu†, husband of Asherah†.

Amrita In Vedic myth the ambrosia of the gods. This nectar, which is referred to in the Churning of the Ocean†, is probably another version of Soma†. The Amrita was stolen by Garuda† from Vishnu† and returned only after a great struggle.

Amset In Egyptian myth one of the four divine sons of Horus†, guardian of the south, and Canopic protector of the liver. He assisted Horus in the mummification of Osiris†. His name is also spelt Imset†, Mestha†, Mesti†. The names of the other three sons were Duamutef†, Hapi†, and Qebhsneuf†.

Amshaspands A name by which the Ameshas†, the Seven Immortal Holy Ones, attendants of Ahura Mazda†, were also known.

Amsu In Egyptian myth alternative name for Min†.

An Alternative name for Babylonian Anu†.

Anahita In Zoroastrian myth a river goddess, at some stage associated with Mithra†. She is the mother goddess of Armenia, and may be equated with Anthat†. She was one of the Yazatas†.

Anaitis In Ugarit myth an alternative name for Anthat†.

Anansi The trickster spider in West African tradition who became the executive or representative of the supreme god, but was eventually put down by the chameleon. Unable to bear the disgrace, Anansi now hides in the corners of houses.

Ananta In Vedic myth a name given to Sesha†, the chief of the Nagas and ruler of Patala.

Anat Sister or wife of Baat†. Alternative name for Anthat† or Atargatis†.

Anatiwa In the Creation Legend of the Karaya† Indians of eastern Brazil the deluge was caused by a malevolent being of this name. The ancestors of the tribe escaped, thanks to Saracura†, the water hen, bringing earth to the hill-top on which they had sought refuge as fast as the fish, sent by Anatiwa, nibbled it away. This legend is shared with the Ges† Indians and seems to be mainly concerned with them, as in another version of the story the ancestors of the Karaya sought refuge in a cavern of safety from which they were brought to the surface by Kabei†. The name given to the hilltop was Tupimara†.

Ancestor Worship The system of ancestor worship practised by the Chinese, and in other parts of the world, is an essential step in the process of creating gods from cultural heroes†. The rank of god was originally a posthumous one, the assumption of divinity by royalty and emperors on their coronation seems to be a later stage of development. For further details *see* Fravashis†.

Andaman Islands Myth *See* Pulug†, the thunder god.

Andarta *See* Adraste†.

Andjeti Early human-headed form of Osiris†, the Egyptian god, in the Nile Delta.

Andraste *See* Adraste†.

Andvari In Nordic myth he was the guardian of the treasures and from him Loki† obtained Draupnir, the magic ring of the Aesir†. He is found in a similar capacity in the Volsung Cycle, the Nibelungenlied, and the Ring Cycle, though known as Alberich† in the last two. He was also the guardian of the Tarnkappe, the garment of invisibility.

Anet In Egyptian myth one of the pair of sacred fish which swam before the boat of Ra† to warn him of danger. It also announced the rise of the Nile. The other was Abtu†.

Angarua Wife of Mokoiro†, co-ruler of Mangaia† Island.

Angiras In Vedic myth one of the seven great Rishis† or Prajapatis†. He was the reputed author of some of the Vedic hymns.

Angra Mainyu *See* Anra Mainyu†.

Ang(u) bodi A Nordic giantess, the wife of Loki†, and mother of Fenrir†, Hel†, and the Midgard Serpent†.

Angus (Oenghus) In Celtic myth son of Dagda† and Boann†. He was the Mac ind Og or the Young God, the Celtic Eros who carried off Etain†, the wife of Midir†. In the story of Diarmaid† and Grainne† he repeatedly saves them from the vengeance of Fionn†. When the Tuatha Dé Danann† were defeated by the Milesians† and were allotting *sidh* or hill forts, to those of their members who remained in Ireland, Angus was forgotten. He eventually managed to displace his father Dagda from his palace at Brugh on the Boyne.

Anhur Human-headed Egyptian war god and sun god of Abydos. At Sebennytus he formed a dual god with Shu†, and was regarded as son of Hathor†. He was also known as Onouris†.

Ani An Etruscan god of the highest heaven, though the etymology of the name is uncertain, and it is not clear whether he was connected with the Roman double-headed Janus.

Anit Egyptian goddess equated with Hather†, and wife of Mentur and mother of one of the Horus† gods.

Anjety *See* Andjeti†.

Ankh Egyptian symbol of life carried by gods and royalty. Shaped like a cross with a loop over the horizontal bar, it is usually held by the loop. For further details *see* Shen†.

Anna-Purna In Vedic myth an aspect of Parvati†, wife of Siva†. The name means 'Full of Food', and it is for her capacity for providing this that she is worshipped. She is depicted seated on a water-lily, holding a dish of rice in one hand and a spoon in the other.

Annwn In Celtic myth the underworld

ruled over by Arawn†. It was from here that one of the magic cauldrons†, with a ridge of pearls round the brim and tended by nine maidens, was acquired by the Celts.

Anotchi The culture hero, learned in medicine and magic, who was responsible for bringing down from heaven the golden stool of the Ashanti from Nyame†, the supreme god.

Anoukis Greek name for the Egyptian goddess Anquet† or Anuket.

Anpu In Egyptian myth an alternative name for Anubis†.

Anqa A bird of enormous size, said by the Turks to inhabit the Caucasus. May be considered as akin to the Roc†.

Anquet (or **Anuket**) Egyptian goddess, third of the Elephantine Triad†, called the Lady of Sati, where she had a temple. She was associated with the fertilizing waters of the Nile. She was also goddess of the first cataract. Usually depicted wearing a head-dress of feathers. The Greek rendering of her name was Anoukis†.

Anra Mainyu In Zoroastrian myth the leader of the forces of evil, usually known as Ahriman†. The spelling Angra Mainyu is also found.

Ansa In Vedic myth one of the Adityas†, or gods of the months of the year.

Anshar and Kishar The second pair of Babylonian gods to arise from the depths of chaos. Their names mean Host of Heaven and Host of Earth respectively.

They were followed by their son Anu†, god of the heavens, by Ea† – who was then called Nudimmud† – and others. Anshar may have been an early form of Asshur†.

Antariksha In Vedic myth the word means 'sky'.

Anthat Goddess of love and war in the Ugarit myths. When her lover Baal† is killed she avenges his death by treating Mot† the slayer thus:
> 'With a sword she cleanses him
> With a pitchfork she winnows him
> With a fire she burns him
> In the millstones she grinds him
> In the field she plants him.'

In Egypt she was worshipped in Thebes in the reign of Thotmes III and called on monuments: 'Lady of heaven and mistress of the gods.' In time she became sufficiently identified with the local gods to have been said to have been produced by Set†. She was also known as Anahita†, Anat† and Anthrathi†.

Anthrathi Egyptian name for Anthat†.

Anti Indian Creation Legends The Creation Legends of the Ipurinas and Yurukares of Bolivia and north-western Brazil have a myth that at the time of some great catastrophe human beings sought refuge in a great cave from which they emerged with great difficulty after the deluge, which succeeded the great conflagration, as the entrance to the cave was blocked. Those who did not seek refuge in the cave were presumably killed, as when the refugees emerged the only living beings were monkeys. The world was repopulated by Titi† and by Ule† and his wife.

Anu 1. Celtic culture heroine and fertility priestess, especially in Munster, where two mountains were known as 'the Paps of Anu'.
2. In Babylonian myth, sky god, son of Anshar† and Kishar†; chief of the great triad of gods, the others being Enlil† and Ea†. Supreme king of heaven, father of the gods, ruler of destiny. One of the most ancient divinities, his name being found on earliest known inscriptions. He was mainly worshipped at Erech and Der. The name means 'Expanse of Heaven', and he may have been an early personification of the Heavenly Father. His counterpart in the lower regions was Kingu†.

Anubis Ancient jackal-headed Egyptian deity, presiding over embalming of the dead; was local god of Abydos; child of Osiris† and Nephthys†, and, after having been exposed by his mother, was found by Isis† with the help of some dogs. He grew up to be her guard and attendant in her wanderings; his name means watcher and guardian of the dogs. With Upuaut†, he presided over the abode of the dead and led them to the judgment hall and supervised the weighing of the heart. His cult is probably older than that of Osiris† and totemistic in origin.

An alternative story makes him the son of Set†; his deification may have been to prevent jackals from devouring the bodies of the dead. Also known as Anpu†, Anup† or Wip†.

Anuket *See* Anquet†.

Anunaki Babylonian gods of the earth created by Marduk† in contrast to the Igigi† or spirits of heaven. They may be the stars of the northern heavens.

Anunitum In Babylonian myth a goddess

with temple at Sippar. Later merged with Ishtar†, although records of her worship continued until the time of Nabonidus, 555–538 B.C.

Anunna (**Anunnaku**) Strictly speaking not a proper name, but a term used to distinguish the pantheon of gods of a given locality of Mesopotamia, as opposed to Igigi†, the spirits of heaven.

Anup In Egyptian myth an alternative name for Anubis†.

Anzety (or **Anjety**) An Egyptian god of Busiris, who preceded Osiris†, and was represented by a human head on a pole, with arms wielding the crook and the flail.

Aoibheall Celtic fairy queen whose activities were centred on Craig Laith in County Clare.

Ao-Kahiwahiwa In Polynesian myth Fiery Black Cloud, one of the children of Tawhiri†.

Ao-Kanapanapa In Polynesian myth Glowing Red Cloud, one of the children of Tawhiri†.

Ao-Nui In Polynesian myth Dense Cloud, ancestor of Tawhaki†, one of the children of Tawhiri†.

Ao-Pakakina In Polynesian myth Wildly Drifting Clouds, one of the children of Tawhiri†.

Ao-Pakarea In Polynesian myth Thunder Clouds, one of the children of Tawhiri†.

Ao-Potango In Polynesian myth Dark

Heavy Clouds, ancestor of Tawhaki†, one of the children of Tawhiri†.

Ao-Pouri In Polynesian myth Dark Clouds, ancestor of Tawhaki†, one of the children of Tawhiri†.

Ao-Roa In Polynesian myth Thick Clouds, one of the children of Tawhiri†.

Ao-Takawe In Polynesian myth Scurrying Clouds, one of the children of Tawhiri†.

Ao-Toto In Polynesian myth an early culture hero or god, one of the ancestors of Tawhaki†. The title in this case means Cloud of Blood.

Ao-Whekere In Polynesian myth Hurricane Clouds, one of the children of Tawhiri†.

Ao-Whetuma In Polynesian myth Fiery Clouds, one of the children of Tawhiri†. The Ao which is found in many names means Cloud or World.

Apason Name given to Apsu† in the Babylonian† Creation Legend of Damascius.

Apep Egyptian snake god, a manifestation of Set†, enemy of Ra† and lord of the Powers of Darkness. As enemy of the sun gods, he was also the enemy of the dead, who could only return to life through his defeat. He is depicted as a great serpent and would appear to be a pre-dynastic storm god, an assumption which is confirmed by his title of the Roarer. He was said to have been slain by Ra at the foot of the sacred sycamore-tree of Nut† at Heliopolis. Every morning Apep menaced the rising sun, but by the recitation of a powerful spell devised by Thoth† the sun was able to render harmless the efforts of Apep. He is also known as Apophis.

Apet Egyptian hippopotamus goddess of Thebes; a local form of Taueret†. She was also known as Opet†.

Apis In Egyptian myth the sacred bull in whom Osiris† was believed to be incarnate. For further information *see* Serapis†.

Apisirahts The morning Venus god of the Blackfoot† Indians.

Aplu Etruscan god of thunder and lighting, though in reality a manifestation of Apollo, taken from the Greek pantheon.

Apo In Zoroastrian myth, one of the Yazatas†, the genius of sweet waters.

Apocatequil Chief priest of the moon god of the Incas, the son of Guamansuri† and the twin brother of Pigueraot†. He was a god of the lightning and statues to him were put up on mountain tops all through the empire of the Incas. After his mother had been treacherously murdered by her brothers, the Guachimines†, he brought her to life again and after having slain them was guided by Ataguchu† to make a hole from the Cave of Refuge by which they were to reach the land of the Incas.

Apochquiahuayan An alternative name for Mictlan†, the lower world of the Aztecs†.

Apophis *See* Apep†.

Apsaras In Vedic myth, one of the celestial nymphs of Swarga, the heaven of Indra†. They appear to correspond to the houris of Islam and the peris of the Persians. They were beautiful fairy-like beings, whose charms were 'the common treasure of the host of heaven'. Associated with them are the Gandharvas†, the heavenly choristers. The greatest Apsaras was Rambha†.

Apsu In Babylonian myth the primeval abyss of sweet water from which sprang all things. She was the Akkadian version of Tiamat†, mother of Ea†, 'The Mother that begat Heaven and Earth'. Later, with the decay of matriarchal ideas, she changed her sex and became the husband of Tiamat†.

Apuat In Egyptian myth an alternative spelling for Upuaut†.

Apu-Hau In Polynesian myth one of the children of Tawhiri†, the god of hurricanes and storms. The name means Fierce Squalls.

Apu-Ko-Hai A fish god of Kanei who occurs in the myths of Mangaia†.

Apu-Matangi In Polynesian myth one of the eleven storm gods who were the children or the bodyguard of Tawhiri†. The word means Whirlwind.

Aqas-Xena-Xenas Hero of a Chinook† story of an Indian boy who reached the upper regions by a chain secured to the end of an arrow; there he reached the abode of the Evening Star and found his family counting over the dead people in Evening Star's game-bag. He marries the Moon, the daughter of Evening Star, and participates in a war with the Morning Star and its daughter the Sun. His

children are Siamese twins and are eventually successfully divided by Blue-Jay†. This appears to be a vague memory of some great cosmic happening of the remote past.

Auquim In Phoenician myth fabulous creations sent by El† to combat Baal† according to the Ugarit texts. Sometimes known as Okelim†. For further details *see* Phoenician† Creation Legends.

Aralu In Babylonian myth Hades, ruled over by Allatu† or Ereshkigal†, queen of the underworld, and by Nergal†. A somewhat depressing reflection of the upper world, those who entered it being doomed to remain for ever in the Stygian gloom, to live on mud and dust. In the Gilgamesh† Epic there would appear to be a superior abode for those slain in batle, who lie on couches and drink pure water. It was customary to provide food and drink for the dead so that they should not have to wander about in search of nourishment. For further details *see* Ishtar's† visit in search of Tammuz†. It was also known as Meslam† and Sekhet Aaru†.

Ararat In the Babylonian† Creation Legends a name given to Amasis† or Masis† as the landing place of the Ark. This name comes from a King Ar, and was only adopted about A.D. 1750.

Araucanian Indians The gods of this tribe of South American Indians included Aka-Kanet†, Epunamun†, Cuccubu†, and Pilan†.

Arawak Creation Legends The myths of this Guiana tribe tell how Makonaima† created the beasts of the forest and placed his son Sigu† over them as king. In the forest was a tree of knowledge which Sigu cut down in order to plant its seeds all over the earth. From the stump, however, water began to gush forth and soon turned into a great deluge. The birds and climbing animals took refuge on the tree tops while the others were led by Sigu into a cave where they remained in safety until the disaster was over.

There are other variants of this myth in Guiana. Aimon Kondi†, who may be taken to be the same as Makonaima, first burnt the world with fire from which those who took refuge in caverns were the only ones to escape. They included Marerewana† and his followers. The Macusis believe that the survivors of the deluge turned stones into human beings to populate the earth. In the Tamanac myth a man and a woman were saved by climbing to the top of a high mountain. The Warrau tribe tell how Okonorote†, their culture hero, led the tribe to earth and how Korobona† was seduced by a water demon and gave birth to the first Carib†. Finally Maiso†, the mother goddess of the Paressis, was the parent of all living things. They share a culture hero Kamu† with the Bakairi† Caribs, the Karayas†, and the Paraguayans†. Details of this myth are given under Tupaya† and Ges Indian Creation Legends.

Arawn King of Annwn who fought the battle of the trees against Amathaon† and Gwydion†, the sons of Dôn†. In the romance of Pwyll† he is a huntsman with a large pale horse pursuing a stag with a pack of white dogs with red ears – the Hounds of Hell similar to Garm†. It was presumably the theft of these that caused the war with Gwydion. A magic cauldron was stolen from his kingdom by Arthur†.

Archons In Manicheism the Sons of the Dark who swallowed up the bright elements of Primal Man.

Ardán Brother of Ainnle† and Naoise† who accompanied the latter when he eloped with Deirdre†.

Argetlam (**Airgedlámh**) 'The Silver Handed', a name given to Nuadha†, the Celtic warrior, on account of his artificial hand. In Britain, Ludd†, who may be taken as being identical with Nuadha, was known as Llawereint† for the same reason.

Arianrhod In Celtic myth she was the daughter of Beli† and Dôn†, and the sister of Gwydion† and Amathaon† and the mother by Gwydion of Lleu† and Dylan†. Her pedigree is given under Lleu.

Arikute Younger of two brothers, heroes of a deluge story in the Tupi-Guarani† Creation Legend. The elder brother was named Tawenduare†. In another version Arikute, the god of night, is daily vanquished by his brother Tawenduare, the god of day. It is a constantly renewed daily combat. See also Irin Mage† and Monan†.

Aritimi The Etruscan version of the Greek goddess Artemis, known to the Romans as Diana.

Armaiti One of the seven Immortal Holy Ones, the attendants of Ahura Mazda†. Armaiti represented modesty and piety, and was the genius of the earth. Sayana, the greatest ancient Indian commentator on the Rig Veda, says the name means 'The Earth'; perhaps it may have been Ara Mater or Mother Earth, which would make her an early mother goddess, though she is the daughter of Ahura Mazda.

Arnaknagsak Alternative name for the Eskimo goddess of food, Sedna†.

Arnquagssaq Alternative name for Arnaknagsak† above.

Aroueris A name by which Horus† is sometimes known in Egyptian myths. *See also* Haroeris†.

Arovac Creation Legend Details of the culture hero Camut† are given under Tupuya† and Ges Creation Legends.

Arsaphes Greek name for Hershef†, the ram-headed Egyptian god. *See also* Harsaphes†.

Arsnuphis Greek form of the name Dedun†.

Arthur An early British culture hero who appears at some time to have acquired the personality and many of the deeds of Gwydion†. That there were several Arthurs is reasonably certain, the last being the military leader mentioned by Geoffrey of Monmouth. The collection of stories known as the Arthurian Legend are to a large extent Christianized versions of early Celtic myth, and, as such, do not fall within the scope of this work.

Artio Early Celtic priestess of a Bear clan who may have been the consort of Esus†. As a goddess she was worshipped in Switzerland at Berne, a name which means 'bears'.

Aruru Babylonian mother goddess who, with Marduk†, created 'the seed of man-

kind'. This is an older tradition than that in which Marduk created mankind from his own blood or from that of Kingu†, which would show that she is pre-diluvial. Zarpanit† (or Zerpanitum†) is possibly another form of this.

In the Babylonian Creation Legend Aruru created Enkidu†, companion of Gilgamesh†, from a piece of clay manufactured from her own spittle.

Aryaman In Vedic myth one of the twelve Adityas†, or guardians of the months of the year.

Asar-Hap In Egyptian myth alternative spelling of Serapis†, the sacred bull of Memphis. The version Usar-Hapi† also exists.

Asari Originally an agricultural god of Syria, who later became confused with Osiris†, the Egyptian god. The version Usire† also exists.

Asārtaiti The 'Swathed One', a title sometimes given to Osiris† in Egyptian myth.

Asasel *See* Azazel†.

Aschochimi Indian Creation Legend This tribe of California Indians tells of a great deluge in which all mankind was drowned. Coyote†, however, created a fresh crop of humans by planting feathers plucked from birds. This type of flood myth usually implies that the survivors of the tribe had to bring in those rescued from other ethnic groups in order that the race might be continued.

Aserah Wife of El†. Also found as Asherah† and Asherat†. *See* also Ashtart†.

Aset Alternative name for Isis† in Egyptian myth.

Asgard The fabled city of the Aesir†, from which Odin† and his followers set forth to battle. It included Valhalla†, the great hall of the castle of Gladsheim†. The Nordic world was divided into Asgard, the home of the Aesir; Jötunnheim†, the home of the giants†; Svartheim†, the home of the dark elves; and Mannheim†, the home of men. It was connected with the outside world by Bifrost†, the rainbow bridge. The word Asgard means the abode of the Ass or Aesir.

Asgaya-Gigagei Bisexual thunder god of the Cherokee† Indians, known as The Red Man or The Red Woman.

Ash In Egyptian myth a three-headed deity – lion, snake and vulture – of foreign origin. His name occurs only five times in inscriptions from the eleventh to the eighteenth dynasties. In the fifth dynasty Ash is called the God of the Land of Tehennu, or Land of the Olive-tree.

Asha One of the seven Immortal Holy Ones, the attendants of Ahura Mazda†. Asha represented righteousness and truth, upholding moral order in the world.

Asherah Alternative spelling of Aserah† and Asherat† in Babylonian myth. *See also* Ashtart†.

Asherat *See* Aserah† and Ashtart†.

Asheratian In the Ugarit texts the Aserah of the sea, wife of El†, and mother of seventy gods and goddesses, including Baal†, Anat†, Kathar-Wa-Hasis†, Athar†. Sea goddess of the northern Semites. Equated with Allat†, Elat†, and Mut†. For further details *see* Phoenician† Creation Legend.

Ashet In Egyptian myth the region of Amenti†, or the Duat†, ruled over by Unneffer†, where lived spirits seven cubits high, and where the wheat, which is three cubits high, was repeated by the Sahu†.

Ashipu A special class of priest in Babylonia to ward off witches, especially Lilith† and other jinn†.

Ashtareth In Babylonian myth an alternative spelling for Ashtart†.

Ashtart (Astarte) Of the various spellings of the name, Astarte† is found in the Tel Amara letters. The Hebrew Ashtoreth† arose when the rabbinical school of the Massoretes in the sixth century decided to adopt a conventional system to compensate for the lack of vowels in written Hebrew, and at the same time to insert in the names of foreign divinities the vowels from the word 'boshet', meaning abomination. Asherah† is the Ugarit version, while by Lucian she is called Syria Dea. The use of the name Atargatis† appears to have arisen from a conflation of Astarte and Anat†.

She was the fertility goddess of the Semitic races, her cult having spread throughout the whole Middle East. In Babylonia she became Ishtar†. By the Greeks she was equated with Aphrodite, who would appear to be the same but in a new setting. As the goddess of the planet Venus she would appear to be a variant of Athar† the South Semitic Venus god. As Ashtoreth† she was a goddess of war in Egypt from 1800 BC until the coming of Christianity. She was known as the lady of horses and chariots, and depicted as lioness-headed and mounted on a quadriga, although it is possible that this is a confusion with Anthat†.

In the Ugarit texts she is also Asheratian (the Aserah of the Sea), wife of El†, creatress of the gods, being the mother of seventy gods and goddesses.

Ashtoreth Hebrew variant of the Babylonian Ashtart†.

Ashushu-Namir In Babylonian myth a being created by Ea† to serve as messenger from the great gods to Allatu†, Queen of Hades, to demand the release of Ishtar†. In her rage at this, Allatu cursed him with a terrible curse condemning him to dwell in darkness and to feed on garbage.

Askr In the Nordic creation myth he and his wife, Embla†, were the first humans, having been carved out of wood or saved from a dug-out canoe by Odin† and his brothers, the sons of Bor†, who may be presumed to have escaped from the Flood by other means. The word means Ash, and is frequently prefixed to Yggdrasill, the tree of life.

Asmodeus Name given in the Book of Tobit to Aeshma†, the Zoroastrian spirit of wrath. The term was possibly derived from Aeshmadaeva, the furry demon. The Median folk story from which the Book of Tobit is derived shows marked resemblances to the Persian original. In the Talmud, Asmodeus is king of the tribe of demons known as the Shedin.

Ass In Egyptian myth a form of Ra†. Later eaten by a monster serpent.

Asshur (**Assur**) Originally an Assyrian moon and war god of the city of that name. Later became head of pantheon, occupying a similar position to that of Marduk†. He may be a later development of Anshar†. His symbol, a god in a horned cap, shooting an arrow from a bow, enclosed in a circle, was the ensign under which the Assyrians marched into battle, and was to be found in one form or another wherever the rule of Assyria spread.

Assorus Name given to Anshar† by Damascius in the Babylonian Creation Legend.

Astar Ethiopic god of heaven.

Astarte *See* Ashtart†.

Asura A name applied in the Vedas to the ruling families of the Naga† civilization, who were defeated by the Hindu invaders. They would appear to have reached a higher degree of culture than their Aryan rivals. The Brahmans attributed to them wealth and luxury, the use of magic, superior architectural skill, and the ability to restore the dead to life. The Asuras included the Daityas†, the Danavas†, the Dasyus†, and Vritra† destroyed by Indra†.

Asvins In Vedic myth, twin gods the sons of Saranyu†. Originally they were cosmic deities, but later, under their individual names of Dasra and Nasatya, were known as the Divine Physicians. They may be taken to have been early Vedic culture heroes, who were raised to divine rank because of their importance.

Asynjor In Nordic myth the attendants of Freyja† or Frigg†.

Ataguchu A god of the Incas† who was involved with Pigueraot† and Apocatequil† in the Inca creation myth in that he instructed them how to get out of Pacari†, the Cave of Refuge, which they had sought during some great disaster.

Atar In Zoroastrian myth, one of the Yazatas†, the genius of fire.

Atar According to the Ugarit Tablets the son of El† and Aserah†, known as The Terrible, chosen to rule the world for a space after the killing of Baal† by Mot†. May be equated to Atter†, the male Venus god of war of the northern Semites.

Atargatis In Babylonian myth corrupt form of Atar'ate, itself a contraction of Ashtart†-Anat†.

Atargatis Derketo Syrian fish goddess of Ascalon, said to be the same as Atargatis†.

Atatarho A culture hero of the Iroquois† who was always attired in a garment of living snakes symbolical of his power as a warrior and as a magician.

Atea Rangi The sky father of the Tuomotuans of Polynesia.

Aten In Egyptian myth the god of the solar disk who was monotheistically worshipped by Akhenaten, a religious theory originating in Heliopolis, which only lasted for one reign. This cult may have been more in the nature of a political move against the priesthood of Amon† in other towns.

Athapasean Indian Creation Legend This tribe of Indians of north-west America have a myth that after the deluge Yetl†, the Great Raven, dragged the earth from the waters and became the ancestor of the tribe and taught the first humans the use of fire.

Athar (**Attar**) God of war and giver of water in South Arabia.

Atharvan In Vedic myth one of the seven great Rishis† or Prajapatis†. He was the reputed author of the fourth Veda, and was said to be the first to open the ways by sacrifice.

Athensic In the myths of the Iroquois† tribes the ancestress of mankind who fell from heaven into the waters of the deluge as it was receding and later she found herself on dry land, which became a continent.

Athtar A god found in the Ras Shamra texts from Canaan, acting as a substitute for Baal†, but when he is unsuccessful in this capacity he descends to become lord of the underworld.

Athyr In Egyptian myth an alternative spelling for Hathor†.

Atius-Tirawa Chief deity of the Pawnees, who figures in their Creation Legend and who endeavoured to destroy the world by fire, the conflagration being put out by the deluge. He was a pre-diluvial culture hero with a knowledge of astronomy as he was supposed to have ordered the movement of the stars and planets. He is sometimes referred to as Tirawa-Atius†.

Atlantide The Basque National Epic, details of which are given under Basque Creation Legend.

Atlas Child of Ouranos† and Gea† in the Phoenician† Creation Legend of Philo Byblos and brother of Ashtart†, Baitules†, Dagon†, El†, Pontus†, and Zeus Demaros†.

Atli (Atilla) A Teutonic word meaning grandfather occasionally applied to Thor†. In the Volsung Saga he was a king who married Gudrun† and was subsequently slain by her. Called Etzel in the Nibelungenlied.

Atmu In Egyptian myth a local deity of Heliopolis. Subsequently became merged with Ra† as Ra-Tem†. At a later date the name Atmu was given to the setting sun. The name is sometimes spelt Atum†. Atmu was a member of the Ennead†. He was the father of Shu† and Tefnut†, and as such dated back to the early stage of Egyptian religion, and was associated with one of the two Deluge Legends of Egypt, the other being given under Ra.

Atraharsis *See* Harsis-Atra†.

Atri In Vedic myth one of the seven great Rishis†.

Attar *See* Athar†.

Atter The male Venus god of war of the northern Semites. The feminine counterpart was Attar†. He may also be equated to Shahar†.

Attis Phrygian vegetation god beloved by Kybele†. In his passion for her he went mad and castrated himself under a pine tree. From his blood spring flowers sprang up.

Atum In Egyptian myth an alternative spelling for Atmu†.

Atunis Estruscan version of the Greek god Adonis.

Auahi-Turoa Australian culture hero who brought fire to men

Audhumla In Nordic myth the mother cow on whose milk Ymir† was fed, and who created Bur† by licking the ice-blocks.

Auf A manifestation of Ra† as the dead sun god during his passage through the underworld.

Aura The first vital form of intelligence in the Phoenician† Creation Legend of Damascius. With Aër† was the parent of Otos†. Daughter of Omiele† by Potos†.

Aurva A name given in Hindu myth to a great volcanic eruption of the past caused by the Rishi Aurva, who created from his thigh a great consuming fire which would have destroyed the world if Brahma† had not assigned it to the ocean to a spot known as the 'mare's mouth'. The fact that this occurred in the sea shows that the story belongs either to the previous occupants of the Indian sub-continent or to the earliest times after the Hindus had arrived there.

Aus In the Babylonian† Creation Legend of Damascius, Aus is given as brother of Anu† and Illinus†, and father by Dauce† of Belus†. He may be equated to Osiris†.

Aust Alternative spelling for Isis† in Egyptian myth.

Australian Creation Legends The Creation Legends of the Australians vary considerably from tribe to tribe. Details are given under the following headings: Auahi-Turoa†, Awhiowhio†, Baiame†, Birral†, Bub-Jil†, Daramulun†, Darawigal†, Imberombera†, Kohin†, Koin†, Kutchis†, Maamba†, Martummere†, Mimi†, Mormo†, Mungan-Ngana†, Muraian†, Mura-Muras†, Nurelli†, Nurrundere†, Pun-Gel†, Tundun†, Twanyrika†, Wyirrawarre†.

Automata The literature of the Near East and of the Mediterranean region includes many stories of automata, usually made of brass, which were produced to the order of various potentates.

King Solomon, who is reputed to have had a fountain of liquid brass in Andaluz – probably a foundry near the Rio Tinto Mines – which played three times a month, and from which were produced various novelties, including a brass throne with two eagles at the back which spread their wings to keep the sun off anybody sitting on it. Another one had two lions' heads on the armrests which opened their mouths and made a noise when the king pressed on them.

In the Arabian Nights there is the story of the City of Brass, in the middle of the desert, where mounted automata cut off the heads of anybody who approached them, and this in spite of the fact that there was nobody left alive in the city. Presumably they were activated by counterweights.

These automata came into use when iron was replacing bronze for weapons, thus leaving the brass founders free to exercise their ingenuity on other things.

Avagdu The ugly son of Ceridwen†, the Celtic fertility goddess and brother of Creirwy†.

Avaiki Alternative spelling of Hawaiki†.

Avalon The Place of Apples in Celtic myth to which Arthur† was taken after being wounded to death. This mysterious island, which may be the Tir-nan-Og† of the Irish Celts, does not appear in Celtic myth before the Arthurian legends, and it is therefore possible that the name may be quite different. The Apple Festival of Allantide† may be connected with this.

Avanc Alternative spelling for Addanc†.

Avatar Pre-Vedic historical or geological periods, adapted to constitute the reincarnations of Brahma† or Vishnu†. A list is given under the latter heading.

Avesta Shortened name of the Zend Avesta†, the Zoroastrian Bible. There is some possibility that this word means fire, and is related to Vesta, the Roman fire goddess.

Awhiowhio Australian god of whirlwinds.

Awonawilona The creator or father god of the Zuñis and the principal figure in their Creation Legend. After the Deluge he spread the waters with a green scum from which arose the earth and the sky.

Awun God of destruction in the Creation Legend of Taiwan.

Azazel The Islamic devil, descended from jinn. He is said to have refused to prostrate himself before God after the creation of Adam, and to have been condemned to death, but to have obtained a respite until the Day of Judgment, when he will be destroyed. The name is not only pre-Islamic, but pre-Jewish. It may have been that of a goat-god of the early Semites, whose worship was accompanied by practices abhorrent to both the Jews and the Mohammedans.

Azhi Dahaka In the Zoroastrian Creation Legend the serpent demon who overthrew Yima†, the first mortal, and cut him in twain. The name Azhi Dahaka appears to have been borne by a dynasty of serpent-worshipping kings of Media which finished with Bevarash, who was overthrown by Faridun† and condemned to be bound to Mount Demavand. This Bevarash has been equated with the Astyages who was overthrown by Cyrus. One of the Azhi Dahaka fought a great battle with Thraetona†, an early Persian culture hero.

Azrael Name given to the Islamic angel of death 'who is charged with you and shall cause you to die' (Koran, Sura 32, ii).

Aztec Creation Legends The myths of the Aztecs as to the Creation tell that the 'first earth' with its inhabitants was destroyed by a great flood caused by Atonatiuh, the water sun, who was subsequently equated with Tlaloc†. The human beings who survived this catastrophe were then exposed to a series of earthquakes caused by the wind sun, and it was the survivors of this latter diaster who were the ancestors of the Mexicans. These stories are a mixture of the disaster legends of two races, possibly the Toltecs and the pre-Toltec aborigines. There is a mother goddess Tlazolteotl† who is described as 'The Woman who sinned before the Deluge', and Nata† and Nena were one of the human pairs who survived the inundation by building themselves a ship. In the same manner Xelhua†, the giant†, survived by climbing to a mountain top. Those who escaped the Deluge and/or the wind storms by taking refuge in caverns handed down the story of Chicomoztoc†. The Cavern of the Seven Chambers is similar to the Tulan-Zuiva† of the Quiches† and may have been the origin of Mictlan†, the Aztec Hades. By the time the Spaniards arrived in Mexico these legends were so ancient as to have been partially forgotten, and the stories of the Deluge seemed to centre mainly around Tlaloc, the rain god, to whom large quantities of children were sacrificed annually in the hope of obviating further diasters of this nature. Other details may be seen under the various Aztec gods and beings, a list of which is given under Aztec Religion.

Aztec Religion It is rarely in the history of the religions of the world that one is encountered which is quite so cruel and sanguinary as that of the Aztecs. To the original festivals of the agricultural deities was grafted on a superstructure of bloody sacrifice such as is without parallel. Tens of thousands of victims had their hearts cut out and thrown on the altars of various gods, or were flayed alive in order to provide garments and masks for the priests.

Details as to the activities of the various gods and beings will be found under the following headings: Aztlan†, Camaxtli†, Chalchihuitlicue†, Chanticot, Chicomecoatlt, Chicomoztoct, Cibolat, Cihuacoatlt, Cihuateteot, Cinteotlt, Citlalinicuet, Coatlicuet, Ehecatlt, Huehueteotlt, Huitzilopochtlit, Huixtocihuatlt, Ilamatecuhtlit, Itzlacoliuhquit, Itzlit, Itzpapalott, Ixtliltont, Lords of the Day and Nightt, Macuilxochitlt, Metztlit, Mictlant, Mictlancihuatlt, Mictlantecuhtlit, Mixcoatlt, Nata and Nenat, Omacatlt, Omeciuatlt, Ometecuhtlit, Opochtlit, Piltzintecuhtlit, Quetzalcoatlt, Tecciztecatlt, Teoyaomiquit, Tepeyollotlt, Teteoinnant, Tezcatlipocat, Tlahuizcalpantecuhtlit, Tlaloct, Tlaltecuhtlit, Tlapallant, Tlazolteotlt, Tloque Nahuaquet, Tocit, Tonacacihuatlt, Tonacatecuhtlit, Tonantzint, Tonatiuht, Tzitzimimet, Xelhuat, Xilonent, Xipet, Xiuhtecuhtlit, Xochipillit, Xochiquetzalt, Xolotlt, Yiacatecutlit.

Aztlan In early Aztect myth Aztlan, 'the Place of Reeds', was given as the country from which the Aztec race started its migration. There is a complete lack of evidence as to where this place might be, but it is possible that it may be linked with Chicomoztoct.

B

God 'B' This Maya god is Kukulcan†, the equivalent of Quetzalcoatl†, and the most important in the pantheon. At times he is a planter of maize, but he is also a water god.

Ba In Egyptian religion the external manifestation of the soul which, in the Book of the Dead, is frequently shown as a man-headed hawk; it might also assume the outward semblance of a flower, a lotus, a serpent, a crocodile, or other object.

Baal Baal is the fertility god of the northern Semites, in eternal conflict with Mot†, the god of death or infertility; he is sometimes victorious and sometimes defeated but always comes to life again. The name means 'Lord' and was applied to the local god of each town. In Babylonia and Assyria the great gods were called 'Bel', the earliest known by this name being Enlil†. The Bel of the Old Testament was probably Marduk†. In Egypt, Baal was equated with Set†.

Baal-Addir 'Mighty Baal' was originally the god of Byblos, a Phoenician town, from where his cult spread to north Africa as the Punic empire expanded.

Baalat A generic term for goddess in the Middle East.

Baalath A generic name for goddess in the Middle East, frequently applied to the titular deity of a particular town. The Baalath of Byblos was Ashtart†. The word itself means lady or mistress, and would seem to be of greater antiquity than Baal†. Baalath was most frequently applied to Ninlil†, consort of Enlil†, but was also given to the wife of Asshur† or as a variant of Ishtar†. In Egypt she was known as Baelthit†. To the Canaanites she was Venus, the evening star.

Baal-Berith 'God of the covenant', who presided over contracts and agreements.

Baal-Biq'ah 'Lord of the plain' was the god of Baalbek, after whom the town was named. He was principally a weather god.

Baal-Hadad 'Lord of the thunder' and rider of the clouds, he was the Syrian god of storm and weather in general.

Baal-Hammon He was the chief god of Carthage, where he was a fertility god. His cult spread into the islands of Malta, Sicily and Sardinia through Punic influence.

Baal-Karmelos He was the god worshipped on Mount Carmel in Canaan, and was believed to deliver oracles.

Baal-Marqod A healing god, though the name means 'Lord of the dance'.

Baal-Melkart Chief god of Tyre, he

went with the Phoenicians to Carthage, where he became one of the chief deities.

Baal-Rammon A manifestation of Baal-Hadad†, meaning 'the thunderer', parodied by the Jews as Rimmon 'the pomegranate'.

Baal-Sapon A Canaanite god whose cult was centred on Mount Sapon in Palestine. He was also known as Baal-Sapan.

Baal Shamain In Babylonian myth the god of the sky. He has been identified by Philo with the sun. He may be equated with Shamash†.

Baal-Shamayim 'Lord of the Heavens' held sway throughout the Phoenician sphere of influence, and was the most serious rival to Yahweh in Israel.

Baalzebul 'Prince Baal' was parodied by the Jewish writers as Beelzebub†.

Baau Wife of Kolpia†, mother of Aion† and Protogonos† in the Phoenician Creation Legend† of Philo Byblos. She may be the same as Ba'u†.

Baba Goddess of Lagash, a Sumerian city, she was regarded as the daughter of An†, the sky god, and the wife of Ningirsu†, god of fertility and irrigation. She was also a healing goddess. Her name is also found as Bau.

Baba-Yaga The witch of East European folktales who is also known as Jezi-Baba†.

Babbar A shortened form of Ashimbab-bar, a name for Nanna†, moon god in the Sumerian pantheon.

Babylon In Babylonian myth, Bab-Ilu, or Gate of God. The Sumerian equivalent was Ka Dingir Ra Ki. Babylon was regarded by Muslims as the fountainhead of black magic.

Babylonian Creation Legends There are three versions of the Babylonian Creation Legend which have come down to us. They are:

1. The story of Berosus (280 B.C.). In the beginning there was an abyss of waters, wherein resided the most hideous beings. This was ruled over by Thalath – meaning the sea, or equally well the moon. Belus† came and cut her asunder, and of one half he formed the heavens and of the other half the earth. At the same time he destroyed all the animals within her.

To populate the world, Belus commanded Kingu† to cut off his head, and from his blood, mixed with earth, were formed men and animals, the sun, the moon and the five planets.

2. The story of Damascius (sixth century A.D.). In the beginning there were Tauthe† and Apason†, Tauthe being the mother of the gods. Their first-born was Moymis†, their second and third, Lakhe† and Lakhus, their fourth and fifth, Assorus† amd Kissare†. From these last two came Anu†, Illinus†, and Aus†. To Aus and Dauce† was born a son Belus†, the fabricator of the world, the Demiurge.

3. The story told in the Creation Tablets in the British Museum, from the library of Ashurbanipal, about 650 B.C. In the beginning there were Apsu†, Mommu†, and Tiamat†. From them sprang two orders of beings, demons

and gods. The gods, in order of creation were Lakhmut and Lakhame; Ashart and Kishart, and then Anut, Eat, and others.

Tiamat, being disturbed by the new gods, consulted with Apsu, and with Mommu, who appears to have been an intermediary between them. As a result it was decided that the gods must be destroyed. This presumably implies that the country was being invaded by peoples bringing new gods with them, and that the representatives of the old religions were refusing to accept this without war. It was in strict accordance with the principles of Dualismt that Tiamat and her associates should become the powers of evil, and Ea the chief of the powers of good.

Ea managed to destroy Apsu by a spell, and Mardukt was born in the place of Apsu. Tiamat called for help from Ummu Khuburt (or Melilit), who became the mother of the six thousand devils, and from the Eleven Mighty Helperst, and the whole force was put under the command of Kingut who was given the Dup Shimatit or Tablets of Fate as his seal of authority.

The next step was that Ea, becoming frightened at this, consulted Anshar and sent Anu as an emissary to Tiamat, but she looked so angry when he arrived that he fled in terror. The gods held a council and after much discussion Marduk was put in command of their forces and invested with magical powers. In Assyria Asshurt took the place of Marduk in all these stories. With the aid of these magical spells Kingu was defeated, and the Dup Shimati were taken, and the body of Tiamat was split in half, one half becoming the dome of heaven and the other the wall to contain the waters. Marduk then cre-

ated man by scrificing Kingu and using his blood. Afterwards Marduk became the Lord of the Gods and of Men.

It appears that the Creation Legends of Babylonia and Assyria are drawn from a source similar to that used by the Hebrews and the Phoenicians and, possibly, the Egyptians. They clearly cannot be memories of the actual creation as such, and may be memories of the emergence of mankind from the effects of some great catastrophe, possibly of a cosmic nature, followed by a flood, and the conflicts between groups of survivors as the effects of the disaster began to disappear. The functions of one of the mother goddesses, whose name may have been Tiamat, Tauthet, Tohut, Tamtut, or Atmut, were attributed to the flood waters, and, afterwards, when the new gods had been established, the old ones were degraded to the rank of demons, in accordance with the principles of Dualismt.

There are two main versions of the Babylonian Deluge Legend, the first of which, taken from the works of Berosus, tells how Xisuthrost, tenth, and last, of the pre-diluvial kings, was warned that there would be a flood by which mankind would be destroyed, and that he should bury all the records of the past at Sippara, and then build a ship into which he could put his family and his friends. The vessel was built and rode the waters of the storm with success. When the flood began to abate Xisuthros sent out birds. The first time they returned, the second time their feet were muddy, and the third time they did not come back. He then found that his ship had stranded on a mountain in Armenia. After building an altar and making a sacrifice Xisuthros vanished, leaving behind instructions for his children.

The other and longer version comes from the Gilgamesh† Epic, and is contained on the tablets now in the British Museum. The hero was Utnapishti† (in the Sumerian and Akkadian versions he was Zindsuddu†, but otherwise the stories are much the same), who was warned by Ea to throw down his house of reeds at Shurippak and build a ship, in which he could house his family. That the vessel was large is shown by references to shipbuilders and a pilot or captain. The flood, when it came, was preceded by violent cyclones, and the waters reached up to the hills, so high that even the goddess Ishtar† was moved to utter a lament to the gods. Eventually the storm ceased and the ship stranded on the mountains of Nisir, where it held fast. On landing Utnapishti built an altar, and was later raised to the rank of the gods.

It may be taken that the Noachic Deluge Legend was drawn from the same sources as these, but whether for that reason Noah is to be equated with Xisuthros, Utnapishti, or Ziudsuddu is by no means certain. The place of landing is variously given as Ararat†, Amasis†, Baris†, Djudi† or Judi†, and Nizir†. The Ark of Noah was said to have been built at a shipyard at Maala, at the foot of the Gebel Shan Sha, near Aden.

Bacabs The Canopic gods of the Mayas, who were also the supporters of the four corners of the earth. Their names, their cardinal points, and their symbolic colours were as follows: Mulac†, north, white; Cauac†, south, red; Kan†, east, yellow; Ix†, west, black. They were also minor agricultural gods, and were included among the attendant gods of Chac-Mool†, to whom they bore the same relationship as the Tlalocs of Aztec myth to Tlaloc† the rain god.

Badb (Badhbh) A Celtic war goddess subordinate to Morrigu†. In Gaul she was known as Cathubodua, 'Crow, or Raven, of Battle'. She may have been a pre-Celtic goddess who was absorbed by Celtic culture.

Badi In the Völundar Kvida he was a giant who was the father of Völund† and Egil†.

Baduh A Semitic spirit who ensures the speedy transmission of messages. He is invoked by writing the numerals 8, 6, 4, 2, representing the letters in the Arabic alphabet forming his name. This practice was still common in Egypt and Iran in 1945.

Baelthi Egyptian name for Baalath†.

Bahamut The enormous fish on which stands Kujata, the giant bull, whose back supports a rock of ruby, on the top of which stands an angel on whose shoulders rests the earth, according to Islamic myth. Our word Behemoth† is of the same origin.

Baiame The name given to the great sky hero in Australia west of the Dividing Range. On the eastern coastal strip he was known as Daramulun†, though the latter was sometimes referred to as the one-legged son of Baiame. In Victoria he tended to be known as Bunjil†, and in the lower Murray river area he was called Nurrundere† or Ngurunderi†.

Baitulos Meaning 'Abode of God' in the Phoenician† Creation Legend.

Bakairi Carib Creation Legend This is given under Tupuya† and Ges Indian Creation Legends.

Bakha In Egyptian myth alternative spelling for Bukhet, the Bull Bouchis. Bakha is a manifestation of Menthut at Hermonthis.

Bala-Ram(a) In Vedic myth the fair-haired twin brother of Krisnat. He was considered to be an incarnation of Seshat, the Nagat chief. From this it would appear that both the brothers were related to the Nagas and that Krisna joined the Hindu invaders while Bala-Rama stayed true to his people. Bala-Rama was also worshipped by the ancient Tamils under the name of Silappadikaram.

Balder In Nordic myth the son of Odint and Friggt, the most beautiful of the Aesirt. Possibly he was the twin brother of Hodert. He was the husband of Nannat and the father of Forsetit. In Balder's Dream it is told how, having been troubled with dreams of death, he reported it to the Aesir in council and Friggt extracted an oath from all things that they would not do any harm to Balder. Lokit, filled with jealousy, ascertained that the mistletoe had not been included in this and persuaded Hoder, who was blind, to throw a sprig at Balder, who immediately fell down dead. Afterwards Hermodt, a son of Odint, took Sleipnirt, the horse of Odin, and rode to Hel to offer a ransom if she would let Balder return. On arriving at his destination Hel said that Balder could return if 'All things in the world, both living and lifeless, weep for him'. Balder then gave Hermod the ring Draupnir which had been placed on his funeral pyre to take back to Odin, and Nanna, who had committed suicide after his death, also sent her magic ring to Fullat. When Hermod returned, every-thing on earth wept for Balder except the giantess Thauktt, and accordingly he did not return.

The alternative version of Saxo Grammaticus makes Hoder the rival of Balder for the affections of Nanna. It would seem, however, that this is a later version. After his death his body was placed on a ship, Hringhorn, which was launched with the aid of the giantess Hyrrokin in strict accordance with northern customs. The fact that Hoder himself was killed some months later may point to Balder having been the divine sacrifice for the saving of the Aesir. The word Balder may be related to the Slavonic Bielbogt, the white god.

Balder's Dream An alternative title for the Edda of the Lady of Vegtamt.

Bali A good Daityat king who, by devotion and austerity, defeated Indrat, thereby extending his power over the three worlds. The other gods appealed to Vishnut for protection, and he appeared as Vamanat, in his fifth or dwarf avatar. He managed to outwit Bali, take back heaven and earth, but left the underworld to him.

Balma The wife of Larat, whose escape from a deluge is told in Celtict Creation Legends.

Balor (Balar) In Celtic myth a leader of the Fomorst and the son of Buarainech. In early youth one of his eyes had been poisoned and it retained the power of striking people to death by a glance; in consequence four men were needed to raise his eyelid in battle. At the battle of Mag Tuireadht he was killed by the Tuatha Dé Danaant.

Banaded, or **Binded** In Egyptian myth a

ram or goat god. The name is a contraction of Ba Neb Djedet. In Greek it is Mendes†.

Banbha One of a trio of goddesses said to have reigned over Ireland at the time of the arrival of the Gaels. The other were Ériu† and Fódla†.

Banshee English spelling of the Irish Bean-Sidhe, or fairy woman. Originally it seems to have meant a princess of the Celtic hill people, and its present use to describe a wailing spectre seems to be the result of a mixture of superstitition and religious animosity.

Baphomet The sabbatic goat of the Occultists. The word is said to come from the Greek *baphemetous*, the appellation of the Pythagorean Pentagon usually found on his head. It is of interest to note that at the trial of the Knights Templars for heresy in 1311 there was only question of a head, said to be that of the Eternal Father at rest, which was stated to come from Gnostics who represented Him as having long hair and a beard, the latter being the beard of truth of the Sephir Dzinioutha. The transformation into a goat's head may be due either to a misreading of the evidence at the trial by later exponents of the magical art, or by confusion with some god of Semitic origin, brought to Europe from the Middle East by the crusaders.

Barbarossa In Teutonic myth Frederick I, the red-haired emperor of Germany, rests asleep in a cavern in the Kyffhauser Mountains awaiting the call to arms. For details of similar stories *see* Sleeping Princes†.

Baris In Babylonian myth a name given

to the landing place of the Ark. The word actually means ship.

Basque Creation Legend A version of the Basque national epic is given in Atlantida†, put together by Verdaguer in 1877–8. The story links Greek myth with the settling of Catalonia and Spain by refugees from Atlantis. Other Basque references are given under Basso-Jaun†, Benzozia†, Maitagarri†, and Orko†.

Basso-Jaun (Basajaun) A Basque forest deity living in the deepest part of the forest or in caves.

Bast or **Bastet (Ubastet)** Egyptian fire and cat goddess of Bubastis†, She was known as the 'Little Cat', as opposed to Sekhmet†, the fire and lioness goddess, who was known as the 'Great Cat'. Both of these goddesses, who are linked with Ptah†, the artificer god, are very ancient.

Battle of the Trees In Celtic myth this was fought between Arawn†, the ruler of Annwn†, against Amaethon† and Gwydion†. The story is told in Taliesin†, where the battle is given its Welsh name of Cad Goddeu†.

Ba'u In Babylonian myth a goddess, wife of Ningirsu†. The festival of their sacred marriage came at the end of the harvest, and ensured success for next year's crops. She gave her name to the first month of the new year, beginning with the autumn equinox. From other calendars of the same period (3000 B.C. or earlier) it is known that the festival fell in the month of Tishrit. She may be the same as Baau†.

Bau *See* Baba†.

Baugi In Nordic myth one of the giants of the Eddas. He was the brother of Suttung† and it is told in the Conversations of Bragi how Odin† tricked him into handing over the secret of the production of Kvasir†.

Beda In Nordic myth one of the Asynjor†, the women grouped around Freyja and Frigg†.

Beelzebub A parody of the name Baalzebul†, meaning 'Baal the prince', which came to be thought of as lord of the flies or dunghill. By New Testament times he had come to be regarded as chief of the demons.

Begochiddy In Navajo† myth the name given to the great god.

Behemoth Originally the name meant simply an animal, but it then came to have a pejorative connotation, and so to be synonymous with Satan. It may in fact have been a hippopotamus.

Bel The Bel of the Old Testament appears to have been the Marduk† of Babylonian myth. He was also Baal† of Phoenician myth.

Belenus A Gallo-Roman god assimilated to Apollo as a healing god, found in northern Italy and southern Gaul, as well as Britain.

Belet It is an alternative spelling for Baalat†.

Beli British name for the Celtic culture hero Bile. He was the husband of Dôn† and the father of Arianrhod† and Amaethon†. The family pedigrees are compared under Lleu†.

Belial Hebrew expression for worthlessness (Beliy Ya'al), meaning the underworld, or the devil.

Belili Sumerian moon goddess, also goddess of trees, love, and the underworld; she was very ancient and preceded Ishtar†. She was the sister and wife of Tammuz†.

Belisama 'Most brilliant', an epithet applied to Minerva, is connected with the fact that at her sanctuary in Britain a fire burned perpetually. This has induced some writers to elaborate a separate Gallo-Roman goddess of this name.

Belisma A Celtic lake or river priestess. Ptolemy gives her name to the Ribble, but inscriptions of it have been found in Gaul.

Belit-Sheri Scribe of the underworld in Babylonian myth. An alternative spelling is Beletseri.

Beltaine The Celtic feast of the spring equinox, held at the beginning of May, the other feasts being Lugnasad†, Oimelc†, and Samhain†. The 'taine' means fire and may be related to Tin†, the Etruscan fire god, while the 'bel' may be Bile†, the ruler of the Celtic underworld. In Ireland this festival was also known as Samradh or Cetsamain, and in Wales it was Cyntefun.

Belus In the Babylonian Creation Legend of Damascius he is the same as Bel†.

Benani In Babylonian myth he was the father by Melili† of the warriors with the bodies of birds and the men with the faces of ravens created by the old gods.

These monsters numbered six thousand, had seven kings, and corresponded to the legion created by Tiamat† for her fight with Marduk†.

Bendigeidfran Full-length rendering of the name of Bran†.

Benin The religion of the inhabitants of Benin is known as fetish worship. The fundamental idea is of a trinity of gods: Maout†, the sun; Lissa†, his wife, the chameleon; and their son Gou†, the moon. Of these the oldest is Lissa, who was the mother goddess. Below this there is a fetish for each tribe, some of the better known being Agassou†, panther; Danh†, snake; Khebieso, thunder; Nesshoue†, river; Sagbata†, smallpox. The individual member of the tribe has, in addition, a personal god, Legba, Legba†, and a personal fate or Fa†, who has to be consulted on all matters of import. The system is an extension of totemism gone wrong, and its final form is to be seen in voodoo† worship in the West Indies. Khebieso was also known as So† and was linked with another god named Bo†.

Bennu The sacred bird of the Egyptians which periodically was re-created by flame, a story which came to western Europe as that of the phoenix. As an emblem of the resurrection it was sacred to Osiris†, but was also known as the head of Ra†. The hieroglyph of the Bennu was one meaning 'water' or 'flood', indicating a link with a flood legend.

Benten Japanese goddess of the sea who resembles Kwannon†, but who was mainly worshipped on the outlying islands. Her shrine was at Enoshim, where she was said to have captivated and

married a dragon which was devouring children of the neighbourhood. She was one of the seven divinities of luck, the Shichi Fukujin†.

Benzozia A mother goddess of the Basque people.

Beowulf The song of Beowulf is mainly concerned with the adventures of a historic king of the Geats, and as such cannot be considered as myth. However, there is a king of a similar name who is mentioned in various king lists as having lived before Odin† or Woden† and it is possible that the dragon-slaying episode of the poem Beowulf belonged to this individual. In the poem is mentioned Sigmund† as slayer of another dragon, and also Sinfjotli, thereby linking this story with the Nibelungenlied.

Bercht (Perchta) Originally a goddess of South German mythology who, under the impact of Christianity, was degraded to the status of a bogy with whom children were threatened.

Berecyntia A goddess of the Gauls, probably the same as Brigit†.

Bergelmir In the Nordic Creation Legends, as told in the Vafthrudnismal, he and his wife were the sole survivors of a deluge which came from the blood of Ymir†. They escaped in a boat and all the other members of the Hrimthursar or ice giants were drowned.

Berouth In the Phoenician† Creation Legend of Philo Byblos he was one of the first gods. He was parent with Elioun† of Gea and Ouranos†.

Bes This bandy-legged dwarf demigod of Egypt was the god of music and pleasure. He may have been a god of birth, as we hear of him as a protector of children.

Besla, Bestla A giantess, daughter of Bolthorn†, wife of Bor† and mother of Odin†, the Nordic culture hero.

Bevarash *See* Azhi Dahaka†.

Beyla The wife of Byggvir† in Norse myth. Her name may be taken from the bee, since honey was used in brewing mead.

Bhadra Vira In Vedic myth a title under which Siva† was worshipped in the Maratha country. He is represented as armed with sword, spear, shield, bow and arrow, with the sun and moon, mounted on Nandi†, and with the goat-headed Daksha† by his side.

Bhaga In Vedic myth one of the twelve Adityas† or guardians of the months of the year.

Bhavani In Vedic myth one of the more gentle manifestations of Parvati†, wife of Siva†.

Bhima In Vedic myth the child of Vayu†.

Bhrigu In Vedic myth one of the seven great Rishis† or Prajapatis†. He was known as 'the Calm-souled'. It was Matariswan†, the messenger of the gods, who brought Agni† to Bhrigu.

B-Iame. *See* Baiame†

Bielbog In Slavonic myth he was the white god, similar to Byelun†, or the power of good as opposed to

Czarnobog†, the black god, or power of evil; a conception of Dualism which may be traced back to ancient Persia. The word may be related to the name of Balder†.

Bifrost In Nordic myth the rainbow bridge or Milky Way leading from the world to Asgard†. In the Ragnarok† it is told how it was broken down by the onrush of the sons of Muspel† led by Surt†.

Bil In Nordic myth a minor Norse goddess and one of the Asynjor†. The version in the Prose Edda is that Bil and Hjuki were returning from the spring with a bucket of water when they were seized by Mani†, the moon god, and afterwards they always followed the moon as it could be seen from the earth.

Bile In Celtic myth an alternative name for Beli. Comparative family trees of Beli†, Bile, and Balor† are given under Lleu†.

Bimbo-Gami Japanese god of poverty.

Binded In Egyptian myth an alternative spelling for Banaded†.

Binzuku Japanese disciple of Buddha who was raised to the rank of god on account of his miraculous powers of healing the sick.

Birral Early culture hero of the Australian tribes who may be equated with Baiame†.

Bishamon Japanese god of war depicted as wearing armour and carrying a spear and a miniature pagoda. He is one of the seven divinities of luck, the Shichi

Fukujin†. He is also one of the guardians of the cardinal points. He was the guardian of the north. He was the brother of Kishijoten†.

Bith and Birren The Adam and Eve of a Deluge story told in Celtic Creation Legends.

Blackfoot Indian Creation Legend This tribe of North American Indians have a legend that at the time of the great catastrophe their ancestors took refuge in a great cave named Nina Stahu†, from which they were led by Napi†, the founder of the tibe. They had a morning Venus god named Apisirahts† and a moon goddess called Komorkis†.

Black Magic At the present day means the use of ritual magic for personal gain or lust, and usually has a strong element of sexuality in it. Earlier it could have been defined as any religious practice appertaining to a superseded or unpopular religion which has not been incorporated in the dogma of an existing and dominating religion. The majority of the practices falling under this heading are to be traced back to the pre-Judaic period in the Middle East, and are vestiges of still earlier ceremonies. The name itself constitutes a recognition of the dualistic† principle of the offsetting of good by evil, which has formed the backbone of many religions, including some Christian heresies. The original definition is ritual practised for harmful purposes, to produce sterility, sickness, or death. While the various phenomena grouped under this designation are frequently difficult to explain by ordinary methods, there would appear to be no reason for describing them as other than 'of the earth, earthy'.

Bláthnad Her name means 'Little Flower', and she was carried off by Cú Chulainn† and Cú Roi†, together with a cauldron and three cows, in a raid into Scotland. Cú Chulainn fails to live up to his promise that Cú Roi would have first choice of the booty, however, so the latter takes all. Bláthnad subsequently betrays Cú Roi, however, in much the same way as did Blodeuwedd†, and Cú Roi is murdered. His poet, Fercherdne†, avenges his death by throwing his arms around Bláthnad as she is standing on the edge of a cliff, and takes both of them to their deaths below.

Blodeuwedd In Celtic myth she was 'Flower Face', the wife of Lleu†, who conspired with Gronw Pebyr† to kill him. As a punishment she was changed into an owl by Gwydion†, the father of Lleu.

Blue-Jay A figure in the Creation Legend of the Chinooks who resembles in character the Coyote of the Californian Indians. He was originally a mischief-making individual who was eventually turned into a zoomorphic being by the gods. This may be a posthumous development. There is a trilogy of stories about Blue-Jay and his sister Ioi which resemble to some extent the initiation ceremonies described in the Popul Vuh. The stories tell how Ioi, Blue-Jay's sister, begs him to take a wife to share her labour. He takes the corpse of a chief's daughter from her grave, and carries her to the land of the Supernatural People, who restore her to life. The chief her father finds this out, and demands Blue-Jay's hair as a recompense, but Blue-Jay changes himself into his bird shape and flies away. His wife dies again. The dead in the land of the

Supernatural Folk then purchase Ioi his sister for a wife, and he sets off in search of her. He finds her surrounded by heaps of bones, to whom she alludes as her relations by marriage. The ghosts resume their human shape but on being addressed by Blue-Jay become heaps of bones once more, and he takes a mischievous delight in reducing them to this condition and in mixing up the various heaps of bones, so that the ghosts have the wrong heads, legs, and arms when they materialize again. There is a similar character in Zambian mythology.

Bn-Ym The son of the sea in the Ugarit texts. He was also known as Khoser-et-Hasis†.

Bo A god of the Ewe peoples of Benin. He was the protector of persons engaged in war and was linked with a god Khebieso† or So† who was the lightning. The priests of Bo carried with them on ceremonial occasions a peculiar axe made of brass and also bundles of sticks from four to six feet long painted red and white. As with the ancient Romans the axe was the symbol of thunder and the fasces, or sticks, that of lightning.

Boann In Celtic myth a queen of Ireland, the wife of Dagda† and the mother of Angus†. Her name was given to the River Boyne and is linked with a flood myth given in Celtic Creation Legends. It is probable that she was the titular priestess of the source of the river, where it is said there lived the salmon of knowledge which fed on nuts dropped from the nine hazel-trees at the water's edge. This sounds very much like the magic cauldron of Annwn which was tended by nine maidens.

Boat of the Soul A vehicle used in Chinese† royal funerals together with the Chariot of the Soul and the Tablet of the Soul, the latter being a piece of thick flat wood five times as long as it is wide, on which the name of the deceased was incribed. This custom may date back to a time when the Chinese were a maritime nation and buried their chiefs in boats.

Bobd A Celtic battle goddess.

Bochica Culture hero of the Muyscayas of Columbia. He brought to them knowledge of building, agriculture, use of a calendar, and a legal code. On his death he handed over the government of the tribe to four chiefs. He is sometimes referred to as Zuhé, Xué or Nemterequeteba. After his death he became a dawn or morning Venus god. Subsequent generations recounted how he carried the world on his shoulders and that when he eased his position there were earthquakes, from which it may be deduced that he lived at a time of great natural disasters.

Bocor Title of the professional sorcerer of the voodoo worshippers of Haiti. The practice of voodoo worship in Haiti resembles that of the fetish worshippers in Benin from whom it appears to have evolved. The slight modifications introduced by local custom and the advent of Christianity do not appear to have brought any great change. In both cases the religious practices appear to be the degenerate remains of an early and somewhat complicated African ritual.

Bodb The Red, a son of Dagda†, who succeeded his father as king of the Tuatha Dé Danann†.

Bod-Baal In the Ugarit texts he was one

of the aids of Baal† in his combat with Khoser† and with Zabel†, the Lord of the Sea, and the Suffete† of the River, on whom he pounces like an eagle.

Bodvild In Nordic myth the daughter of King Nithud†, who was seduced by Völund† in revenge for his ill treatment at the hands of her father.

Bog A generic term for God in the Slavonic languages. It comes from the Persian *bagi*, and the Sanskrit *bhaga*, implying richness and power.

Boí (or **Buí**) A Celtic divinity known as the queen of the Limerick fairies, whose activities reached into Scotland. She was the wife of the god Lugh†, and had a reputation for passing repeatedly through the cycle of youth and age.

Bolthorn A northern giant, father of Besla†, the wife of Bor†, and grandfather of Odin†.

Bomazi A divine figure who came from heaven to found the various peoples of the Bushongo and related tribes in the Congo. This light-skinned man appeared to a childless elderly couple and predicted that the wife would give birth to a daughter. When the child grew up, Lord Bomazi married her, and their five sons became the chiefs of five tribes.

Book of the Dead *See also* Egyptian† Creation Legends and Egyptian† Religion.

An aspect of early religious thought peculiar to the Egyptians was the custom of furnishing the dead with detailed instructions, with the aid of which they could overcome all difficulties on their way to the Elysian Fields, the Sekhet Aaru† (*see* Sad El†). At first these instructions were painted on the inner walls of pyramids and on sarcophagi and coffins, being known as pyramid texts, but by the eighteenth dynasty the formulae had become so large that it became necessary to put them on papyrus rolls, extant copies of which range between 50 and 135 feet in length. The Arab tomb robbers called these rolls 'Kitab al Mayit', meaning 'Book of the Dead Man', a name which is now generally applied to them.

The earliest texts were taken from the Pertemhru or 'Coming forth by Day', which seems to have been evolved in the earliest dynastic or even pre-dynastic period. Although it was in use for over three thousand years, nothing appears to have been taken from it, the only changes being in the nature of increases. There were three main recensions, at Heliopolis, Thebes, and Sais, differing mainly in the naming of Amon† Ra or Osiris† as chief god. These collations of prayers, religious texts, magical spells, hymns, evocations, and detailed instructions faithfully reflected the religious feeling of their time, but with the general decline in Egyptian religion the meaning of many of the texts had obviously been forgotten.

The author of the Pertemhru was generally assumed to be Thoth†, the scribe of the Ennead†, the Great Company of the Gods, and the recording angel of paradise, and it was upon his advocacy that the Egyptian counted for the securing of his acquittal on the Day of Judgment, so that he might enjoy the fruits of a virtuous life. The underlying assumption of the whole work, as was the case for the whole religion of Osiris, was that the dead came up for moral judgment, before a tribunal of the gods.

The accused entered the antechamber, and repeated an affirmation of his good conduct during life, and was then admitted for trial before Osiris. Near him were the scales, watched over by Anubis†, and in a state of expectant waiting was Amemait†, the devourer of the hearts of the wicked. After addressing the assembled gods, the heart of the accused was weighed by Thoth balanced against the Maat† or feather of truth. If the balance was exact the heart became as the heart of Osiris, and he was admitted into the other world, or Amenti†, the Land of the West, as a Sahu† or spirit body.

Bor In Nordic myth, son of Bur† and father, by the giantess Besla†, of Odin†, Wili† and We†, the slayers of Ymir†, the first of the frost giants or Jotunns†.

Bormanus (Bormo or Boryo) An early god of the continental Celts, associated with hot springs. His consort is Damona†.

Borve In Celtic myth a king who was involved in the dispute between Llyr† and his second wife Aeife, who turned the children of his first wife into swans. For this act she was changed by King Borve into a demon. There is a Borvo† who was a deity of the continental Celts associated with hot springs who may possibly be the same person.

Borvo A god of hot springs associated with the continental Celts, equated by the Romans with Apollo. He seems to have arisen as the son of an earlier goddess Sirona† or Dirona†. The word borvo means to boil.

Bouto (Buto) Greek name for Uadjit†, the Egyptian serpent goddess.

Bouyan An island paradise of the Slavs. On it was the sacred stone Alatuir†, from beneath which flowed a river whose waters healed all ailments. Here dwelt the king of the snakes and Zarya† the beautiful priestess. It resembles Falias†, the City of the North of Celtic myth, from whence came the Stone of Destiny, and seems to indicate an intermingling of Slavonic and Celtic myth at some early stage. Bouyan also resembles Murias† in being the City beneath the Waters. Even after the revolution Bouyan continued to occupy an important place in Slavonic† myth, and is akin to Raj†.

Bragi In Nordic myth one of the Aesir† and husband of Iduna†. In the Braga Raedur, or 'Conversations of Bragi', one of the Eddas, he tells Aegir† the stories of Iduna and her apples; of the peace treaties between the Aesir and the Vanir† sealed by spitting in Odherir, the magic cauldron; of the murder of Kvasir† by the dwarfs; of the liquor of poetic inspiration brewed by the giant Suttung† from the fermented blood of Kvasir, and how Odin† steals the recipe by seducing Gunnlauth†.

Brahma In later Vedic myth the senior god of the Great Triad with Vishnu† and Siva†. He was said to be born from the golden egg called Narayana†, which floated on the waters. He divided himself into two halves, a male half called Purusha†, and a female half called Satarupa†. In view of the fact that Purusha is also described as a primeval giant from whose dead body the world was created, it would seem possible that at some very early stage Satarupa may have been the mother goddess from whom Brahma developed. The whole conception of Brahma as the universal all-pervading deity appears to have arisen comparatively late in the structure of Vedic religion, and to be rather a theological concept than an expression of popular opinion. The Matsya†, Kurma† and Varaha† avatars of Vishnu have also been attributed to Brahma.

The Kalpa, or Day of Brahma, was supposed to cover the entire period from the creation of the universe to its final destruction. Brahma is represented as red or gold coloured, robed in white, and seated on a swan. He has four heads and four arms. In his hands he holds a rosary, a vessel containing Ganges water, a portion of the Vedas, and a sceptre. His city is Brahmapura on the summit of Mount Meru. Although Brahma is the most familiar name in the Hindu pantheon, he has receded so far into the background as to be almost outside the field of popular worship.

Brahmanaspati In late Vedic myth the lord of prayer. This purely abstract deity appears to have arisen as part of the general polytheistic tendencies of Brahmanism.

Brahmapura In Vedic myth the city of Brahma†, situated on the summit of Mount Meru†.

Brân Hypocoristic form of Bendigeidfran†. In Celtic myth he was the son of Llyr† by Iweridd† and was the brother of Branwen†. After his sister had married Matholwch†, the King of Ireland, her husband's continued ill treatment of her forced Brân to invade Ireland and he was killed in a battle, only seven of his followers surviving. After the death of Brân, his head was cut off

and carried by the seven to Tower Hill in London, where it was buried.

Brandan or **Brendan** An apocryphal Irish voyager who was reputed to have lived in the fifth century. His tour of a whole series of mysterious islands is a hotch-potch of ill-digested information of earlier voyages put together by monks who had, in all probability, never been on a sea voyage of any extent and who did not realize that both climate and geography had to be taken into consideration. His visits enumerate twelve islands. Other Irish voyagers were Corra† and Maeldune†.

Branwen In Celtic myth the daughter of Llyr† by Iweridd†. She was one of the three matriarchs of Britain and became the wife of Matholwch†, the King of Ireland, and had one son, Gwern†. Her continued ill treatment by her husband caused her brother Brân†, the King of England, to invade Ireland and kill her husband with most of the Irish nobility. Her son was murdered by Evnisien†, her stepbrother.

Bregon In Celtic myth the father of Bile†, a leader of the Milesians†. He was also the father of Ith†.

Breidablik The zodiacal house of Vali† and Vidar†.

Bress (Bres) In Celtic myth the son of Elthan†, chief of the Fomors†, and the most beautiful being in Ireland. After the deposition of Nuda† he was made king of the Tuatha Dé Danann† as a move towards peace between the two nations. He was a most unpopular king and eventually was himself deposed in favour of Nuda, after he had fallen ill following a magical satire written about him by Caipret.

Brian In Celtic myth one of the three sons of Tuirennt the murderers of Ciant who, as a penalty, had to seek and find what subsequently became the treasures of the Tuatha Dé Danannt. His brothers were Iuchart and Iucharbar.

Brigantia Goddess of the Brigantes; she was a northern Celtic variant of Brigitt.

Brigindo Name given to Brigitt by the Celts of eastern France.

Brigit The Celtic goddess of fire, of the hearth, and of poetry, who was also known as Brigantiat, and Brighid. With the advent of Christianity she became St Brigit or Brigid. She was said to be the daughter of Dagdat and dates back to the earliest periods of Irish history.

Brihaspati *See* Brahmanaspatit and Vrishaspatit.

Brisingamen In Nordic myth the fiery necklace of Freyjat, which she broke in her fury on hearing that the giant Thrymt had demanded her hand as a reward for the return of the hammer of Thort. Later Freyja lent the necklace to Thor, who disguised himself as the bride and went in her stead. Other details of the story will be found under Thrym. The tale that the necklace was made by the dwarfst, and that it was only by surrendering herself to four of them that Freyja obtained it, seems to refer to some dispute between the mother goddess and the dwarfs settled by payment of a necklace. In the same manner Odin'st bribing of Lokit to steal it must relate to a dispute between the invading Aesirt and the goddess. To recover it Heimdallt fought Loki daily until he killed him at Ragnarokt. It is possible that the necklace was a magic one as an enchantress of the name of Brisin is mentioned in the Arthurian legends. In Scaldic literature it is called Sviagris.

Brownie A kindly Scottish goblin similar to the elvest and the koboldst of continental tradition. There was an altar to a brownie in Scotland until recently, from which one may conclude that he was a pre-Celtic god who had been degraded by time. To some extent he resembles the Fenodryeet, or the Cornish piskyt.

Brynhild, Brunhild In the Volsung Cycle a Valkyriet who is awakened from a charmed sleep by Sigurdt, to whom she becomes betrothed. Later, Sigurd, having lost his memory, impersonates Gunnart to enable him to win Brynhild. To do this he rides through a wall of flame (initiation ceremony), as in the case of Mengladt and Skirnirt. When Brynhild discovers the treachery of which she has been the victim, she turns against Sigurd, and has him killed and then takes her own life.

In the Thidrek Saga, her betrothed Siegfriedt marries Grimhildt, for reasons of policy. The rest of the story is similar to the above.

In the Nibelungenlied she is a queen of Iceland, who can only be wed by one who could defeat her in three trials of strength. Siegfried, her betrothed, wearing the Tarnkappe, the helmet of invisibility, defeats her, thus enabling Gunthert to wed her. Because of this she has Siegfried murdered by Hagent.

Buanann A warlike Celtic goddess known as 'The Lasting One' or 'Mother of Heroes', who taught the martial arts to heroes.

Buddha Gautama Buddha, to whom in the western world the name Buddha is usually applied, was according to the traditions of the faith the twenty-fifth in order of a series of great religious leaders who preached the gospel to mankind. On each occasion, however, men forgot the truth and fell away into ignorance and sin, and a new Buddha arose. Gautama was born about 560 BC to a princely family of the Sakyas, rulers of portions of Oudh and Nepal. Before his birth his mother Maya dreamt she beheld the future Buddha descending from heaven and entering her womb in the form of a white elephant, for which reason the elephant is a sacred animal to Buddhists. At the time of his birth earthquakes and miracles of healing took place, flowers bloomed out of season, and heavenly music was heard. It was prophesied that at the age of thirty-five he would become a Buddha, after seeing the four signs: a decrepit man, a sick man, a dead man, and a monk.

In spite of precautions the four signs were manifested and Gautama, at the age of twenty-nine, abandoned his princely life, his wife, and his son, and proceeded to a life of six years of austeries, after which he sat alone under the sacred Bo Tree, and after a successful battle with Mara†, the tempter, he became a Buddha, the Enlightened One.

After forty-five years spent in teaching the Buddha died at the age of eighty.

The religious system which he initiated spread to Tibet, China, and Japan, where it still survives, although in India itself it has largely been displaced by Brahmanism and Islam.

The doctrine of the Noble Eightfold Path, sometimes called the Middle Path because it avoids both bodily indulgence and asceticism, has been made known to the western world largely through the activities of the Theosophical Society and kindred bodies.

The adoption in Vedic religion of Buddha as the ninth avatar of Vishnu† was due to the necessity for some compromise between the two faiths.

Buddhist Creation Legend According to Buddhist myth our universe is divided into three regions: Kama Loka, the world of desire; Rupa Loka, the world of form; and Arupa Loka, the world of the spirit. In Tibetan Buddhism there is yet another region above the Arupa Loka, that of the Five Celestial Ginas or Dhyani Buddhas, crowned by the realm of Adi Buddha, the primeval Buddha. The Kama Loka is divided into six regions, beginning with that of the four maharajas, the guardians of the four cardinal points, situated on the top of Mount Meru†; the Trayastrinska, the abode of Indra† and of the thirty-three subordinate divinities; the kingdom of Yama†, the realm of the dead; Tushita, the home of the Boddhisattvas; the Nirmanarati, the abode of the creative gods, and at the top, Paranirmita-Vasavartin, the abode of Mara†, the great tempter.

Below this and still forming part of the Kama Loka are, in descending order, the world of men, that of the Asuras†, that of animals, that of ghosts, and at the very bottom the various hells.

For further details see Buddha†, Hsi-Yu-Chi†, Karma†, Kuan-Yin†, Nirvana†, Sakyamuni†, Sun-Houtzu†, and Tripitaka†. The Japanese Buddhist deities were Amida†, Binzuku†, Dainichi†, Emma-Ō†, Fudo†, Jizō†, Kompira†, and Kwannon†.

Buí *See* Boí†.

Bukhe In Egyptian myth, a name given to the Bull Bouchis, a manifestation of Munt† or Menthu-Ra† at Hermonthis. An alternative spelling is Bakha†.

Bun-Jil (Bunjil) A culture hero of the Wurunjerri and Kulin tribes of Australia. He is said by the first to have made men of clay and endowed them with life, and by the second to have taught them the art of life. Later he ascended to the sky land. He is of a similar type to Baiame†, Daramulun and Nurrundere†.

Bur In the Nordic creation myth he was the first man, the father of Bor† and the grandfather of Odin†.

Buriash (Burijash) Kassite god of storm, corresponding to Adad† and Teshub†.

Bushes, Sacred The Lithuanians worshipped sacred bushes, a practice which appears to have been similar to the worship of Djin†, the woodland spirits of Albania and Serbia.

Bushmen Creation Legends The bush-men of South Africa believe that in the beginning men and animals were endowed with speech. There existed a quarrelsome being named Hochigan† who hated animals; he eventually disappeared, but with his departure the animals lost the power of speech. They also believe in a being as mischievous and full of tricks as the Coyote† of North America; his representative on earth is the praying mantis. He is named Kaggen†, or, alternatively, Cagn†.

Bussumarus A god of the continental Celts, whom the Romans identified with Jupiter. The name signifies 'the large-lipped'.

Buto A transcription made by the Greeks of Per Uadjit, for 'the dwelling of Uadjit', for the town in the Delta of Egypt, and also for the goddess worshipped there. Originally a snake goddess, she helped Isis† to protect the baby Horus†. *See also* Uadjit†.

Byelun A Slavonic† deity similar to Bielbog†, the name meaning 'the white one.'

Byggvir A tiny figure in Norse mythology who is represented as chattering into the ear of Freyr†. His name means 'barley', and his wife is Beyla†, possibly connected with bees.

C

God 'C' All that is known about this Maya god is that he is associated with astronomical signs. He may possibly be an equivalent of Mixcoatl†, the Aztec god of stars and numbers.

Cabraca In Maya mythology the younger son of Vukub-Caquix†.

Cad Goddeu The Welsh name for the Battle of the Trees†.

Cagn A culture hero of the African Bushmen. He may originally have been the head of a tribe with a mantis totem. He is to be identified with Kaggen.

Caillech Bhérri Another name of Buí† or Boí†.

Caipre (Coirbre) In Celtic myth the son of Ogma† and bard to the Tuatha Dé Danann†. On being rudely treated by King Bress† he composed a satire so virulent that it caused the king's face to come out in red blotches, a disfigurement which enabled the Tuatha to demand his abdication. Later his satires broke the morale of the Fomors† in the war with the Tuatha.

California Indians The Creation Legends of the California Indians are told under Achomawi†, Aschochimi†, and Maidu† Creation Legends.

Camaxtli Aztec† war god of Tlaxcala sometimes merged with Mixcoatl†.

Camazotz Bat god of Xibalba mentioned in the Quiche Creation Legend as told in the Popul Vuh. In the battle between Hunapú† and Xbalanque† and the rulers of Xibalba, Camazotz cut off the head of Hunapú with his claws, but thanks to the aid of a tortoise Hunapú was restored to life and Camazotz was defeated. He is the same as Zotzilaha Chimalman†, the bat god of the Mayas.

Camu A culture hero of the Arovacs† who in all probability corresponds to the Kamu† or Tamu† of the Caribs†.

Camulos In Celtic myth a king of the Tuatha Dé Danann† who has been fused with some early heaven god. It is possible that he may have been the Cumhal, the king warrior who was the father of Finn† and original King Cole†, hero of nursery rhyme.

Canopic Jars In the process of embalming as practised in Egypt, the intestines and other internal organs were removed, cleaned, wrapped in linen with powdered spices, etc., and placed in jars named Canopic Jars. The name is said to have arisen from the old legend whereby Canopus, the pilot of Menelaus, was buried at Canopus, and there worshipped in the shape of a jar with small feet, thin neck, swollen body, and a round back. As far back as the sixth dynasty these jars were dedicated to the

---

four cardinal points, and from about the seventeenth dynasty they bore the heads of the four sons of Horus† (or of Osiris†): Amset†, Hapi†, Duamutef†, and Qebehsenuf†, who also became gods of the cardinal points, protecting the liver, lungs, stomach, and intestines respectively. Traces of a similar custom have been observed in the Americas. For details *see* Bacabs†.

Carib Creation Legend This now extinct tribe of the Antilles had a myth that after the Deluge the founder of the race created mankind by sowing stones in the soil from which sprang men and women. Their earth mother goddess was called Mama Nono†.

A Creation Legend of the Bakairi Caribs is given under Tupuya† and Ges Creation Legends, dealing with the adventures of their culture hero Kame†. Another Carib Creation Legend whose heroine is Korobona† is given under Arawak† Creation Legends.

Cashinaua Indian Creation Legend This tribe of Indians of western Brazil have a myth of torrential rains drowning everything on the earth, which was followed by the bursting of the heavens and the crashing to earth of huge fragments of rock.

Caswallawn In Celtic myth the son of Beli† who, thanks to a cloak of invisibility, succeeded in taking possession of the lands and power of Manawydan† while he was away at the wars with his brother Brân†. His wife was Fflur, the daughter of a dwarf†. The stories about him are so ancient that they had mostly been forgotten by the time that Celtic mythology was being put into writing.

Cathubodua A name meaning the war fury given to Badb† in Gaul.

Cato Indian Creation Legend This tribe of California Indians have a myth that the old world was bad and needed re-creating, and so the highlands were set on fire and the world blazed until the thunder god put the fire out with a great rain storm which drowned vast areas of the earth.

Cauac One of the four Bacabs, the Maya gods of the cardinal points. He represented the south and his colour was red.

Ceithlenn In Celtic myth the wife of Balor†. Her detailed pedigree is given under Lleu†.

Celebes Islands Creation Legends The Melanesian† Toradja tribe have a story that after the Deluge had subsided rice, their staple cereal, was salvaged and the tribe were thus enabled to survive. They have a culture hero and sun lord named Laseo†, a sky god named Puang Matowa†. The Minehassas have a culture heroine Luminu'utt† and a sun priest named To'ar†.

Celtic Creation Legends 1. An Irish myth tells how Bith†, his wife Birren, their daughter Cesara† with her husband Fintan†, their son Lara† with his wife Balma†, escaped to Inisfail in a ship, at the time of the Deluge. Later there was a large red moon, with bright expanding clouds breaking up into hundreds of pieces, and the whole family were killed, leaving the land uninhabited. Another legend tells that a woman had a magic cask which, when opened, flowed for so long that that water covered the earth.

Boann†, the wife of Dagda†, is also linked with a Flood myth, concerning the overflowing of the Boyne. Badb† prophesied after Mag Tuireadh† that there would be a disaster involving the gods similar to Ragnarok†.

2. In Wales, the Deluge myth tells of the overflowing of Llyon-Llion†, from which Dwyvan† and Dwybach alone escaped. There is a Druid myth telling how fire and water prevailed over the earth.

Cenn Cruaich In Celtic myth 'the Lord of the Mound' to whom firstlings were sacrificed in Ireland. His effigy was stated to have been of gold surrounded by twelve stones.

Cephalonia The Lost Island, so called because even those who had been there were able to find it again only by chance.

Ceridwen An early British fertility goddess mentioned in the Mabinogion. She was the possessor of a magic cauldron called Amen†. She was the wife of Tegid† and had three children, of which Creirwy† was the most beautiful girl and Avagdu† the ugliest boy. To compensate him for this she prepared a magic draught made from six plants and named 'greal' – which has some affinity with the Grail† – and which when drunk was to give inspiration and science. The process of making took a year and a day, and Gwion† was ordered to stir it when three drops splashed from the cauldron named Amen on to his fingers, and on his sucking them to stop the pain he suddenly became possessed of all knowledge. The liquor resembled the Kvasir† of the northern races.

Ceridwen on discovering what had happened pursued Gwion. He changed into a hare and she became a greyhound; he became a fish, she became an otter; he became a bird, she became a hawk; he became a grain of corn, she became a hen, and ate him. Later she gave birth to a child who became Taliesin†, the most famous of the Welsh bards. The myth resembles various initiation ceremonies, and may well relate to the rites connected with the appointment of a bard or Druid†.

Cermait The Honey-mouthed, a name given to Ogma†, the Celtic god of literature.

Cernunnos A Celtic deity portrayed in a seated position with antlers on his head. Although the name, which means 'The Horned (or peaked) One', is only found on one of the sculptures that are extant, the title Cernunnos is applied to all such depictions as a type, for example the Gundestrup Cauldron.

Cesara, Cessair In Celtic myth the daughter of Bith† and Birren, who escaped with her husband Fintan† in a ship to Inisfail (Ireland) at the time of the Deluge. The story, which is detailed in Celtic† Creation Legends, shows traces of the matriarchy, the worship of strange gods inspired by the approach of disaster, and details of what appears to be a lunar catastrophe. Cesara, who was also known as Cessair, was pre-Celtic.

Cethe In Celtic myth the son of Dianchecht†, the Celtic god of medicine, and brother of Cian† and Cu†.

Chac A rain and thunder god of the Mayas who became a personification of the four Bacabs whose personal names were Kan†, Cauac†, Mulac†, and Ix†, words meaning yellow, red, white, and black.

Chac Mool An attendant of the Toltec rain god Tlaloc†, the Mayan Chac†, depicted holding a shallow dish in which to catch the rain.

Chalchihuitlicue Aztec water goddess, the wife of Tlaloc†, and known as 'the Goddess of the Jade Petticoat'. There may be some connection between her and Xochiquetzal† as in one instance she is referred to as 'Macuilxochiquetzalli', meaning 'Five Times Flower Feather'. She was the lord of the third hour of the day and the sixth hour of the night. She preceded Chac† the Maya rain and thunder god, and may have been his mythical mother, and goddess 'I'†.

Chandra In Vedic myth, as Soma†, one of the eight Vasus†, the divine attendants of Indra†. The word means moon, and is probably the name of some pre-Vedic moon god. The fact that Chandra was produced at the Churning of the Ocean in the Kurma† avatar would indicate a cosmic catastrophe of some import, which was remembered by the Vedic races.

Chantico Aztec† fire goddess of the domestic hearth.

Chemosh War god of the Moabites in their wars against Israel. He was the Shamash† of the Babylonians.

Chernobog *See* Czarnobog†.

Cherokee Indian Creation Legends The main deities of the Cherokee Indians of North America were Asgaya Gigagei†, Oonawieh Unggi†, and Tsul 'Kalu†. They had also a Deluge legend which included a ship of refuge in which the ancestors of the race escaped from the great waters.

Cherubim Biblical equivalent of the Assyrian Kherebu†.

Cheyenne Indian Creation Legend The Great Medicine created the earth, the animals, and then humans. There were three kinds of men, hairy men, white men, and red men, and they lived in a land where it was always spring, but later the red men left this earthly paradise.

Chhih-yu In Chinese mythology the inventor of war and weapons, the son of Shen-nung†. He was depicted as being ox-headed, with horns, a forehead of bronze and a skull of iron.

Chia Moon goddess of the Muyscaya (Chibcha) Indians. In their creation myth she was once supposed to have flooded the whole world.

Chibcha Indian Creation Legend Details of this Creation Legend are given under Muyscayas†.

Chicomecoatl Aztec maize goddess dating from Middle Culture times known as 'Seven Snakes'. She was probably of Toltec origin and has been equated with Tonacacihuatl†.

Chicomoztoc In the Aztec† Creation Legend the first of their race emerged from Chicomoztoc, the Cavern of the Seven Chambers, the place of refuge of the race during some period of natural disaster, possibly situated in Aztlan† or alternatively somewhere to the north of Mexico. In the first case this would fit in with the story of their departure by boat for Mexico, bringing with them their chief god Huitzilopochtli†. Whether the seven cities of Cibola† can be integrated into this picture is not clear. It seems possible that Mictlan†, the Aztec Hades, was derived from this, while the Tulan Zuiva† of the Quiches† may well be the same place.

Children of Don In British Celtic myth the equivalent of the Tuatha Dé Danann†.

Chimalmat In the Quiche Creation Legend as told in the Popul Vuh she was the wife of Vukub-Caquix†, a giant, and the mother of two sons, Zipacná† and Cabraca† 'Earth Heaper' and 'Earthquake'.

Chimini-Pagus In the Creation Legend of the Muyscayas and Chibchas light, which existed before all things, was brought to earth in a casket called Chimini-Pagus from which blackbirds distributed the shining matter in their beaks. An alternative spelling is Chiminigagua.

Chinese Creation Legend From primeval chaos matter was formed which eventually divided into Yang† and Yin†, the male and female principles. From these arose Pan-Ku†, a giant†, from whose body the world and our solar system were composed.

Shang-Ti† and Tien†, the heaven gods, appear to have been imported from northern China about 2000 B.C. Their relationship to the Creation is purely abstract. The Deluge myth of

Kung-Kung† tells how he caused the Deluge by butting down the pillars of heaven with his head, thereby causing the collapse of the firmament.

Other references to Chinese myths are to be found under Boat† of the Soul, Chung-Yung†, Chun-Tsiu†, Confucianism†, Dragons†, Enlightener† of the Darkness, Hou-Chi†, How-Too†, Hsi Wang-Mu†, Hsi-Yu-Chi†, Kuan-Ti†, Kuan-Yin†, Kung-Kung†, Kwei†, Li-Ki†, Lun-Yu†, Meng-Tsze†, Miao Yachio†, Pan-Ku†, Puhsien†, Sakyamuni†, Shang-Ti†, Shen-nung†, Shi-King†, Shu-King†, Sien-Tsan†, Sun Houtzu†, Ta-Hsuch†, Taoism†, Tien†, Tou Mu†, Tripitaka†, Tsin King†, Wen Tschang†, Yang†, Yangwu†, Yen-Wang†, Yih-King†, Yin†, Yuh-Hwang-Shangte†.

Chinook Indian Creation Legend The Chinook Indians, who were also known as the 'Flat Heads' because of their extensive practice of artificial cranial deformation, have a creation myth in which Italapas†, or Coyote†, drove the waters of the Deluge away from the prairies and enabled mankind to start life anew. There are also stories resembling the Popul Vuh† dealing with the adventures of Blue-Jay† and his sister Ioi†. Memories of some cosmic catastrophe are found in the story of Aqas-Xena-Xenas†.

Chinvat Peretu In Zoroastrian myth the bridge over the abyss which the souls of the dead had to cross. For the good it was broad and pleasant; for the wicked it was narrow and impassable: with the result that they fell into the clutches of the demons waiting beneath. The name means 'Bridge of the Gatherer' and it resembles the Islamic Sirat†.

Chiriguano Indian Creation Legend
This tribe of Indians of south-eastern Bolivia have a legend that after the Deluge receded a great expanse of fetid mud covered the earth. The survivors were two children who had floated to safety on a raft.

Chnoumis (Khnoumis) Alternative spelling for Khnemu†, the ram-headed creator potter god of Egyptian myth.

Choctaw Indian Creation Legend The myth of this tribe is related under Creek† Indian Creation Legend.

Chousorus Child of Oulomos in the Phoenician† Creation Legend of Mochus.

Chu-jung The Chinese spirit of fire.

Chung-kuei The Chinese god of examinations. He was also revered by travellers as protector against the evil spirits – *kuei* – who haunt the roads.

Chung-Yung The eighth of the nine authoritative works on Confucianism†. The name means 'Doctrine of the Mean'; it is in fact chapter xxxi of the Li-Ki† and with its commentary is regarded as the most complete account of Confucian philosophy, and is said to have been done by the grandson of the Master himself. The preceding work is the Ta-Hsuch† and the following work is the Meng-Tsze†.

Chun-Tsiu The fourth of the nine authoritative works on Confucianism†. The name means 'Spring and Autumn', and the work itself, which is a history of the Chinese state of Lu from 772 B.C. to 484 B.C., is usually regarded as having been written by Confucius himself. The style, however, is rather that of the Anglo-Saxon Chronicle, a sequence of factual statements of events. The preceding work is the Shi-King†, the following work is the Li-Ki†.

Churinga A name given to sacred tablets of wood or stone containing the souls of members of Australian† tribes. After death these tablets are hidden in trees or clefts until such time as a suitable mother for the reincarnation of the soul appears in the vicinity when the soul leaves the tablet and follows her to her home.

Churning of the Ocean In Vedic myth the Churning of the Ocean, which is described under Kurma†, is a peculiar mixture of a Deluge legend, a cosmic diaster, an early sea battle with the Asuras†, and the treasures which the Vedic tribes had as their legendary heritage.

Cian In Celtic myth the son of Dianchecht†, the husband of Ethne† and the father of Lugh†, the leader of the Tuatha Dé Danann† against the Fomors†. He was murdered by the three sons of Tuirenn†, and as a penance they had to bring to Lugh the eight wonders of the Celtic world, which became the treasures† of the Tuatha. He may be equated with MacKinely†. Comparative pedigrees are given under Lleu†.

Cibola, The Seven Cities of Legendary cities from which the first Aztecs† originated. It is possible these may be the same as Chicomoztoc†.

Cihuacoatl Aztec mother goddess ruling over childbirth known as 'Serpent Woman'. She was also styled Tonantzin†, meaning 'Our Mother'. She was the mother of Mixcoatl†.

Cihuatetee In Aztec† myth these goddesses were the spirits of women who had died in childbirth and who lurked at cross-roads inflicting evil on passers by. Originally they would appear to have been priestesses of one or other of the fertility cults whose transformation into forces of evil may have taken place at the time of some religious change.

Cinteotl Aztec maize god, the son of Tlazolteotl† and the husband of Xochiquetzal†. He is probably the same as the Mayan God 'E'†. In his earlier stages he may have been a maize goddess. He was the lord of the fourth hour of the night.

Citaltonac Another name for Ometecuhtli†.

Citlalinicue 'Star Garment'. Secondary name of Omecihuatl† or Ilamatecuhtli†, ancient Aztec fertility goddess.

Clíodna An Irish fairy queen whose centre of activity was Carraig Clíodna in Cork.

Cluricane In Celtic myth an Irish elf of evil disposition, noted for his knowledge of hidden treasure; he generally assumed the appearance of a wrinkled old man. An alternative spelling is Cluricaune.

Coatlicue Aztec earth goddess known as 'Serpent Skirt' who was associated with spring sowing festivals. She was the mother by Mixcoatl† of Huitzilopochtli†, the Aztec god of war.

Cocidius A North British Celtic deity equated with Silvanus† the Hunter.

Coem In the Tupi-Guarani† Creation Legend one of three brothers, the others being Hermitten† and Kriment†, who escaped from the Deluge by climbing trees or by hiding in caves.

Coirbre *See* Caipre†.

Cole British name for Camulos†, the Celtic culture hero.

Comanche Indian Creation Legend The myth of this tribe is found under Shoshonean† Indian Creation Legend.

Conchobar In Celtic myth he was the child of Fathach and Nessa† and the brother of Dechtere†. On the death of his father his mother persuaded the then King of Ulster, Fergus†, to allow her son to occupy the throne for a year, at the end of which time the nobles refused to allow Fergus to return. Conchobar married first Medb†, and after she had left him for Ailill† he married her sister Eithne. He appears to have been a wise and successful king. The story of Deirdre† and Naoise†, one of the most tragic of the Celtic love stories, is intimately linked with him.

Confucianism The doctrines of Confucianism are expressed in nine books. Confucius himself was mainly a political and social reformer and his doctrines are in the main rather a system of ethics than a religion. The actual name of Confucius was Kung-Fu-Tsze.

As was the case with Taoism, the ancient cosmological dualistic doctrine of the Yang and the Yin became an important part of the background of Confucianism.

Copacati Inca† lake goddess whose worship was mainly centred round Tiahuanaco†, where she was said to have overthrown temples put up to other gods, or to have submerged them beneath the waters of Lake Titicaca.

Corb In Celtic myth a god of the Fomors†, possibly Iberian.

Corra (or **O'Corra**) The earliest of the legendary Irish voyagers, the others being Brandan† and Maeldune†.

Couvade A ritual custom, common all over the world, whereby after the birth of a child the father takes to bed for ten to twelve days. It has been suggested that this is a form of Geasa†, Tabu, or Novana†, whereby individuals, or even whole tribes, have applied to them the same preclusion and precaution as are imposed on the mother of the (presumably) royal child. An alternative explanation is that the practice is intended to obviate the ritual sacrifice of the firstborn, which formed such an important part of the religious background of many peoples, including the Hebrews. A Basque family living in the south of France practised the couvade as recently as September 1952. *See also* Maiso†.

Coyolxauhqui The name means 'Golden Bells', and she was the moon lady of the Aztec pantheon. Her brother was Tezcatlipoca†.

Coyote A figure common to the culture myths of many of the North American Indian tribes, including the Achomawi, the Aschochimi, the Maidu, the Navajo, the Sia, the Tuleyone, the Yana, the Yokut, etc. He is usually depicted as being cunning and resourceful, mischievous and malicious, and corresponds to some extent to the Loki† of Nordic myth. In the Tuleyone Creation Legend,

however, he appears as Olle, the saviour of the world, his part as the agent of destruction having been taken by Sahte. He resembles the Blue-Jay† of the Chinooks, and the Cagn† or Kaggen of the African bushmen.

Craosa In Zoroastrian myth the good opponent of Aeshma†, the spirit of wrath. Alternative spellings art Craosha and Sraosha†.

Credne (**Creidhne**) The bronze worker, a culture hero of the Tuatha Dé Danann who, together with Goibniu† and Luchtaine†, made the weapons with which the Fomors† were defeated.

Cree Indian Creation Legend This tribe of Knistenaux Indians of North America have a myth that the flesh of the generations which perished in the waters of the Deluge was changed into the deposits of red clay which were found after the waters had subsided.

Creek Indian Creation Legend The Creation Legend of this tribe, which was common to other members of the Muskhogean family such as the Choctaws and the Seminoles, begins with the Sea of Waters after the Deluge out of which arose gradually a great mountain, Nunne Chaha†, on which Esaugetuh Emisee† resided. As the waters receded he moulded mankind out of clay and when this had dried in the sun it became endowed with life. These were the ancestors of the tribe. This is an interesting variant of the usual North American Deluge legend as there is no question of the waters having been preceded by a great fire. It is possible that this particular tribe originated in an area different to that of the majority of their neighbours.

Creirwy In Celtic myth the daughter of Ceridwen† and sister of Avagdu†.

Cronos *See* Kronos†.

Crow Indian Creation Legend In the beginning all was water and the Old Man created the world from the mud which emerged from the waters, and afterwards he created a living couple who were the ancestors of the tribe.

Cu In Celtic myth the son of Dianchecht†, the Celtic god of medicine, brother of Cethe† and Cian†.

Cú Chulainn In Celtic myth one of the greatest heroes of the Ultonian Cycles. His mother was Dechtere†, the sister of King Conchobar† of Ulster. The accounts of his youth have a certain resemblance to that of Hercules but this is in all probability due to the tendency of unrelated myths to attach themselves to the persons of great men. He was the great enemy of Ailill† and Medb†, the rulers of Connaught, with whom he was constantly at war. On one occasion on the battlefield he saved Conchobar from death. On one of his expeditions he stole the magic cauldron of Mider† with the aid of Blathnad†, his daughter. He was eventually slain by the King of Leinster.

Culhwch The story of Culhwch and Olwen tells how Arthur† and his retinue hunted a magic and venomous boar called Twrch Trwyd through parts of Ireland, South Wales and Cornwall, and has many echoes of the Irish story of Finn†.

Culture Hero It should be noted that while it is quite possible for culture heroes to become gods it is rare that gods become culture heroes. The reason for this is that most gods appear to have started as abstract conceptions and their relationship with mankind was limited to the personalities of the priest or priestess who became identified with the god. The process of deification of the culture hero is relatively common and tends to occur even nowadays with outstanding personalities. It is akin to that of ancestor worship†.

Cú Roí In full his name is Cú Roí mac Dáiri. After the defeat of the Tuatha Dé Danann† he was killed by Cú Chulainn† thanks to the treachery of his wife Bláthnad†.

Cyhiraeth A Celtic goddess of streams who degenerated into a spectre haunting woodland brooks and whose shriek foretold death.

Czarnobog In Slavonic myth the black god as opposed to Bielbog†, the white god. This dualistic system of organizing the heavens appears to have originated in Persia before the Great Migration. His name was also spelt Zcernoboch†.

D

God 'D' A moon god of the Mayas, he may possibly be equated with Kukulcan†—Quetzalcoatl†. He may represent the endless cycles of death and rebirth.

Da-Bog (Dabog) Slavonic sun god, also known as the Son of Svarog†. The name is composed of the words Dazh meaning 'give', and Bog meaning 'god'. He was one of the group of gods whose statues stood in the castle of Kiev. The other three gods with whom he was associated were Khors†, Peroun†, and Stribog†. His idols were of wood with a silver head and a golden moustache. It is of interest to note that in Serbia he had been degraded to the rank of demon. Alternative spellings were Dajdbog†, Dazhbog†.

Daeva *See* Deva†.

Dagan An early Assyrian and Babylonian god who ranked with Anu† as one of the chief deities. He has been confused with Dagon† the son of Ouranos and Gea of Phoenician myth.

Dagda (Daghdha) In Celtic myth Dagda was a king of the Tuatha Dé Danann†, the husband of Boann† and the father of Angus†, Brigit†, Mider†, and Ogma† . He was a successful campaigner against the Formors† and may be described as an agrarian leader. His magic cauldron known as Undry later became one of the treasures of the Tuatha.

Dagon (Dagan) *1.* One of the gods of the Phoenician Creation Legend of Philo Byblos, child of Ouranos and Gea. He was known as Baal† Dagon, or Siton, and although related to the Ouranos group, later acquired a maritime character. In spite of the fact that Philo considered him to be a corn god, the description in 1 Samuel v. 4, and the Graeco-Roman coins found at Abydos, would indicate that he was related to the Chaldean fish god Oannes†. He was also the Baal of Arvad.

2. In the Ugarit epics Ben Dagon, son of the above, fought on the side of Baal against El†.

Daikoku The Japanese god of wealth, who is usually depicted as armed with a magical hammer bearing the sign of the male and female spirit, thereby showing that he was a pre-Buddhist creative deity. His manifestation was a rat, which is often depicted as playing with the hammer. Once the Buddhist gods sent Shiro to get rid of him, but the rat drove Shiro away with a branch of holly. He was the father of Ebisu†, the god of labour, and was one of the seven divinities of luck, the Shichi Fukujin†.

Dainichi The personification of purity and wisdom, one of the great Buddhist trinity of Japan. By some authorities he is identified with Fudo†.

Dainn In Nordic myth one of the

51

dwarfs† and also one of the harts that ate the buds of Yggdrasil†. The others were Davalin†, Duneyr, and Durathror.

Daityas In Vedic myth the Titans who fought against the gods. They were the sons of Diti†. It is told that at the Churning of the Ocean they endeavoured to seize the ambrosia of the gods but were defeated and fled to Patala. In reality they appear to have been the culture heroes of the races who were defeated by the Vedic invaders in their conquest of India. The descriptions of fights would therefore have been related to actual battles. They are one of the tribes of the Asuras†, who were defeated by Indra†. Haya-Griva†, the villain of an early Deluge legend, was a Daitya, as was also Hiranyaksha†.

Dajdbog In Slavonic myth a variant of Da-Bog†.

Dakota Indians The two principal figures in Dakota myth are Untunktahe†, the water god, and Waukheon†, the thunder bird.

Daksha In Vedic myth one of the early gods who eventually became subordinated to Siva†. Daksha was an Aditya†, a Prajapati†, and a Rishi†. He was the father of Uma†, the wife of Siva, and Diti†, the wife of Kasyapa†. There was a great quarrel between Daksha and his son-in-law, during which Siva, infuriated at not being invited to a great sacrifice which Daksha had organized, sent a monster, Vira-bhadra†, which cut off the head of Daksha. Subsequently the parties were reconciled but it was only possible for Daksha to be given a goat's head in place of his own. This story was originally told of Rudra†. His

twenty-seven daughters were brides of Chandra†.

Dalhan In Islamic myth a ferocious species of cannibal jinn†, living on desert islands, and feeding on shipwrecked sailors. Is usually seen as a man riding on a camel.

Damara Creation Legend This South African tribe believed that the progenitor of men and cattle was Omumborombonga†.

Damkina Pre-diluvial Babylonian goddess, wife of El† and mother of Marduk†. Sometimes known as Ninella or Damku†.

Damku Alternative form of Damkina†.

Damona The goddess of a Celtic tribe. She is 'The Divine Cow', and the consort of Bormanus†.

Danavas In Vedic myth they were descendants from Danu† by the sage Kasyapa†, giants who fought against the gods.

Danh Snake god of the fetish worshippers of Benin†.

Danu *1.* Culture heroine of the Tuatha Dé Danann†, sister of King Math† and mother of Gwydion†, Amathaon†, and Arianrhod†. Her husband was Bile†, but she was also known as Dôn†, the wife of Beli†. The pedigree of her descendants is given under Lleu†. She was also known as Anu†.
2. An Indian serpent god, also known as Kabandha†.

Daramulun In Australian myth a culture hero of the distant past now become one of the sources from which medicine men draw supernatural power. This power may be used to take the lives of their enemies or to enable them to fly through the air, even to the land of ghosts, the sky land. He is of a similar type to Baiamet, Bunjilt, Nurrunderet, and Ngurunderit.

Darawigal In Australian myth the force of evil as opposed to Baiamet, the force of good.

Dar el-Jannah The Islamic paradise, divided into eight stages: Jannatu el-Khuldt, the Garden of Eternity; Daru el-Salamt, the Dwelling of Peace; Daru el-Qarart, the Dwelling which Abideth; Jannatu el-'Adnt, the Gardens of Eden; Jannatu el-Ma'wat, the Gardens of Refuge; Jannatu el-Na'imt, the Gardens of Delight; Illiyunt; Jannatu el-Firdaust, the Gardens of Paradise.

Daru el-Bawar Islamic hell, or abode of perdition, divided into seven stages: Jahannamt, Lazat, Hutamaht, Sa'irt, Saqart, Jahimt, Hawiyaht. The seven stages of hell were borrowed from the Jews and the Magians, and were later to be encountered in the works of Dante.

Daru el-Qarar Third stage of Islamic paradise, Dar el-Jannaht, the Dwelling which Abideth, symbolized by green chrysolite.

Daru el-Salam The Dwelling of Peace, or second stage of Dar el-Jannaht, the Islamic paradise, symbolized by white pearls.

Dasan In the Pomot Indian Creation Legend he and his father Makilat, lead-

ers of a bird clan, came over from the waters and brought civilization with them.

Dasyus In Vedic myth one of the races of the Asurast who were defeated by Indrat. They appear to have been a dark-skinned Aboriginal people. Later their name was given to the fourth non-Aryan caste.

Dauce Parent with Aust of Belust in the Babyloniant Creation Legend of Damascius.

Davalin In Nordic myth a dwarft who is father of one or more of the Nornst. The name is that of one of the four harts which ate the buds of Yggdrasilt, and may indicate that they were the original guardians of the sacred tree. The others were Daint, Durathror, and Duneyr.

Dazh-Bog In Slavonic myth a variant of Da-Bogt.

Dechtere (Deichtine) Sister of Conchobart and mother of Cú Chulainnt in Celtic myth.

Ded In Egyptian myth a symbol of Osirist. In the Ani papyrus it is represented as a pillar with cross-pieces, with human arms holding the flail and the crook – the emblems of sovereignty. It is thought to represent the backbone or skeleton of Osiris returned to life, in which case the horizontal cross-pieces may be ribs. An alternative assumption is that it represents the tree trunk in which the body of Osiris was hidden by Isist. It was, after the eye of Horust, the most popular amulet in Egypt. Alternative spellings are Tatt and Tett.

Dedun A Nubian god worshipped in Egypt. His Greek name was Arsnuphist†.

Deirdre In Celtic myth she was the beautiful daughter of one of the bards at the court of Ulster, of whom it was said that she would grow up to be the most lovely woman in the world but that she would bring death to many and much sorrow to Ulster. Conchobar†, the King of Ulster, hid her away, intending to make her his wife, but before he could do this she ran away with Naoise†. Later, after many adventures, they were permitted to return to Ulster, but were treacherously attacked, Naoise and his two brothers being killed. Deirdre died of grief a few hours later.

Dekans A group of thirty-six Egyptian war gods having their temple in Heliopolis.

Deluge Myths These will be found under the Creation Legends of the appropriate mythic or racial groups.

Demares The same as Zeus† Demares in the Phoenician† Creation Legend.

Deng A Dinka deity, held by some traditions to be the father of this Sudanese people, but by others a god of lightning and thunder, thus bringing rain and, ultimately, fertility.

Desire In the Phoenician† Creation Legend the same as Potos†.

Deva The word Deva or Daeva has different values in the various religions of the East. In the Vedas it means any of the gods; in the Zend-Avesta† it means an evil spirit, while in Buddhism it may mean hero or goblin. The reason for this is that the original value of the word was preserved in the Vedas, but by the time it had become incorporated in the Zend-Avesta it had become degraded by the process of Dualism. The Zoroastrians declared: 'I cease to be a worshipper of the Devas'; in Buddhism the religion had grown so far away from the ancient gods that they were no longer of import either for good or for evil.

Devaki In Vedic myth wife of Vasudeva† and mother of Krishna†.

Dhanus In Vedic myth the Bow of Victory, which was produced at the Churning of the Ocean† in the Kurma† avatar.

Dhanvantari In Vedic myth the physician of the gods and, possibly, the inventor of Amrita, the ambrosia of the gods. He was produced at the Churning of the Ocean in the Kurma† avatar. Alternative spelling Dhanwantari.

Dhatri In Vedic myth one of the twelve Adityas† or guardians of the months of the year. He must have been an early post-catastrophe god, as he was said to have 'formed the sun, moon, sky, earth, air, and heaven as before.' Later he became a minor deity concerned with healing and domestic felicity.

Di *See* Shang-di†.

Dianchech (**Dian Cécht**) The Celtic father of medicine, father of Etan, Cian, Cethe, Cu, Miach, and Airmid†. At the battle of Mag Tuireadh he bathed the wounded in a stream with healing properties.

Diarmait (Diarmaid) In Celtic myth the lover of Gráinne†, the betrothed of Finn†, by whom he was subsequently allowed to die, in spite of the efforts of Angus† to save him. His full name is Diarmait na Duibhne.

Dilmun Site of Sumerian paradise, residence of Ziusudra†.

Dings (Mars Thingsus) Teutonic name for Tiwaz† or Tyr†. The word means thing or popular assembly over which the god was lord. It may therefore be linked with Forseti†. From this comes *Dienstag*, the German for Tuesday. He was the regimental god of Frisian troops stationed on the Roman Wall.

Dirona Alternative spelling for Sirona†, the Celtic goddess.

Dis Caesar called the transcendent god among the Celts 'Dis', but it is difficult at present to determine exactly what god or goddess regarded as the racial ancestor of the Gauls was thus referred to.

Disir Strictly speaking a collective term for goddesses, or merely supernatural female beings in Norse mythology. The Norns† and the Valkyries† come within its scope, and Freyja†, as Vanadis†, was 'Dis of the Vanir'†.

Diti In Vedic myth the daughter of Daksha†, the wife of Kasyapa†, the mother of the Daityas†, and also of the Maruts†. Originally she was akin to Aditi† and represented illimitable space. She desired to have a son who would have power to slay Indra†; certain conditions of piety and purity were imposed on her in order that her wish might be fulfilled; she failed in one item of ceremonial purity, whereupon Indra† divided the embryo in her womb, and created the Maruts from the several portions.

Djehuti In Egyptian myth one of the names of Thoth†.

Djin Generic term for woodland, lake†, and mountain spirits in Serbia and Albania. The use of the Arabic term was due to Turkish influence. The Djin of Riyetchki Kom, near the northern side of the lake of Skutar, surrounded any passer-by who touched even a leaf in the green woods on the mountain-side with a dense fog in which terrifying visions were beheld. This story is presumably linked with local atmospheric conditions. In pre-Islamic myth it is an alternative spelling for jinn†.

Djudi In Islamic myth the landing place of Noah (Koran, Sura xi, 46). Mohammed placed this in Arabia, but later writers agree that it was in Armenia. It is also spelt Judi†. Other details are given under Babylonian† Creation Legends.

Domnu Goddess of the Fomors† in Celtic myth. The original name of the Fomors would appear to have been the Fir Domnann, or the people whose goddess was Domnu, a name which Rhys reports as linking with two peoples of Roman Britain situated on the Severn and on the Forth. She was the mother of King Indech†.

Dôn In Celtic myth the wife of Beli†, who may be said to be the same as Danu† the wife of Bile† and Ceithlenn† the wife of Balor†. The pedigree of her descendants is shown under Lleu†.

Donar The thunder god of the Teutons. He was of inferior status to Woden†. He was strong, brutal, and simple-minded, in all essentials a god of the peasants rather than of the warriors. He was akin to Thor†. To the Anglo-Saxons he was known as Thunar or Thunor†.

Dongo A celestial spirit revered by the Songhay people of the upper Niger. When he threw his axe there was a lightning flash and some men on earth were killed. His grandfather told him to fill his mouth with water and spray it over the men, and they would be revived. Dongo told the human beings that the men had originally died because no one had praised him. He then taught them a prayer spell that would avert danger when there were future storms.

Dontso In Navajo† myth a name given to the messenger fly.

Dragons In Chinese myth dragons play an important part. Before the advent of Buddhism they were mainly beneficent producers of rain or representatives of the Yang† principle. Imperial dragons had five claws on each foot, other dragons four only. There are five sea dragon kings who are all immortal, and many others concerned with inland rivers and lakes. Another dragon myth is given under Enlightenment† of the Darkness.

Draupnir In Nordic myth the magic ring of Odin†, one of the treasures of the Aesir†. It was originally obtained by Loki† from Andvari† the rock dwarf. The fact that Draupnir was also the name of another rock dwarf shows some confusion; perhaps it may be the name of the original maker. It was placed by

Odin on the pyre of Balder† and multiplied itself daily for several days.

Druids The word Druid, which occurs so frequently in Welsh myth, may possibly come from 'derroydd' or 'oak seer' and may also be related to the Fathi† of the Irish Celts. At this stage it is somewhat difficult to determine the main features of the Druidical religion, but it would appear that the Druids themselves, who may have been of pre-Celtic origin, occupied a position similar to that of the Magi†. While all the excesses attributed to them by the Romans may not be true, there seems to be no reason for assuming that their religious practices were any milder than those of their contemporaries. The cutting of the mistletoe from the oak would appear to commemorate the emasculation of the old king by his successor. References to them in classical literature include Tacitus, Diogenes Laertius, and Sotion of Alexandria.

Druj Nasu A corpse demon in Iranian mythology who personifies the spirit of contagion and impurity, corruption and decomposition.

Dua In Egyptian myth a god whose name means Today. He also washes and shaves the King.

Dualism This conception of religion, where the power of good was balanced by the power of evil, may have required a long period of gestation before it finally became established. Its beginnings may be linked with the custom of degrading gods of conquered peoples by calling them the powers of evil and setting against them the gods of the victors as powers of good. It may also be linked with the supersession of the mother goddesses by the father gods, and the attempt to degrade them to the status of witches or evil spirits as with Allat†. Other references to Dualism are to be found under Ahriman†, Bielbog†, Black Magic†, In† and Yo†, Keji-Ki†, Mithraism†, Taoism†, Yang† and Yin†, and Zoroastrian†.

Duamutef In Egyptian myth one of the four divine sons of Horus†. Guardian of the East and Canopic protector of the stomach. The others were Amset†, Hapi†, and Qebhsneuf†. The name means 'Praiser of his Mother.'

Duat Egyptian abode of the dead, referred to as Amenti† and Tuat†.

Dulachan In Celtic myth a malicious elf† or goblin† of foreign origin resembling the cluricanes†.

Dumuzi *See* Tammuz†.

Dup Shimati The Tablet of Destinies, similar to the 'Preserved Tablet' of the Koran (Sura x. 62), held by Tiamat† in the Babylonian† Creation Legend.

Durga (Durgha) In Vedic myth a name given to Parvati†, wife of Siva†, in her aspect as Kali†. The name is that of the giant whose decapitated head she bears in her hand.

Du'uzu The fourth month of the Babylonian year (June), named after Tammuz†.

Duzzakh The purgatory of the Zoroastrians, a place where the Devas might seize the soul of the sinner and plunge it into cleansing flames, which would,

eventually, free it from Ahriman† the leader of the evil ones.

Dwapara In the Hindu† Creation Legend the third of the four Yugas† of the current Mahayugas†, having a length of 2,400 divine years.

Dwarfs in Celtic, Teutonic, Slav, and Vedic Myth The role played by dwarfs in the myths of these races is considerably less important than with the Nordic races. Below are given some of the more oustanding names:
  Celtic: Gavida†, Goibniu†, Govannon†, Leprechaun†, Luchorpan†, Luchtaine†.
  Teutonic: Kobold†.
  Slav: Karliki†, Ljeschi†, Lychie†.
  Vedic: Tavashtri†, Vamana†.

Dwarfs in Nordic Myth In Nordic myth the dwarfs play a very important part in that they are the artificers, the craftsmen, and the inventors. Both the Aesir† and the Vanir† appear to have maintained amicable relations with the dwarfs, and in return for this they made such things as Brisingamen†, the necklace of Freyja; Draupnir†, the ring of Odin†; Gungnir†, the sword of Odin; Hringhorn†, the ship of Balder†, and Skidbladnir†, the ship of Freyr†; and the wig of Sif†. Many of these are included in the list of treasures†. In practice the dwarfs appear in the same relationship to the Scandinavians as to the Celts and the Slavs and there seems but little doubt that they were a short, round-headed central European tribe possessing the art of working in bronze and iron in addition to precious metals. In the following is given a list of the more important dwarfs mentioned in the Eddas†: Ai, Alfar†, Alfreikr (elf king

Albericht), Althjofr, Alvisst, An, Andvarit, Annar, Austri, Baumbur, Bavor, Bivor (the Tremulous), Dainnt, Davalint, Dolgthasir, Dori, Draupnirt, Dufr, Duneyr, Durathror, Durinn, Eikinskjaudi, Fili, Fith, Fjalart, Frosti, Fundin, Galart, Gandalfr, Ginnar, Gloinn, Harrt, Hepti, Hljodalfr, Hogstari, Ivaldi, Kili, Liturt, Mjodvitnir, Moin, Naglfart, Nain, Nali, Nar, Nibelung, Nipingr, Nordri, Nori, Norori, Nyi, Nyr, Nyradr, Oinn, Ori, Radsvithr, Regint, Sjarr, Skandar, Skirvir, Sudri, Thekkrt, Thorinn, Thrort, Throrinn, Veigur, Vestri, Vindalfr, Virvir, Vithur, Yingi.

Certain of these names are also names of Odin, thereby showing the close relationship between the Aesir and the dwarfs. Further details will be found under Alfheimt, Elvest, Fayst, Lovart, Yggdrasilt, etc.

Dwyvan and Dwyvach In the Celtict creation myth the man and woman who built Nefyed Nav Neviont, the Welsh Ark, in which with an assortment of animals, they escaped from the deluge caused by the Addanct, a monster who dwelt by Llyon-Lliont, the Lake of the Waves. This legend is pre-Celtic but has suffered from Christian additions.

Dyaush-Pitir Primitive Aryan sky father who may be equated with Zeus and Jupiter although the adventures of both

of them clearly belong to the history of the Mediterranean Sea. By the time the Vedast were written Dyaush had already receded into the background. It is possible that Dyaush-Pitir may originally have been a sun-mother goddess. Alternative spelling is Dyaus-pitri.

Dyavo In Slavonic myth the demons of Serbia, in whom it is just possible to recognize the Devast of the Vedic and Zoroastrian myths.

Dylan In Celtic myth a sea god, the brother of Lleut. As soon as he was born he was said to have plunged into the sea and swum like a fish, and accordingly was called Eilton (Eil Don)t, or son of the wave. The word *dile* is an old Irish term for flood, while, according to Wormius, Endilt was another name for him as a sea god. Dylan was eventually slain by Govannont, whose relationship to him seems to have been purely mythological, Dylan being a chief of the Celtic invaders from the sea, and Govannon being an artificer, possibly a dwarf and a member of the pre-Celtic clans of Britain. His daughter was Vivianet.

Dyrnwyn The sword of Rhyddereh Hael. *See* Treasurest.

Dyu In Vedic myth the word means heaven, and may have some affinity with Dyausht.

E

God 'E' Mayan maize god who is probably the same as the Aztec Cinteotl†. His head-dress is an ear of corn and he may be either Ghanan† or Yum Kaax†.

Ea Ea, who was known as Nudimmud†, or Nidim, was the first of the Babylonian new order of gods, as opposed to Tiamat†, Apsu†, and Mommu†, in the Babylonian Creation Legend. Ea, as the champion of purity, fought and defeated Apsu and Mommu by the utterance of a powerful spell. He then divided Apsu, who was his mother and whose name means 'the Fresh Water Sea', into chambers and made a resting place for himself. Later, when Tiamat assembled the forces of evil to avenge the death of Apsu, Ea called in the aid of Anshar†, who appointed Marduk† as champion of the new gods. From the blood of Kingu†, the defeated leader, he created mankind. Ea was the water god of Eridu, and also the god of wisdom whose jealousy deprived humanity of eternal life. He was third of the Great Triad of Gods with Anu† and Enlil†. One of his daughters was Nina. He is the same as the Sumerian Enki†.

Ear One of a series of names given in south Germany to Tiwaz or Tyr†.

Easter Island Creation Legend The earliest myths of Easter Island refer to struggle for supremacy between the 'Big Ears' and the 'Small Ears'. It is not now possible to say where the 'Big Ear' people, the prototype of the statues, came from; but there are elements of Melanesian culture which appear to be similar. The colossal stone statues of long-eared people wearing pumice-stone hats have long been a mystery to archaeologists; they possibly represented a link with some vanished culture of the Pacific. Unfortunately it has not been possible to decipher the petroglyphs or to interpret the drawings of birds and birdmen, which seem to relate to some unusual form of worship. The native name for Easter Island is Rapanui†. They had a creator god, Meke Meke†, who may have been Tangaroa†, the Polynesian god.

Ebisu Japanese god of labour, the son of Daikoku†. He is usually depicted with a fishing rod, and a fish under his arm, and may originally have been a god of the fishermen's clan. He was one of the seven divinities of luck, the Shichi Fukujin†.

Eblis *See* Iblis†.

Edaín A Celtic goddess whose full title is Edaín Echraidhe, where the second half means horse-riding. This aspect implies a parallel with the Gaulish Epona†, who enjoyed a particular popularity among the Roman cavalry.

Eda Male Twin idols, male and female,

used by the Ogoboni tribe of the Yorubas† in their initiation ceremonies.

Eddas The Eddas, the source books of Nordic myths, have come to us mainly in three texts. The oldest of these is the Elder Edda or Codex Regius, considered to have been drawn up by the Icelandic historian Saemund about the year 1090. The next is a Christianized version by Saxo Grammaticus written in 1190 and included in the Gesta Danorum. Unfortunately this version has been so modified in accordance with the existing religious sentiments as to be almost valueless. The third and last version is the Prose Edda drawn up by Snorri Sturlason in 1220. The vast majority of the stories and myths of the Scandinavians have come to us from the Elder and the Prose Eddas. The fact that both these codices were discovered in Iceland seems to prove that the disintegrating impact of Christianity only reached that country after the legends had been reduced to writing, and was therefore too late to be fully effective. The stories of the Eddas are independent of the great body of Celtic myth, although there are certain points, particularly in the treasures†, where they tend to overlap. They bear the impression of the early struggles of at least four racial groups involved in the development of the Northlands. These were the giants†, whom we take to be the first hyperborean inhabitants (the Frost Giants may have been the heroes of the Kalevala† and the Hero of Estonia†), and the dwarfs†, who were eventually dominated by a combination of two invading groups, the Vanir† and the Aesir†. In a similar manner to the Celts the Norsemen appear to have been incapable of working metals and were forced to rely upon the services of the dwarfs†, who may be considered to be a tribe of short, sturdy, Central European stock specializing in metal working and other crafts. An aphabetical list of the works included in the Elder and the Prose Eddas is given below. Details about them will be found under the appropriate headings.

Aegisdrekka or Lokasenna (Aegir's† Carousal or the Taunting of Loki†); Alvis-Mal (The Lay of Alviss†); *Braga Raedur (The Conversations of Bragi†); *Eptirmati; Fjol Svinnsmal; *Formali; Grimis-Mal (The Lay of Grimnir†); The Magic Lay of Groa-Galdur; *Gylfa-Ginning (The Deluding of Gylfi†); Harbards-Ljod (Lay of Harbard†) * Hattatal†; Havamal†; Hrafna'Galdur† Odins (Odin's Raven Spell); Hymiskvida (Lay of Hymir†); Hyndlu-Ljod (The Chant of Hyndla†); Rigs-Thula (The Lay of Rig†); *Skaldskaparmal†; Skirnis-For (Skirnir's Quest†); Solar-Ljod†; Thryms-Kvida (The Lay of Thrym†); Vafthrudnis-Kvida, Vafthrudnismal (The Lay of Vafthrudnir†); Vegtams-Kvida (The Lay of Vegtam†); Volsung† Cycle; Völundar-Kvida (The Lay of Völund†); Völuspa†.

The Chant of Hyndla and the shorter version of the Völuspa are in the Flatey Book†. The Yngling Saga† and the Yngling Atal† are not included in the Eddas.

N.B. Titles marked * are in the Prose Edda.

Efé First man among the mythology of the Pygmies of Africa, who was taken back into heaven by the supreme being as a hunter, but eventually returned to earth bringing spears and other presents to his fellows.

Efrit The second most powerful class of jinn† in pre-Islamic myth.

Egg In the Phoenician† Creation Legend of Philo Byblos, Mot†, the primeval egg, was the child of Wind† and Desire† (Potos).

In the Phoenician Creation Legend of Mochus, the egg was produced by Oulomos† and when broken gave rise to Ouranos† and Gea†.

The Ghaddar† and certain other jinn† are said to have sprung from an egg: this may be a distorted Arabian version of the Creation Legends.

See also Narayana†, Ghaddar†, Egyptian† Creation Legends, Khnemu†.

Egil (Eigil) In Nordic myth the brother of Völund†, who at the court of King Nithud† shot with an arrow an apple off the head of a young boy, a feat later attributed to William Tell. Later he assisted his brother to escape. He was the son of Badi†.

Egyptian Creation Legends There is a great similarity between the Creation Legends of the Nile Valley and those of the Fertile Crescent. In all of them the beginning was a primitive chaotic mass of waters known to the Babylonians as Tamtu†, Tiamat†, or Tiawath†, and to the Hebrews as Tohu† or Tehom†. One would therefore expect the Egyptian chaos monster to have had a name fitting into this common pattern, but instead he is called Nun, or Nu†. However, there is also a primeval god called Atmu†, who is said to have caused the Deluge, from which it would appear that he or she was the original mass of waters, and that at some later date Nun or Nu was installed in this position.

There are several alternative versions of the actual creation process, of which the simplest is that the sun arose from the waters, and that when the light had made a rift between the earth and the sky, four pillars, marking the cardinal points, were erected to hold up the heavens. At Hermopolis, however, Thoth† was the mind and intelligence of Nu, and, with the aid of Khnemu† and Ptah†, created several pairs of gods, including Heru† and Hehut, Kekui† and Kekuit, Qeh and Qerhit, and afterwards the remainder of the universe.

At Sais, Neith†, the self-created virgin goddess, became the mother of Ra†, from whom sprang the gods. At Hermopolis, Khepera†, the scarab beetle god, created Geb† and Nut†, the parents of Osiris† and Isis† and of other gods. At Elephantine it was Khnemu†, the potter god, who created the universe, made the cosmic egg† from the mud of the Nile, and shaped man on his potter's wheel, while at Memphis the same part was played by Ptah†, who in the process of development seems to have absorbed Tenen†, an early creator god.

Contrary to general opinion, there are at least two Egyptian Deluge legends, of which the earliest says that the god Atmu caused the waters of the great deep to overflow and drown everybody, except those who were with him in his boat. This would indicate that when Atmu, as mentioned above, was deposed from the post of god of the mass of waters, he, in turn, took over the functions of the Egyptian Noah or Utanapishti†, whose name may some day be discovered.

The other Deluge legend tells how Ra, being offended with his subjects, ordered Hathor† and Sekhmet†, the fire goddess, to destroy them all. After they had partially completed their work, and were wading in human blood, Ra relented, and, being unable to persuade them to desist, flooded the world with beer, which the goddesses drank to such an extent that they forgot all about their dreadful mission. This rewriting of an early myth of volcanic catastrophe followed by flood is rather different to those of the countries to the north-east, where there are references mainly to floods. There may also be a faint recollection of a flood in the hieroglyph of the Bennu† bird. Also there is Manetho's story of Thoth† setting up the Siriadic Columns†, before the Deluge, in order that the records of the past should not be lost.

Egyptian Religion It is not possible to give more than the briefest outline of Egyptian religion in the space available. The original basis appears to have been the totems of the pre-dynastic tribes, many of which were female, and later became metamorphosed into goddesses and gods. In the earliest stages these birds, beasts, and fishes were recognized for what they were, but later, with the advent of the polytheism which is the sure sign of religions in decay, they all were endowed with the functions of actual gods.

Later came the divine kings, originally perhaps the object of sacrifice, but later to emerge as supreme rulers. The story of the murder of Osiris† is clearly that of the death by sacrifice of a barley king. Such beings as Amt†, Anquet†, Hathor†, Isis†, Maat†, Nephthys†, Ptah†, Set†, and Thoth† may have been kings and queens, priests and priestesses, who were deified after their deaths; while the stories of the fights between the gods are obviously memories of intertribal wars, in which Set, Osiris, Horus†, Isis, and Nephthys were the names of leading personalities involved.

As it is obvious that no human beings were actually present at the Creation, in whatever manner it may have occurred, the Creation Legends of the Egyptians, in common with those of other countries, must be made up of memories of some great disaster from which mankind only emerged with great difficulty, combined with priestly ideas as to what might possibly have occurred in the beginning.

The gradual change of Osiris from being the god of a most depressing nether world into the potential saviour of the soul must have taken a long time, and is intimately linked up with the story of his resurrection by Isis and of his begetting Horus in the interval before he became ruler of the Kingdom of the Dead. The somewhat excessive preoccupation of the Egyptian with the problems of the next world must have been fostered by the dry climate which made mummification relatively easy, and also by the fact that the system of regulated agrarian life left long periods for leisure and contemplation. The trend towards monotheism, which came to its zenith with the worship of Aten†, appears always to have been that of the ruling classes, as the vast bulk of the populace preferred the potential delights of the Osirian paradise to the somewhat impersonal joys of accompanying Ra† in his sun boat.

The problem of life in the after-world is revealed by the number of parts of the body and personality which had to be considered. They were the Khat† or physical body; the Ka† or double; the Ba† or soul; the Khu† or aura; the Khaibit† or shadow; the Sekhem† or vital force; the Ren† or name, the Ab† or will, symbolized as a heart; the Hati† or physical heart; the Sahu† or spirit body; and the Ikh† or final spiritual state.

The Egyptians may take credit for having evolved the first Holy Trinity of Father, Mother, and Child (Osiris, Isis, and the Child Horus), and also for conception of the future life directly related to the moral value of conduct on this earth, and, finally, the first abstract monotheism, in the worship of Aten, in 1375 B.C., which arose at a time when the Hebrews were still struggling in Canaan.

For further details *see* Book of the Dead†, Egyptian† Creation Legends, and references to named goddesses and gods.

Ehecatl Aztec wind god, sometimes equated with Quetzalcoatl†. He may possibly be God 'K'† of the Mayas.

Einherjar In Nordic myth the name given to heroes who fell in battle and who were chosen in the great hall, Sessymir, for admission to Valhalla.

Eir In Nordic myth third of the Asynjor†, noted as a healer.

Eithne In Celtic myth the sister of Medb†, the first wife of Conchobar†. After Medb had left him Eithne became his wife.

Ek Ahau Probably God 'M'† of the Maya.

Ekchuah Black-skinned travellers' deity of the Mayas, particularly concerned with the cacao planters. He is probably God 'L'†.

Ekhi A personification of the sun among the Basques.

Ekhi A variant of Sut† or Set† in Egyptian myth.

El Semitic term for god. When 'El' stands alone, the term means 'God', the supreme being. El lived, not in heaven, but in the region which was 'The source of the rivers', and his title of 'Bull' indicates his significance is a fertility god.

Elagabalus Known also as Heliogabalos, a sun god who was worshipped at Emesa as a variant of Baal†. His image was a black stone.

Elat Semitic goddess, wife of El† and considered to be the same as Asheratian†, the sea goddess. Also akin to Allat†. She would appear to have preceded El by some thousands of years, and to have been the original mother goddess of the Semitic tribes.

Eldhrimer ('Firefrost') Another name for Odherir†, the magic cauldron of the Aesir†, applied to it on the occasion of the boiling of the flesh of the wild boar, in all probability Sachrimnir.

Elephantine Triad Composed of Anquet†, Khnemu†, and Sati†, whose shrines were at Yebu (Elephantine), southern frontier city of Ancient Egypt.

Eleven Mighty Helpers In Babylonian myth they were enrolled by Tiamat† in her fight against Marduk†. They were the Viper, Lakhmu† the Shining Snake, the Great Lion, the Ravening Dog, the Scorpion Man, the Storm Winds, the Fish Man, the Goat Fish. They were armed with the Thunderbolt, the invincible weapon, and commanded by Kingu†.

Elioun In the Phoenician† Creation

Legend of Philo Byblos, one of the first gods, and parent with Beroutht of Gea and Ouranost.

Elivagar In Nordic myth the frozen river of Hvergelmirt, the source of twelve rivers called Elivagar from which came the drops of venom which turned into the giant Ymirt, whose sweat while sleeping engendered the Frost Giantst.

El-Khadir The Old Man of the Sea of Muslim legends and the Arabian Nights. The name is derived from Xisuthrost, which in its turn has been transformed from Hasisatrat. He is greatly venerated in the part of Syria inhabited by the Alaouites (formerly the Nosciris). El-Khadir has many points of resemblance to Elt, the god of the northern Phoenicians, who occupied the land of the Alaouites 3,000 years ago.

Elli In Nordic myth the giant crone of old age with whom Thort wrestled without success, as told in the Lay of Skrymirt.

Elom Name given to the moon by the southern Hebrews. Variants of Elom were Erah, Eterah†, Ilmaqah†, Jerah†, Shahar†, and Terah†.

Elthan (Elatha) A chief of the Fomors† and the father of Bress†, who for a short period became King of Ireland.

Elves In Nordic myth the elves were the dwellers in Alfheim†, the dwelling place of Freyr†. There were also black elves who dwelt in Svartheim†, but whether this differentiation was one of actual complexion as between two of the tribes of dwarfs or whether it was merely a term of derogation applied to those who were not friendly with the Aesir† is not clear. The question is gone into in greater detail in the article on dwarfs†.

Allied with the elves are the brownies†, cluricanes†, the Dulachans†, Fenodyrees†. In Celtic myth Ailill† may be an elf or dwarf†.

Embla In the Nordic Creation Legend the wife of Askr† created out of a tree. The fact that her name was not Eskga, which would have paired with Askr, makes it appear that the combination results from the fusion of two different legends.

Emma-Ō Japanese Buddhist god who was the lord of Yomi, the other world, and who sat in judgment on the dead. Also known as Emma-ten.

Emrys In Celtic myth the city of Dinas Emrys, a name given to Myrddin† or Merlin†. It has been identified as a fortification called Broich y Ddinas on the summit of Penmaen. Emrys is also a Welsh rendering of the late Roman name Ambrosius.

Endil A marine deity of the Celts who may be the same as Dylan†.

Enigorio and Enigohatgea In the Iroquois† Creation Legend these were the twin brothers, Enigorio having been the benign creator of rivers, fertile plans, and fruitful trees, and his brother Enigohatgea endeavouring to neutralize all these activities by the creation of deserts, harmful plants, and natural catastrophes. They are the equivalent of Tsentsa† and Tawiscara† in the Huron† Creation Legends.

Enki Babylonian god of fresh water and god of wisdom and magic. He is the same as Ea†.

Enkidu He was companion of Gilgamesh† and enemy of Humbaba†.

Enlightener of the Darkness In Chinese† myth we are told that this dragon† produces light by opening his eyes and causes darkness by shutting them. His serpent-like body is a thousand miles long and of a filthy colour. He never rests and his breath causes wind and cold weather. He can assume nine colours and his breath descends as a rain of water or fire. Gold is the congealed breath of white dragons, crystal the spittle of purple dragons, and glass solidified dragon breath.

Enlil Sumerian god addressed as 'the Great Mountain' and 'Lord of the Storm'. He was also known as Rimn (wild ox). He was son of Anu†. His wife, in some versions, was Ninlil†.

Enmesharra Babylonian god of the underworld Aralu, or Meslam. Ministered to by a special kind of priest called Kalu.

Ennead Name given to the 'Paut' or great company of nine Egyptian gods of Heliopolis: Atmu†, Shu†, Tefnut†, Geb†, Nut†, Osiris† and Isis†, Set† and Nephthys†. To this list Ra†, Horus†, Uadjit†, Hu†, Saa†, and Khenti Amenti† were sometimes added.

Enurta The name of the Sumerian god of war Ninurta† is sometimes spelt Enurta. He was the son of Enlil†, and the husband of Gula†.

Enzu Alternative name for Nannar†,

the Babylonian moon god. He may be equated with Sin†.

Eostre Teutonic goddess of the dawn who gave her name to Easter. The word may have evolved from Ishtar†, as her festival has some resemblance to the Babylonian spring festival.

Epact Name given to the five extra days added to the Egyptian year as a result of the gamble between Thoth† and the moon, whereby the latter lost one seventy-second part of each day, thereby enabling not only Osiris† but also Horus† the Elder, Set†, Isis†, and Nephthys† to be born, these days being celebrated as the birthdays of the gods. In actual fact the date of the introduction of the change in the calendar must have been at a time when the heliacal rising of Sirius coincided with the rise of the Nile, which cannot have taken place later than 4231 B.C., as by the next rising of Sirius in 2871 B.C. the calendar was already in use. It may even have been changed before the mentioned date.

Epona Goddess of a continental Celtic tribe, having a horse totem. She is usually shown riding on horseback, sidesaddle.

Epunamun Supreme Being of the Araucanian Indians. Probably of Inca origin. Also known as Guinemapunt.

Erah *See* Jerah†.

Erchtag A variant of Ear†, a name for Tiwaz†.

Ercildoune, Thomas of An English nobleman who is said to sleep with his knights in a cavern in Eildon Hill. Fod details of similar stories *see* Sleeping Princes†.

Ereshkigal Alternative name for the goddess of the underworld, the wife of Nergal†, in Babylonian myth.

Ériu One of a trio of goddesses said to have ruled over Ireland at the time of the coming of the Gaels, and now preserved in the name of Eire.

Ernutit Alternative spelling for Renenet†, the Egyptian goddess of birth and child-bearing.

Erra The Babylonian god of plague.

Esaugetuh Emissee Chief god of the Creek Indians. He was a wind deity and his name means Lord of Wind. In the Creek† Creation Legend it is told how he took up his residence on Nunne Chaha† as the waters of the flood receded and there proceeded to make the ancestors of the tribe out of wet clay.

Eset Alternative spelling of Isis† in Egyptian myth.

Eshmun God of healing in Phoenicia. He is equated by some classical authors with Asclepius, the Greek god of medicine.

Eshtan The Hattic version of the sun god known as Ishtanu† in Hittite.

Eshu Divine messenger in the mythology of the Yoruba peoples of Africa. He is similar to the Legba† of the Fon people.

Eskimo Myths The Eskimos have a chief deity, known as Tornarsuk†, and a goddess of food, known as Sedna† or Arnaknagsak†.

Estanatlehi A goddess of the Navajo who played a part in the creation of her people and then became ruler of their underworld.

Estonia *See* Hero of Estonia.

Esus Eponymous agricultural god of the Essuvi who may possibly have been the husband of Artio†. Alternative spellings are Essus and Hesus†.

Etain (Edaín) In Celtic myth the wife of Mider†, who was stolen from him by Angus†.

Etan In Celtic myth the daughter of Dianchecht†, the Celtic god of medicine, and wife of Ogma†, the god of literature, and mother of Caipre†.

Etana Babylonian king of the earliest Kish dynasty who subsequently became a god. He became merged with Etana, the hero of an early myth, who was taken to heaven on the back of an eagle to obtain a herb needed for the safe birth of his son. Etana reached the dwelling of Anu†, but failed to reach that of Ishtar†, which was higher, and fell to earth. The end of the story is lost, but Etana appears to have survived, as he was mentioned in the Gilgamesh† epic.

Eterah In the Ugarit texts a name given to El†, the moon god, as husband of the sun goddess. Other spellings are Érah, Jarih†, and Terah†. Eterah was a Semitic word meaning moon.

Ether In the Phoenician† Creation Legend of Mochus, Ether and Aër are the parents of Oulomos†.

Ethne In Celtic myth the daughter of

Balor† who, having been warned that he would be killed by his grandson, imprisoned her to prevent her marriage. In spite of his precautions she married MacKinely†, or Cian†, and had a son Lugh†, who ultimately killed his grandfather. She may be taken to be the same person as Arianrhod†, the daughter of Beli†. Comparative pedigrees are given under Lleu†.

Etruscan Religion Owing to the fact that the mystery of the Etruscan language is still only partially solved, much of their religious background is still unknown. Such details as are available come mainly from classical writers, from monuments, and from mirrors.

There were twelve great gods, six of each sex, who were called 'the Senators of the Gods' and 'the Penates of the Thunderer Himself'. Their chief was Tin†. They were fierce and pitiless deities whose name it was forbidden to utter, but they were not deemed eternal but supposed to rise and fall together. Above the great gods were the 'Shrouded Gods', who ruled both gods and men. In practice, however, the three gods of greatest importance were Tin, Uni†, and Menrva†. The Thunderbolt-hurling Gods, such as Summanus† and Sethlans†, were subordinate to these.

Besides these there were Voltumna†, mother goddess; Feronia†, Horta†, Ilythyia-Leucothea†, Thalna†, and Turan†, who were fertility goddesses; Nortia†, the goddess of fortune; Losna†, the moon goddess; and Fufluns†, the Bacchic god. Finally there were the guardians of Hades, Mantus† and his wife Mania.

Eus-os The wife of Ra†, also known as Iusas†, Uert-Hekeu† and Rat†, a feminised version of his name.

Euwe Peoples They had two gods Bo† and So†, who was also known as Khebieso†.

Evnisien In Celtic myth the son of Penard'un† by her first marriage, and stepbrother of Brân†, King of Britain, and Branwen†. By spite he caused the hatred between them and Matholwch†, and later, when a reconciliation was on the point of being arranged, he burnt his nephew Gwern†, the son of Branwen and Matholwch, to death, and killed himself by jumping into Llassar's Cauldron† of Rebirth. In another version he received the cauldron from Brân and proceeded with it to Ireland as an emissary. There he allied himself with Mathlwch and slew his stepbrother in the ensuing war. The story of the embittered hatred of the displaced heir to the throne, for his stepbrother, the King of Britain, and his stepsister, the Queen of Ireland, has within it a tragic element of historical truth.

F

God 'F' Mayan war or sacrifice god similar to the Xipé† of the Aztecs. He is frequently represented with vertical marks on his face.

Fa The god of destiny of the fetish worshippers of Benin. This god has a special name for each follower, and is consulted through his priests on every occasion of import. The basic assumption is that human destiny is fixed only within certain limits, and that by consulting one's Fa one can obtain advice as to which course of action is the less likely to have ill effects.

Fafnir In Nordic myth, as expressed in the Volsung Cycle, the Nibelungenlied, etc., he was the guardian of the treasure. He and his brother Regin†, killed their father, Hreidmar† and Fafnir turned himself into a dragon. He was later slain by Sigurd† or Siegfried†, who then killed Regin.

Falias In Celtic myth the city of the north, one of the four from which originated the Tuatha Dé Danaan†. From it came the Lia Fail, or Stone of Destiny, which was one of the treasures of the Tuatha, and which may be the stone in the Coronation Chair at Westminster Abbey. The other cities were Finias†, Gorias†, and Murias†. Note resemblance between this and the story of Bouyan†.

Fand In Celtic myth wife of Manannan†, whom he deserted.

Faran A hero of the Songhay people and several others in the immediate vicinity of the Niger, who confounds the river spirit, Zin-kibaru†, in a series of encounters.

Farbauti Father of Loki†, the Nordic Merlin†. His wife was Laufey or Nal, and his other children were Byleifstr and Helbindi†.

Faridun In Persian myth an early king who overthrew Bevarash†, the last of the Azhi Dahaka dynasty of serpent-kings, and condemned him to be bound to Mount Demavend.

Fathach In Celtic myth the poet king of the Firbolgs†. The word may be related to Fathi† – Irish equivalent for Druids†. He was the husband of Nessa† and the father of Conchobar†.

Fathi Irish equivalent of the Welsh Druids†. The word may be related to Fathach†, the poet of the Firbolgs†.

Fati (or **Fadu**) In the Society Islands myth, the moon, the son of Roua† by Taonoui†.

Fays While most fairy lore belongs to a period considerably later than that covered by this work, their origin appears to be linked with the priestesses of the pre-Celtic matriarchal races. In the majority of early accounts the fays are women only, but there are a few accounts of fairy men which are not irreconcilable with the foregoing, and the visitor is able to stay in their realms for quite long periods of time without seeing any men, which would indicate either a clan of priestesses as suggested, or alternatively that the men of the tribe were away hunting and would only return for the spring or the autumn fertility festivals, the approach of which would automatically terminate the stay of any outsider who hoped to survive. That they were pre-Celtic is indicated by their not knowing the use of iron and by their inability to count above five. Whether they are to be linked with the dwarfs† or not is not clear, but it is significant that there are few references to women in stories about the dwarfs.

Feather Cloak of Freyja This magic garment, named Valhamr†, which is mentioned in the Nordic stories of Thiassi† and of Thrym†, appears to have given the user the power to fly through the air. Unfortunately no further details about it are available.

Fei Lien Chinese god of the wind. He is also associated with drought, through his ability to dry up the soil and so prevent the growth of crops. He keeps his winds in a large sack, from which he lets them escape in the direction he chooses. In his human form he is known as Feng Po†.

Feng Po The anthropomorphic form of Fei Lien†, god of the wind, as an old man. There is also a female version, Feng Pho-pho. At other times Feng Po may appear as an animal that is a cross between a bird and a dragon, with a stag's head and a serpent tail.

Fenodyree A name for a hairy being, or satyr, similar to the dwarfs† of Nordic myth and the elves†, brownies†, and cluricanes† of the Celts. In actual fact it appears to be a memory of the pre-Celtic and pre-Teutonic inhabitants of western Europe.

Fenrir The Fenris Wolf of Nordic myth, one of the monsters spawned by Loki†. As it could not be restrained by any force of the Aesir†, they asked the dwarfs to make a suitable cord to fetter it, which they did from 'the noise of the footfall of a cat, the beards of women, the roots of stones, the sinews of bears, the breath of fish, and the spittle of birds'. It was as light as silk but strong enough to hold the monster, although in the act of binding him the hand of Tyr† was bitten off. He remained captive until Ragnarok, when he killed Odin† and was slain by Vidar†.

Fercherdne The poet of Cú Roi† who avenged his master's death by leaping to his death and taking the unfaithful wife, Bláthnad†, with him.

Fergus (Ferghus) An early king of Ulster who fell in love with Nessa†, the mother of Conchobar†, who consented to marry him on condition that he should hand over to her son the sovereignty for a year, at the end of which time his people refused to restore him to the kingship. Later, while in exile he acted as tutor to a nephew of Conchobar named Cú Chulainn†, one of the greatest figures of early Irish history.

Feronia An Etruscan fire and fertility goddess.

Fimbulvetr The Great Winter of Nordic

Mythology, when Hrimthursar†, the Frost Giants, bring with them the ice, while the Fire Giants pour down lava on the land before them. The real point of interest in this is that the tale goes back to the onset of the last great Ice Age which ended soon after 10,000 BC, and must date back at least twenty thousand years before then. This does not imply that the Scandinavian races had spent the intervening period in northern Europe but rather that they had always dwelt in the most northerly latitudes and that when the ice age set in they had been obliged to retreat southwards in order to survive. And, later, as the ice glaciers receded, the ancestors of the Norsemen moved northwards and occupied the lands vacated by the ice-fields. The ensuing disaster, Ragnarok†, completes the destruction of the first Nordic culture.

Findrina A metal known to the Irish Celts as lying between bronze and silver and having some resemblance to the orichalcum of the Greeks.

Finias In Celtic myth the city of the south and one of the four from which came the Tuatha Dé Danann†. From here they brought the sword or spear of Nuda†, later one of the treasures† of the Tuatha. The other cities were Falias†, Gorias†, and Murias†.

Finn (Fionn) In Celtic myth the son of Cumhal or Camulos†, a king of the Tuatha Dé Danann†. As a child he was apprenticed to a magician of the same name who was fishing for the salmon of knowledge in the pool at the source of the Boyne or Boann. When the salmon was caught Finn burnt his thumb on it and on sucking it to ease the pain

became possessed of all knowledge. The story of his betrothed Gráinne† who eloped with Diarmait† is told under those headings. He was the father of Ossian†, and is also known as Fingal.

Finno-Estonian Creation Legends Details of these, which greatly resemble each other, are given under Hero† of Estonia and Kalevala†.

Finola In Celtic myth the eldest daughter of Llyr†.

Fintan Husband of Cesara or Cesair, and father of Lara in a Deluge myth given in the Celtic Creation Legend.

Fionnuala *See* Finola†.

Firbolgs (Fir Bholg) In Celtic myth the third dynasty of ancient Ireland following those of Nemed† and Partholon†. It is possible that they occupied portions of Ireland simultaneously with the Fomors†, but the tendency of early myth has been to keep them separate. The Fir Domnann (Dhomhnann) and the Gailioin appear to have been subdivisions of the same tribe, and their last king was Eochaidh mac Eirc, whose wife Tailtiu became the foster-mother of Lugh† after their defeat by the Tuatha Dé Danann†.

Fire One of the three children of Genos† and Genea in the Phoenician† Creation Legend of Philo Byblos, the others being Flame† and Light†. From Fire came the giants†, including Hyposouranios† and Ousoos†.

Fjalar In Nordic myth one of the dwarfs† – the other being Galar† – who murdered Kvasir† and the giant Gilling†. Suttung†, the son of the giant, was going to drown them in the sea when they purchased their lives with the secret of the beverage made from the blood of Kvasir which was afterwards known as Suttung's mead.

Fjol Svinnsmal An obscure dramatic dialogue poem in the Prose Edda†.

Fjörgynn In Nordic myth the giant mother of Frigg†, and wife of Odin† and mother of Thor†. She was one of the Asynjor†.

At some later stage a husband was devised for her with the name Fjorgyn.

Flame Brother of Fire† and Light† in the Phoenician† Creation Legend of Philo Byblos.

Flatey Book A fourteenth-century manuscript, containing, in addition to long lists of Norwegian kings, two of the Eddic poems, the Chant of Hyndla† and the shorter version of the Völuspa†.

Fódla One of the three goddesses who reigned over Ireland at the coming of the Gaels.

Folkvangr In Nordic myth the 'folk meadow' or dwelling of Freyja† and also her zodiacal† house.

Fomors (Fomhoire) In Celtic myth the fourth dynasty of ancient Ireland, succeeding that of the Firbolgs† and preceding that of the Tuatha Dé Danann†. They appear to have developed from the Fir Domnann, who were one of the subdivisions of the Firbolgs. Like the Firbolgs they were a maritime race and it is possible that in both cases there were many expeditions to Ireland before a settlement was attempted. They were eventually defeated by the Tuatha at the battle of Mag Tuireadh. (Magh Tuiredh)

Forseti In Nordic myth one of the Aesir† and the son of Balder† and Nanna†. He was the dispenser of justice and seems to have been a Frisian deity who became absorbed into Scandinavian culture at some early period. His home was Glitnir.

Fravashis In Zoroastrian myth the guardian ancestor spirits of the believers. They data back to the very earliest periods and are specifically omitted from the Dathas, or fundamental statements of doctrine in the Zend-Avesta†. They constitute a form of ancestor worship† and are of interest as they show a stage in the process whereby the great ones of the past acquire divine or semi-divine rank.

Freyja In Nordic myth one of the Asynjor† and wife of Odin† and mother of Hnossa. She appears to have been originally a moon goddess and to have travelled in a chariot drawn by two cats, and also to have been priestess of a clan having a hawk totem. This element of confusion may have arisen from the fact that by the time she was taken over by the Aesir† her cult was so ancient that it had already acquired certain portions of other cults. She lived in Folkvangr, and received half the dead slain in battle. Her marriage to Odin was a purely mythological one. Her personality tended to become merged with that of Frigg†, who may well have been a different entity. In the later stages of Scandinavian religion she was the goddess of love, of marriage, and of fertility. Her necklace Brisingamen and her feather cloak, Valhamr, are included in the treasures of the Aesir. On two occasions the giants tried to get her away from the Aesir; on the first she was demanded as payment for the building of the wall of Asgard and was saved by Loki†, and on the second her hand in marriage was asked for by Thrym†, and on this occasion she was saved by Loki and Thor†. The word Freyja means lady in the same way as Freyr means lord.

Freyja was also known as Gef(jo)n†, Horn†, Mardoll†, Mengladf† or Menglod, and Vanadis†. Her partial supersession by Freyr was probably a stage in the replacing of the early fertility goddesses by gods.

Freyr In Nordic myth the son of Njord† and Skadi†, who resided in Alfheim, from which it may be presumed that he was related to the dwarfs. He had a ship Skidbladnir, built by the dwarfs, which could contain all the Aesir†, but which could be folded up. His sword, which rendered him invincible, was given by him to Skirnir† in return for his services in persuading Gerd†, a giantess, to marry him. Owing to this he fell to the arms of Surt† at Ragnarok.

Adam of Bremen identifies him with Frikka, the husband of Frigg†, which is quite possible, although it is not clear whether this might not make him a Teutonic rather than a northern character. He is found associated with the boar, two of which, Gullinbursti† and Slidrugtanni, drew his chariot, from which it may be assumed that he was originally the chief of a boar clan of the Vanir† who later became merged with the Aesir. Later he became one of three gods who shared the great temple at Upsala. He is always known as the brother of Freyja†

and his promotion to the rank of god may be yet another case of the supersession of a goddess by a god occurring after the end of the matriarchy. The attempts to fuse the personalities of Freyr and Yngvi, or Ingr, the chief of the Ingaevones, as put forward in the Ynglinga Saga, do not appear to have any solid foundation.

Frigg In Nordic myth Frigg appears to have usurped the place of Freyja† and to have become not only the wife of Odin† but also the chief of the Asynjor†. She was a Teutonic mother goddess, and while she may originally have been the same as Freyja, by the time she was brought into contact with the Aesir† she presented a strong element of competition. She had a residence called Fensalir, 'the Halls of the Sea'. By Odin† she was the mother of Balder†.

Frikka Name meaning lover or wooer given by Adam of Bremen to Freyr†.

Frimla A Nordic virgin goddess who wore gold ribbon in her hair. At some period she was absorbed into the Asynjor† as a personal attendant of Frigga†. She may be the same as Fimila.

Frost Giants *See* Giants† and Kalevala†.

Fruits Magical fruits such as the apples of the Hesperides are listed under Treasures†.

Fuchi Fire goddess of the Ainu of Japan from whom Fuji-Yama, the now extinct volcano near Tokyo, takes its name.

Fudo Japanese Buddhist god of wisdom who may be identified with Dianichi†.

Fufluns The Etruscan Bacchus god.

Fu-hsi A serpent-bodied deity, first of the Three Sovereigns, who taught the Chinese how to fish, domesticate animals and breed silkworms. He was also responsible in great part for the invention of writing and music.

Fu-hsing Chinese god of happiness.

Fujin A minor Japanese divinity usually found associated with Raident, the Japanese thunder god.

Fukurokuju Japanese god of wisdom and longevity depicted with a long head and attended by a crane, a deer, or a tortoise. He is one of the seven divinities of luck, the Shichi Fukujint.

Fulla In Nordic myth the sister of Friggt and custodian of her magic casket and also her slippers. She was one of the Asynjort and appears to have been an early mother goddess whose original functions had been partially forgotten. After the death of Nannat she came into possession of her magic ring.

Futsunushi Japanese fire or lightning god. He was one of the emissaries sent by Amaterasu to force the abdication of Onamujit in order that Ninigit could come to the throne. His associate in this work was Takemikadzuchit, the thunder god.

G

God 'G' The sun god of the Mayas who is in all probability Kukulcan†. He can be recognized by the snake-like tongue obtruding from his lips.

Gaea Alternative spelling for Gea†.

Galar In Nordic myth one of the dwarfs† the other being Fjalar† – who murdered Kvasir† and the giant Gillingt†.

Gandharvas In Vedic myth the heavenly choristers of Swarga, the heaven of Indra†. They are usually found associated with the Apsarasest†, the celestial nymphs of Swarga. They were said to have a great partiality for women, and the word Gandharva was used to describe a marriage 'from affection without any nuptial rite'.

Ganesa In Vedic myth the god of wisdom and the patron of literature. He is usually depicted with the head of an elephant. The story goes that his mother, Parvati†, showed him to Siva†, whose glance destroyed his head, which was replaced by that of an elephant. As Ganesa is corpulent, it is possible that his designation as an elephant may have been due to his bulk and to his rank as the leader of the armed forces of Siva, in which case the elephant's trunk would be a later addition.

Ganga Goddess of the Ganges River. In Vedic myth the Ganges was the most sacred of all the rivers in India. It was formerly the custom for pilgrims to start from the source of the river at Gangotri and to walk down the left bank to the mouth at Ganga-sagara, and then to return to the source by the right bank. This pilgrimage, which takes six years to accomplish, is called Pradakshini, and great merit was acquired by it. The guide to persons undertaking these pilgrimages was known as a Gangaputra. The sacredness of this river is due to the belief that it flows from the toe of Vishnu†. Its waters are said to hold great curative properties.

Garang Among the Dinka of the Sudan, the first man, made out of clay, together with Abuk†, the first woman. Garang also has a role as a divine influence that falls on men from the sky.

Garm In Nordic myth the hell-dog slain at Ragnarok by Tyr† in a terrible conflict in which both participants died. It is the same as the moon hound of Teutonic myth, and the white dogs with red ears of Arawn†, which are included in the treasures of Britain.

Garuda In Vedic myth the divine bird, the attendant of Narayana† (a manifestation of Vishnu†). Mythologically he was the son of Kasyapa† and Vinata†. He is often shown with Vishnu riding on his back.

Gatumdu(g) Local Babylonian mother

goddess to whom a temple was built at Lagash by Gudea, the Sumerian king, following a dream in which Ningirsu† appeared.

Gaunab Among the Hottentots a mythical chief, possibly even a personification of death itself, who struggled with the hero and rain god Tsui-goab†, but who was eventually defeated.

Gavida In Celtic myth the smith, the brother of MacKinely†, who may be taken to be the same as Goibniu† or Govannon†.

Gayatri In Vedic myth a milkmaid whom Brahma† is said to have taken to wife in place of Sarasvati†. As a consequence of this the goddess put a curse on him that he should only be worshipped on one day in a year. The name is also that of a sacred verse of the Vedas containing an address to the sun.

Gayomart In the Zoroastrian Creation Legend the first man who was slain by Ahriman†, but whose twin children, Mashya† and Mashyane, born posthumously, were the ancestors of the human race.

Gbeni The chief masked spirit of the Poro society in West Africa.

Gea *1*. Mother Earth, the first goddess of pre-diluvial Athens.
2. The earth in the cosmogony of the early Egyptians. One of the four children of Ra†, the husband of Nut† and the father of Osiris†, Isis†, Set†, Horus† the elder, and Nephthys†. He is represented as lying prone while his brother Shu† supports the heavens over him. One of the great company of Heliopolis.

Egyptian spelling was Geb†; alternative spelling Gae. Among his titles was the Great Cackler, with the goose as his symbol, as he had laid the cosmic egg. He is figured as a man with a goose on his head.

Geasa Forms of religious and secular taboos imposed on the Celts, usually to persons of high rank only. The singular of the word is geis. Form of Geasa may be the Couvade† and the Novena†.

Geb Egyptian name for Gea†, the earth. One of the Ennead†.

Gefjon In Nordic myth one of the Asynjor†, a protector of girls who died unwed. She may be the giantess of whom it was related in the prose Edda that she was promised by King Gylfi† of Sweden as much land as she could plough in a day and a night, upon which she ploughed up a large piece with her giant oxen and dragged it over to Denmark. The kinship of Freyja† with the giants is shown by the fact that one of her names was Gef(jō)n.

Geh and Gerhit Two of the gods created by Thoth† mentioned in the Egyptian† Creation Legends.

Geirrod The story of Geirrod and his encounter with Odin† is told under Grimnir†.

Genos and Genea Children of Aion† and Protogonos† in the Phoenician† Creation Legend. They were the first to worship the sun. Their children were Light†, Fire†, and Flame†. The word *genos* means race.

Gerdi In Nordic myth a giantess, daughter of Gymir and Agurboda, and one of the Asynjor†. The story of her wooing by Skirnir† on behalf of Freyr† is told in the Eddic recital of Skirnir's quest.

Ges Indian Creation Legend This is given under Tupuya† and Ges Indian Creation Legends.

Ghaddar In pre-Islamic myth jinn† found in the Yemen and in Upper Egypt, who enticed men and tortured them, or just terrified them, and then left them. They are said to be the offspring of Iblis† and his wife; they came from an egg which may have been the cosmic egg†.

Ghanan Maya† agricultural god who may be God 'E.'†

Ghul In pre-Islamic myth female jinn† opposed to travel. The male of the species is the Qutrub†. From Ghul comes the modern word ghoul. They were cannibals, and often appeared to men in the desert, and, occasionally, prostituted themselves to them.

Giants Mythology and fable are full of stories of giants, and it is felt that these may be divided into two groups. The first group, of which the Jotunn† are typical representatives, is composed of people who are slightly taller and larger than the tellers of the stories, in the manner that a Scandinavian may seem a giant to an Italian. These differences are merely of a racial character and do not necessitate more than the interminglings of peoples at the time of the great migrations.

Giants in Celtic Myth Lassar†.

Giants in Nordic Myth The following

are the more important of the giants and giantesses encountered in the Eddas†: Angurbodi†, Badi†, Baugi†, Bergelmir†, Besla†, Bolthorn†, Elli†, Fjörgynn†, Gefjon†, Gerd†, Gilling†, Gullveig†, Gunnlauth†, Hlodyn†, Hraesveglur†, Hrimthursar†, Hrungnir†, Hymir†, Hyndla†, Hyrrokin†, Jarnsaxa†, Jord†, Mimir†, Njord†, Nott†, Orgelmir†, Sif†, Skadi†, Skrymir†, Surt†, Thauk†, Thiassi†, Thrym†, Vadi†, Vafthrudnit†, Ymir†. The generic name for the giants was Jotunn†, and they lived in Jötunheim† or Utgard†.

Gibil (Girru) Babylonian fire and light god; he represented the sacred fire of sacrifice, and was also the god of metal workers. He was similar to Nusku†. He appears to symbolize a stage in the evolution of a pure fire god caused by the discovery of metal founding.

Gilbert Islands Creation Legend The Nurunau tribe on these Polynesian† islands have a myth of universal darkness followed by a deluge. The deluge was considered of such import that they have a deluge god.

Gilgamesh This epic hero of Sumeria, whose adventures are told in the epic bearing his name, appears to have lived at a time when the activities of the Mesopotamian tribes were cohering to a point when the state was beginning to emerge. This period can be set back to the fourth millennium BC, if not earlier.

Gilgamesh is recorded as having been the fifth divine King of Erech after the Flood, his immediate predecessor having been Tammuz†. The record of his adventures was put into writing at about the same time that Homer was composing the Greek Epics.

Gilgamesh was the son of Lugalbanda†, the third king and Ninsun†, a minor goddess of Erech. When he reached manhood he recaptured his native city after a long siege, and his initial period of rule was marked by unwonted severity. To distract his attention the inhabitants brought to him Enkidu†, the natural man, with whom Gilgamesh contracted a great friendship. They go together to the mountains to secure cedar wood for the city and its temples and the support of the god Shamash† is secured for the venture. The giant Humbaba†, guardian of the forests, is subdued only with the help of Shamash. But Humbaba is the liege man of Enlil†, with unpleasant results later. After victory the triumphant king is desired by Ishtar†, and in revenge for the flouting of her wishes she conjures up the Bull of Heaven, which causes a seven years' drought and which has eventually to be killed. After this decisive victory Humbaba asks for mercy but Enkidu refuses this, and because of this and other offences the gods decide that one of the two must die. The lot falls on Enkidu and Gilgamesh is left alone.

Gilgamesh then goes to seek the wisdom of his forefathers and has numerous adventures, including the slaying of the lion, whose skin he is frequently depicted as wearing. He then comes to Mount Mashu, where he meets the Scorpion Man†, who allows him through the pass. He crosses the ocean and meets Utnapishti†, who tells him the story of the Deluge, the same as in the Babylonian Creation Legends and in the Book of Genesis. He then returns home.

The conflict with the Bull may refer to the bringing of bull worship into the Fertile Crescent. In general it is clear that all the races in this area shared the same creation and flood legends, although the names of the chief protagonists varied according to the political situation at the time. Gilgamesh seems to have been an actual king to whom were attributed the deeds of earlier generations, a process encountered elsewhere, as with King Arthur† of Britain.

The city of Erech is also known as Uruk.

Gilling In Nordic myth a giant, father of Suttung†. Together with his wife he was murdered by two dwarfs, Fjalar and Galar, who had become drunk on the blood of Kvasir†.

Gishzida Babylonian god, who intervened together with Tammuz† on behalf of Adapa†. Alternative spelling is Gizidu.

Gjallar In Nordic myth the horn of Heimdal† with which the gods were called to their last great battle as described in Ragnarok†. The name means 'resounding'. It is included in the treasures† of the Aesir†.

Gladsheim In Nordic myth Odin's† castle at Asgard†. The name means the glad home. It was also his zodiacal† house.

Glitnir The zodiacal† house of Forseti†

Glunen In Celtic myth the son of Taran† and one of the survivors of the battle between Brân† and Matholwch†.

Gluskap Benign culture hero of the Algonkian Indians as opposed to his twin brother Maslum†. In the Creation Legend of the Algonkians is told how after the death of their mother Gluskap formed the solar system and the human race out of her body, while his brother made things which would be hurtful to mankind. Gluskap, whose name means 'the liar', a title bestowed on him because he was more crafty than his brother, carried out many contests with him before finally defeating him. He also defeated powerful sorcerers known as Wimpe, Pamola, the Kewawkqu, and the Medecolin before going to the other world.

Gna In Nordic myth the messenger of the Asynjor†.

Gog and Magog In British mythology the only survivors of a group of giants killed by King Brute. They were made to act as porters on either side of the door of the royal palace in London. They are recalled today by the statues at Guildhall in London. In the Bible they are mentioned in both the Old and New Testaments, generally with threatening implications.

Goibniu (Goibhniu) The smith of Celtic myth who together with Credne† and Luchtainel† made the arms which enabled the Tuatha Dé Danann† to defeat the Fomors†. He is the same as Gavida† or Govannon†, and was the uncle of Lugh† or Lleu†.

Gondul In Nordic myth the manifestation of Freyja† as a Valkyrie†.

Gorias In Celtic myth the city of the east, one of the four from which came the Tuatha Dé Danann†. From it came the lance of Lugh†, one of the treasures† of the Tuatha. The other three cities were Falias†, Finias†, and Murias†.

Gou (Gu) In Benin, the god of metal; the son of Lissa†, and Maou†.

Govannon (Gofannon) In Celtic myth the son of Dôn†, the brother of Amathaon† and of Gwydion†, the smith of the gods, the British equivalent of Goibniu†. He was the slayer of Dylan†.

Grail The story of the Grail as told in Athurian legend is a christianized version of the legend appertaining to Amen† the magic cauldron† of Ceridwen†, and the *greal*, the liquor which it distilled. This would not in any way invalidate its religious value but would remove it from the orbit of the Christian Church as having originated considerably earlier. There are possible links with Kvasir† and Soma†.

Gráinne In Celtic myth the betrothed of Finn†, who ran away with Diarmait†.

Grannus Early continental Celtic god of mineral springs. Several localities in France are named after him, notably Aix-la-Chapelle (Aquae Granni), Graux, and Eaux Graunnes. An inscription to Grannus has been found at Musselburgh, near Edinburgh.

Great Company of the Gods Nine Egyptian gods known as the Ennead†.

Grimhild *See* Krimhild†.

Grimnir Grimnis-Mal in the Edda tells how Odin† disguised himself as Grimnir, 'the Hooded One', and went to visit his foster-son Geirrod†. He is harshly treated on his arrival and then while awaiting the dawn he tells Geirrod the story of the gods. Geirrod eventually realizes that his guest is really Odin. He accordingly commits suicide by falling on his sword.

Groa In Nordic myth the magic lay of Groa or Grou Galdur is a collection of spells and incantations in the Poetic Edda†.

Gronw Pebyr In Celtic myth the lover of Blodeuwedd†, who plotted with her to kill her husband, Lleu Law Gyffes†. In the end, however, Lleu killed his rival.

Gros-Ventre Indian Creation Legend In the myth of this tribe of the Algonkian† Indians it is told how their god Nichant† destroyed the world by fire and subsequently by water.

Gu *See* Gou.

Guachimines In Inca† myth the brothers-in-law of Guamansuri†, whom they treacherously mudered. Later, after the birth of her twin children Apocatequil† and Pigueraot†, they also murdered their sister. She was recalled to life by Apocatequil, by whom the Guachimines were all slain.

Guamansuri In the Inca† Creation Legend the first mortal to descend to earth. He seduced the sister of the Guachimines† and was killed by them. His posthumous children were Apocatequil† and Pigueraot†.

Guanche Mythology The Guanches of the Canary Islands appear to have been refugees from the mainland who exterminated the original inhabitants. They had an all-encompassing male deity named Abora in Palma, Achaman in Tenerife, Acoran in Gran Canary, and Eraoranzan

in Tenerife. The Grand Canary name shows marked traces of Muslim influence.

Guaracy In the Tupi-Guarani† Creation Legend the sun, the creator of all animals on the earth. His fellow creator gods were Jacy† and Peruda†. He corresponds to Torushompek†.

Guayami Indian Creation Legend This Costa Rican tribe have a myth that as the waters of the Great Deluge receded Nancomala† waded out and there found floating on a raft Rutbe†, whom he married. These two were the ancestors of the tribe.

Gucumatz Feathered serpent god of the Popul Vuh, the sacred book of the Quiches, who may be considered to be the same as Quetzalcoatl†, the Aztec culture hero.

He is linked with Hurakan† and Xpiyacoc and Xmucane in the work of creation. He also appears as the Wind of the Nine Caverns in the Mixtec Creation Legend.

Gudrun In the Volsung Cycle the daughter of Krimhild†, who became the wife of Siegfried†, thanks to a magic draught. In the Thidrek Saga her place is taken by Grimhild (Krimhild†). In the Nibelungenlied she is the sister of Gunther† (Gunnar†), and is known as Gutrune†.

Guecubu (Guecufü) A malicious deity of the Araucanian Indians. The name means 'the Wanderer Without' and it is possible that under the dualistic system he may have been the evil twin of Aka-Kanet. All the misfortunes which occur to man are presumed to have been caused by Guecubu.

Guinechén or **Guinemapun** Supreme Being of the Araucanians of Chile. The first name means 'Master of Men' and the second 'Master of the Land'.

Gula A Babylonian goddess of healing, the wife of Enurta†. Her symbol was a dog.

Gullinbursti The boar with golden bristles made by the dwarfs for Freyr†.

Gulltoppr In Nordic myth the horse with the golden mane on which Heimdall† rode to the funeral of Balder†.

Gullveig In Nordic myth one of the Vanir†, probably a sorceress who was ill-treated by the Aesir†, who speared her and tried three times to burn her without success. The news of this brought about the war between the Vanir and the Aesir, which ended in the victory of the former. In the Völuspa the name Gullveig is given to the Völva, or sibyl, after whom the book was named. The name means 'Goldbranch', She also appears to have been a giantess.

Gulu The Buganda king of heaven.

Gungnir In Nordic myth the sword of Odin†, one of the treasures† of the Aesir†.

Gunnar In the Volsung Cycle the brother of Gudrun†, who marries Brynhild†, with the assistance of Sigurd† (Siegfried), who crosses the ring of fire to win her. Later, after the murder of Sigurd, Gunnar himself is murdered.

In the Thidrek Saga Gunnar orders Hagen† (Hagru) to murder Siegfried†, while in the Nibelungenlied he allows Hagen to commit the murder on the orders of Brynhild†.

Gunnlauth In Nordic myth the daughter of Suttung† the giant, who was seduced by Odin† in the endeavour to obtain the secret of the manufacture of Kvasir†, the intoxicating mead brewed in Odherir, the magic cauldron. The story is told in the Conversations of Bragi.

Gunther In the Nibelungenlied a name given to Gunnar†.

Gutrune *See* Gudrun†.

Gwal, the Son of Cud In Celtic myth the unsuccessful suitor of Rhiannon†. He was eventually trapped in a bag and beaten.

Gwalu (C'balu) Rain god of the Yoruba† tribe.

Gwern In Celtic myth the son of Branwen† and Matholwch† who was burned to death by his step-uncle Evnisien† after the great battle between his father and his uncle Brân†. It is possible that this murder may have been some form of a ritual sacrifice.

Gwigawd A magic cauldron which formed part of the treasures† of Britain. It may have been Amen†, the cauldron of Ceridwen†.

Gwion In Celtic myth Gwion Bach was the name of the boy who stirred Amen†, the magic cauldron of Ceridwen†, and who subsequently was metamorphosed into Taliesin†.

Gwri 'He of the Golden Hair', the name given to Pryderi†, the son of Rhiannon† by his adopted father Teyrnon Twry Bliant†.

Gwyddno One of the heroes of British Celtic myth, also known as Longshanks. He was the possessor of the magic basket or cauldron which formed part of the treasures of Britain and which was capable of feeding one hundred people if food for one was put in it. He was the Prince of Cantref y Gwaelod, a city which was submerged by the sea and now lies under Cardigan Bay.

Gwydion The bard, magician, King of the British Celts who studied wizardry with Amathaon†, with whom he sided in the Battle of the Trees against Arawn†, the King of Annwn. He is an early British culture hero who may to some extent be equated with Ogma† and, at a later date, many of the stories of his adventures were absorbed into the general body of Arthurian myth and credited to Arthur† himself. He was the son of Dôn† and Beli†, and by his sister Arianrhod† was the father of Lleu† and Dylan†. The comparative family trees of Lleu and Lugh† are given under the first named.

Gylfi An early ruler of Sweden who is used by Snorri in the Prose Edda as an excuse for the detailed outline of Nordic myth known as *Gylfaginning* (Deluding of Gylfi). The story goes that to find out about the Aesir† he disguises himself as an old man and proceeds to Asgard, he then asks a series of questions covering all the main stories of the Elder Edda. The answers form a useful check for the text of Saemund, particularly that of the Völuspa.

H

God 'H' An unknown Maya serpent god, possibly Kukulcan–Quetzalcoatl in his serpent form.

Hachiman The Shinto god of war in Japan. Before deification he was Ojin, son of the Empress Jingo.

Hadad Alternative form of spelling for Adad†, the Babylonian storm god.

Hagen In the Nibelungenlied the murderer of Siegfried† at the order of Brynhild†. He was later killed by Krimhild†. He also occurs in the Volsung Cycle under the name of Högni†, and in the Thidrek Saga under his own name (Hagru).

Hakm Early Arabian name for the moon.

Hammarsheimt In Nordic myth 'the Homecoming of the Hammer', an alternative title for the Lay of Thrym†, one of the stories in the Edda†.

Hanuman In Vedic myth the general of the monkey-king referred to in the Ramayana. He facilitated the assault on Ceylon by building a bridge or causeway over which Rama and his troops crossed to rescue Sita† from the clutches of Ravana†. Hanuman would appear to have been the leader of some south Indian tribe who was immortalized for his bravery. He was the son of Vayu†.

Haokah In Sioux† myth the thunder god, who employed the wind as a stick to beat the thunder drum. He wore horns showing that he was also a hunting god and had the gift of crying when he was cheerful and of laughing when he was unhappy, and of feeling heat as cold and cold as heat.

Haoma In Zoroastrian myth the Soma† was worshipped under this name. It was considered as the purifier of the Place of the Sacred Fire, as the destroyer of demons and tyrants, and as the provider of husbands for spinsters.

Hapi Alternative spelling for Serapis†, the Egyptian bull god.

Hapi Androgynous Egyptian god of the Nile. He wore a crown of papyrus plants in the north, and one of lotus plants in the south. His fertility was indicated by pendent breasts. The Nile, over which Hapi presided and which was called by his name, formed a part of the great celestial stream over which the boat of Ra†, the sun god, sailed daily. It encircled the earth, from which it was separated by high mountains. At one place, however, was the throne of Osiris, near to a fissure through which the waters reached the earth. The other end of this aperture was said to be near the first cataract between two mountains near the islands of Elephantine and Philae. Owing to the dominating role played by the Nile in the life of Egypt, Hapi gradually increased in importance until he joined the Great Company of Gods†.

Hapy One of the four sons of Horus†, the others being Amset† (Imset), Duamutef† and Qebhsneuf† (Qebehsenuf), who guarded the four cardinal points and protected the viscera. Hapy was guardian of the north cardinal point and protected the lungs. He is shown with the head of a dog.

Hara In Vedic myth a name given to Rudra† or Siva†. Harit-Hara is the name given to the dual personality formed by the combination of Siva and Vishnu†.

Harakhtes The Greek rendering of Harakhte, meaning 'Horus of the Horizon'. When Ra† became pre-eminent, he assumed the title of Ra-Harakhte†.

Harbard Harbardsljod, or the Lay or Harbard, in the Edda†, tells how Thor† and Harbard, who is Odin† in disguise, have an argument at a ferry which Thor desires to cross and during the course of which they both boast of their exploits.

Hari In Vedic myth a name given to Vishnu†, or alternatively Krisna†. Hari-Hara† is the name given to the dual personality formed by the combination of Siva† and Vishnu.

Harmakhis See Hermakhis†.

Haroeris A variant of the Egyptian god Horus†.

Har-pa-neb-taui Title of Horus† as 'Lord of the two lands'.

Harpakhrad Alternative name for Horus† in Egyptian myth.

Harpokrates Alternative version of Harpakhrad†, the infant Horus†.

Harr 'The Old One' (or 'the High One'?). In Nordic myth one of the rock dwarfs listed in the Eddas. The name, with those of Thekkr and Thror, was claimed by Odin†, which would show that his kinship rested at some point upon a relationship with the dwarfs.

Harsaphes See Hersheft†.

Harsiesis Name of Horus† as the infant avenger of his father.

Harsomtus (Heru-Sam-Taui) Title of Horus† meaning 'Horus who united the two countries'.

Hartomes Title of Horus† as 'Horus the Lancer', who pierces his opponents.

Hashje-Altye In Navajo† myth a name given to the talking god.

Hasis-Atra (Atraharsis) Another name for Utnapishti†.

Hathor In the Egyptian Creation Legend goddess of love and beauty, often identified with most of the other goddesses, including Sekhmet†. Her name means 'House of Horus'; she was guardian of the cemeteries of the dead. As a mother goddess, she was cow–headed, and was subsequently linked with Isis†, Mehueret†, Meskhenit†, and Qedeshet†: At Sebennytus she was mother of Anhur†. The name is sometimes rendered as Athyr†.

Hati The physical heart of the Egyptian, as opposed to Abt, the symbolic heart, in Egyptiant Religion.

Hatif A species of jinnt in pre-Islamic myth that is heard but not seen; usually communicates advice, directions, and warnings.

Hattatal A treatise on prosody, with metrical examples, included by Snorri in the Prose Eddat. It has no mythological value.

Haumea In Hawaiian mythology mother of Pelet, patroness of childbirth, and sometimes even regarded as the first woman.

Haurvatat One of the seven Immortal Holy Ones, the attendants of Ahura Mazdat. Haurvatat represented integrity and health. He was the genius of the waters and may have been an early river or lake divinity. He was one of the Yazatast.

Havamal 'The Sayings of the High One.' A poem in the Poetic Eddat. This collection of precepts, resembling parts of Ecclesiastes, contains one hundred and forty verses attributed to Odint and a runic section of some twenty verses of a later date. It is in this poem that Odin tells how he 'hung on the tree for nine nights, wounded with a spear. . . . I gathered up the runes . . . nine chants of power I learnt . . . I won a draught of the famous mead.'

Hawaiki In Polynesian myth the traditional homeland of the Polynesians, from which they set forth to colonize the Pacific Islands. The Mangaians believed that it was a vast coconut shell containing Varit and Take, the root of all existence, which sustained the universe. An alternative spelling was Avaikit.

Hawiyah Seventh stage of the Islamic hell, Daru el Bawart, a bottomless pit for hypocrites.

Haya 'Goddess of Direction', a title given to the Babylonian goddess Nin-lilt.

Haya-Griva In Vedic myth a demon of the Daityast who stole the Vedas and was defeated by Vishnut in the form of a fish, a story linked with the Matsyat avatar. Vishnu was aided by Satyavratat, a king of Dravidia. A similar story is told of Hiranyakshat.

Hebat Hurrian chief goddess and sun goddess, wife of the weather god Teshubt.

Hefeydd the Old In Celtic myth the father of Rhiannont.

Heimdall In Nordic myth one of the Aesirt. The story of how he repopulated the world after some disaster is told in the Edda of Rig. In a poem called 'Heimdall's Incantation' in the Prose Edda it is reported that he was the son of nine virgins, i.e. of a group of priestesses, which would show his royal descent. His function was to act as guardian of the Bifrost bridge against the assault of the giants, being in effect a warden of the outer marches. He was famous for Gulltopprt his horse, Höfud his sword, and Gjallar his horn. His traditional dislike of Lokit crystallized in a long-drawn-out series of combats for Brisinga-men, the neckace of Freyjat. At

Ragnarok he finally defeated his enemy. His home was Himinbjorg, the name of his actual residence, on the borders of Asgard at the end of the Bifrost bridge.

Heket Egyptian goddess with the form of a frog. She was a goddess of childbirth, and was regarded as the mother of Haroeris†. *See* Hequet†.

Hel The goddess of the dead in Nordic myth and her dwelling. She was said to be the child of Loki† and to have been cast by Odin† into Niflheim. It is possible that Hel was a sibyl dwelling in a cave, an idea which is supported by Odin's consultation with her about the death of Balder†. The comparison of her domain with the Christian hell is of more recent date.

Helblindi In Nordic myth the son of Farbauti† and brother of Loki†. It was also a name given to Odin†, which seems to show that it may refer to some important personage who existed earlier.

Helgi A hero of Nordic mythology who was protected by the Valkyrie Svava†.

Heliopolis Company of the Gods Nine Egyptian gods known as the Ennead†.

Heng-o Chinese goddess of the moon. Younger sister of Ho Po†, she lived in a palace made out of cinnamon trees for her by her husband Yi†, the Divine Archer.

Hequet In Egyptian myth a frog-headed goddess of birth, mother of one of the forms of Horus†. *See* Heket†.

Hercle Herakles or Hercules in Etruscan mythology.

Heres Canaanite name for Shamash†, the sun god.

Herfjoturr One of the Valkyries whose name means 'War-fetter'.

Herdesuf A form of the Egyptian god Horus†.

Herhkhty Originally a form of the Egyptian god Horus†. *See* Harakhtes†.

Hermakhis In Egyptian myth a name for Horus† on the Horizon, i.e. the rising or setting sun. Another variant is Horakhti†. The term is sometimes applied to Ra†. Alternative spelling Harmakhis†.

Hermes Trismegistus Greek name for the Egyptian god Thoth†.

Hermin *See* Irmin†.

Hermitten In the Tupi-Guarani† Creation Legend one of three brothers, the others being Coem† and Krimen†, who escaped from the Deluge by climbing trees or by hiding in caves.

Hermod In Nordic myth a son of Odin† who rode to Hel on Sleipnir†, the horse of Odin, in the endeavour to ransom Balder† from death.

Hero of Estonia The Estonian national epic, having many points of resemblance to the Finnish Kalevala†. Its principal hero is Kallevipoeg†, who is the Finnish Kullervo†; while Vanemuind†, the god of music, is the Väinämöinen† of the Finns.

Hershef Known as Terrible Face, a ram-headed Egyptian god worshipped at Heracleopolis Magna.

The Greek version of the name is Arsaphes† or Harsaphes†.

Hertha Alternative form of Nerthus†, the Teutonic fertility goddess.

Heru and Hehut Two of the gods produced by Thoth† from Chaos†, mentioned in the Egyptian† Creation Legend. The use of this word in connection with Horus† may indicate the merging of the two gods.

Heru-Sam-Taui In Egyptian myth one of the many names applied to Horus†. It means 'Horus who united the two countries'.

Herusmatauy In Egyptian myth the son of Horus† of Edfu and Hathor†; also known as Ahy (or Ihy)†.

Hest A variant of Isis†, the Egyptian goddess. Also Aset† or Eset†.

Hesus War god of the Gauls akin to Teutates†. Also Esus†.

Hey-Tau of Nega Egyptian god of the Byblos region, known from the period 3000 B.C. by Egyptian texts. He was transformed into a pine-tree, and can to some extent by equated with Tammuz† and Osiris†. Pepi I (sixth dynasty, 2400 B.C.), in his funerary inscription, compares himself to Hey-Tau, in his wooden sarcophagus.

Himingjorg The zodiacal† house of Heimdall†.

Hildisvin The name of the boar belonging to Freyja†, and later that of a helmet of one of the early Swedish kings.

Hildur The name of one of the Valkyries.

Hina (or **Ina**) Alternative name for Sina†, the Polynesian moon goddess.

Hindu Creation Legend In Hindu myth the world is now in its fourth Yuga† or age. The first of these lasted 4,000 divine years, being preceded and followed by twilights of 400 divine years. The second lasted 3,000 divine years with twilights of 300, the third 2,000 with twilights of 200, and the fourth 1,000 with twilights of 100 divine years. The four Yugas together cover a period of 12,000 divine years or 4,320,000 human years. This period is named a Mahayuga†. A thousand Mahayugas make a day of Brahma†, this being the length of time separating the Creation from the end of the world. The day of Brahma, or Kalpa†, is divided into fourteen periods, named Manvantaras†, each of which is ruled over by a Manu†. (As a thousand cannot be divided by fourteen without remainder, it is probable that the stories of the Manus belong to some different faith.) The present Manu is the seventh, which would put the world about mid career. *See* Vedic Sacred Writings.

Hinun The thunder god of the Iroquois† Indians, who with the aid of his brother the West Wind overcame the Stone Giants, the aboriginal inhabitants of the land.

Hiranya-Garbha In the Hindu Creation Legend the primeval germ from which Brahma† was born. An alternative name is Narayana†.

Hiranya-Kasipu In Vedic myth a demon of the Daityas† related to Ravana†, who is slain by Vishnu† in his fourth avatar as the man-lion, Narasinha†.

Hiranyaksha In Vedic myth a Daitya† who occurs in Narasinha the story of the man-lion avatar of Vishnu†. He is also the villain of a Deluge legend akin to Haya-Griva† in that he dragged the earth to the depths of the ocean. Finally he, or his brother Hiranya-Kasipu†, is the same as Ravana†. This confusion may arise from the name having been a family one in the Daitya dynasty.

Hirihbi King of Sumer in the Ugarit stories, and messenger to Yarih (or Yerah)† from Nikkal†.

Hlodyn A Nordic giantess who was mentioned in the Völuspa as the mother of Thor†. She may be identical with Hludana, a name found on Frisian and Rhineland inscriptions.

Hmin In Burmese myth the demon of ague, who afflicted all travellers.

Hnossa In Nordic myth one of the Asynjor†. She was the daughter of Freyja† and was so beautiful that the word 'hnosir' was subsequently used to describe things of beauty.

Hochigan Quarrelsome being in the Bushmen† Creation Legends. In the beginning animals were endowed with speech. Hochigan hated animals. He disappeared one day and with him the power of speech was lost to animals.

Hoder In Nordic myth one of the Aesir†. He was born blind and was the accidental cause of the death of Balder†. In some stories he is stated to have been sacrificed at the next festival, but in the

Völuspa he is said to have survived Ragnarok. The death of his twin brother Balder† may well have been the ritual sacrifice of one twin, as with Romulus and Remus. The story of Hagen† may be drawn from this source.

Hoenir In Nordic myth one of the Aesir†, a brother of Odint†, may originally have been Willi† or We†. His Scandinavian descent is shown by his description as fair, tall, and fleet of foot. When the Aesir made peace with the Vanir† he was sent to them as hostage. He appears both in the Nordic Creation Legends and in Ragnarok.

Höfud The wonderful sword of Heimdall†, one of the treasures† of the Aesir†.

Hogahn In Navajo† myth this word is applied indiscriminately to a purification ceremony, or to the house in which the ceremony is held. As, however, the house god is known as Hashje-Hogahn, it would appear that the name originated with the building rather than the ceremony.

Högni In the Volsung Cycle, a name given to Hagen†.

Holle, Holda, Hoide The Frau Holle of German folklore was the German lunar goddess of witches and sabbath. In summer she was to be surprised bathing in forest streams, while in winter she shook down the snowflakes from the trees. Holle or Holda or Hoide would appear to be generic terms for priestesses of the lunar cult amongst the Teutons.

Hopi Indian Creation Legend In the myth of this tribe the two Huruing†

Wuhti mother goddesses having survived the Deluge waited for the rays of the sun to dry up the mud banks left behind by the receding waters, and when the soil was in suitable condition they proceeded to create human beings. One sister lived in the east and one in the west; there was a third mother goddess, Ragnot, who lived by herself but did not take any recorded part in the proceedings.

Ho Po Count of the River in Chinese mythology, and brother of Heng-ot, the moon goddess. He is also known as Ping-it.

Horakhti-Ra In Egyptian myth a name of Horust on the Horizon. Another variant is Hermakhist. These names are sometimes applied to Rat. Alternative spelling Harakhti-Ra.

Horbehudet In Egyptian myth a variant of Horust.

Hormazu In Zoroastrian myth an alternative name for Ahura Mazdat, or Ohrmazdt.

Horn In Nordic myth one of the names of Freyjat and also that of one of the members of the Asynjort.

Horn of Amenti One of the boundaries of the Egyptian Elysian Fields.

Horns Drinking and hunting horns are listed under Treasurest.

Horses of the Aesir To the northern peoples the difficulty of securing horses as opposed to ponies must have been very great, as is shown by the specific mention by name of all the horses that

occur in the Eddast. In the following are listed twenty of them: Alsuid, Arvar (the sun god), Blodighofi, Falhofnir, Gardrofa (dam of Hofvarpnir), Gils, Gladr, Glaer, Gultopprt (the horse of Heimdallt), Gyllir, Hamskerpir (sire of Hofvarpnir), Hofvarpnir (the horse of Gnat), Hrimfaxi (the horse of Nottt), Lettfeti, Silfrintoppr, Skeidbrimir, Skinfaxi, Sleipnirt (the horse of Odint), Svadilfari, Synir. The horse of Balder was burnt on his funeral pyre.

Horta Etruscant goddess of agriculture from whom a town of Etruria derived its name.

Horus Son of Isist and Osirist, nephew of Nephthyst and Sett, grandson of Nutt and Geat or Nut and Rat, father of the four Canopic gods: Amsett, Duamuteft, Hapit, and Qebhsneuft, and member of the Enneadt. There are several manifestations of Horus, which tend to overlap, and the problem of disentangling them is not always easy, as Horus may well have been the name of a whole series of pre-dynastic rulers or priests. Another difficulty arises from the habit of the ancient Egyptians of combining two or three gods into dyadic or triune deities, which was frequently done with Amont, Horus, Osiris, Ptaht, and Ra.

The more important manifestations of Horus were:
1. Horus the Elder, or Haroerist, a falcon-headed sky god, of pre–dynastic origin, who may possibly have been the high priest or ruler of a tribe having a falcon totem. The story of his fight, as god of the sun, god of day, god of light, god of life and of all good, with Set, as god of night, god of darkness, god of death and of all evil, was already current

in the earliest dynastic periods. According to this, Horus had two eyes, the sun and the moon, of which Set managed to steal the sun, but was attacked by Horus, who inflicted a deadly wound in one of his thighs. Thoth†, acting as mediator, made a treaty between them, allotting the day to Horus and the night to Set, and making them of equal length. Set, however, continued to persecute Horus, by cutting off pieces from his other eye, the moon, for a fortnight in each month, until there was none of it left. Thoth managed to frustrate him by making a new moon each month. This is an interesting earlier variant of the Osiris-Set conflict, and seems to relate to a dispute between two sun and sky gods, Set having been a sun and sky god originally, combined with memories of some cosmic event of great import.

Horus the Elder was known by many names, including Aroueris† and Heru-Sam-Taui†.

2. Horus of Edfu, or Horbehudet†. A war god of Edfu, whose deeds were commemorated on the walls of the temple there.

3. Horus on the Horizon, or Herkhty†. A manifestation of Ra, the sun god, on the horizon, i.e. the rising or setting sun.

4. Horus the infant sun god, who was reborn every morning, and was also a manifestation of Ra.

5. Horus the Child, or Harpakhrad†. The son of Isis and Osiris, who is usually shown as being suckled by his mother. He was conceived when Osiris had been brought back from the dead by Isis, a point which later allowed Set to oppose his claim for the throne of Egypt.

6. Horus the son of Osiris. He is sometimes shown as a man with a falcon's head, wearing the double crown. He was the avenger of Osiris, and as such protagonist in the battles with Set, where we have another version of the story of the loss of an eye, only here Thoth brought it back and restored its sight by spitting on it. Horus then gave the eye to Osiris, who ate it and became filled with vital powers sufficient to enable him to take over the kingship of the dead.

7. Harpokrates. A son of a Horus god, another form of Horus the Child.

Hotei Japanese god of laughter and contentment. He is usually depicted as being extremely fat and carries on his back a linen bag (*ho-tei*) from which he derives his name. He is one of the seven divinities of luck, the Shichi Fukujin†.

Hou-Chi Early Chinese culture hero who at some stage became linked with the Chou dynasty. He was of royal descent, as is shown by the legend of his virgin birth, and was later raised to the rank of god for having brought the knowledge of agriculture to the Chinese, in which he resembles Shen-nung†.

Houri (Hur) The damsels with 'retiring glances whom nor man nor jinn hath touched', who await the faithful in the Islamic paradise Dar el-Jannah†.

How-Too Chinese† earth monster god manifested in mountains and rivers. To him were sacrificed domestic animals, whilst prayers written on silk or parchment were buried before his effigy.

Hraesveglur In Nordic myth a giant†, head of an eagle totem clan, who is referred to in the Prose Edda† as guardian of the gates.

Hrafna Galdur Odins A somewhat obscure poem forming part of the Poetic Edda† entitled Odin's† Raven Spell.

Hreidmar In Nordic mythology the father of Fafnir† and Regin†.

Hrimfaxi The horse of Nott† in Nordic mythology.

Hrimnir A giant in Nordic mythology whose daughter Frigg† sent to earth with an apple which she dropped into the lap of the wife of King Rerir so that she might conceive a child.

Hrimthursar In Nordic myth the ice giants, sons of Ymir† or Hrim. When their father was slain by Odin†, helped by Vili† and Ve†, all were drowned in his blood, except Bergelmir† and his wife, who escaped in a boat. Another version of the story in Ragnarok† refers, however, to the sailing of the hosts of the frost giants in the ship Naglfar†, steered by Hrim. Details are also given under Nordic† Creation Legends.

Hringhorn In Nordic myth the ship of Balder† which was described as being larger than either Naglfar† or Skidbladnir†. After his death it was used as his funeral pyre, being launched for this purpose by Hyrrokin† the giantess.

Hrist The name of one of the Valkyries.

Hsi Wang Mu In Chinese mythology the royal Mother of the Western Paradise. She changed from being a fearful demon in earlier times to a beautiful goddess and guardian of the herb of immortality in Taoist literature.

Hsi-Yu-Chi A record of a journey to the western paradise to procure the Buddhist scriptures for the Emperor of China. The work is a dramatization of the introduction of Buddhism into China, and contains within it many myths and legends, including that of Sun-Houtzu†.

Hrungnir In Nordic myth one of the giants, killed by Thor.

Hu A child of Ra†, an Egyptian god occasionally included in the Ennead†, who appears in the Boat of the Sun at the Creation, and later, at the Judgment of the Dead.

Huahuantli Alternative name for Teoyaomiqui†, the Aztec god of dead warriors.

Hubur Primordial mother goddess in Babylonian mythology who spawned a brood of monsters to aid Tiamat† in her battle against Marduk†. It also denotes a river in the underworld akin to the Styx in Graeco-Roman mythology.

Hu Gadarn Early culture hero of the Celts who was the ancestor of the Cymry. It was his team of oxen that dragged the Addanc† from the lake of Llyon-Llion†.

Huehueteotl 'The Old God', a name occasionally given to the Aztec fire god Xiuhtecuhtli†. Alternative spelling Huehuecoyotl.

Huginn ('Mind' or 'Thought'). In Nordic myth one of the raven messengers of Odin†, who was also a raven god, the other being Muninn†.

Huitzilopochtli The humming bird

wizard, the war and sun god, the chief god of Tenochtitlan, the Aztec city. He was the son of Coatlicue† and brother of the southern star gods. He appears to have been a later development of Opochtli, a culture hero of the Tenochtitlan period, who later became promoted to the rank of a god of fishing and bird snaring. The story of his being brought to Mexico by boat may be related to Chicomoztoc of the Aztecs.

Huixtocihuatl Aztec† goddess of salt considered as the elder sister of Tlaloc†, a fact which would indicate that she may have been a pre-Aztec mother goddess.

Humbaba Nature god of the Gilgamesh Epic, enemy of Enkidu†. Alternative spelling Huwawa.

Hunab-ku Abstract, invisible, and supreme god of the Mayas.

Hunapú In the Quiche Creation Legend as told in the Popul Vuh he was a great culture hero and the brother of Xbalanqué or Ixbalanqué†. He is chiefly famous for his visit to Xibalba, the Quiche Hades, when his head was cut off by Camazotz†.

Huncame In the Quiche† Creation Legend as told in the Popul Vuh† he was the co-lord of Xibalba†, the cavern world. After murdering Hunhunapú and Vukub-Hunapu† he and his fellow sovereign Vukubcame† were destroyed by Hunapú and Xbalanqué†.

Hunhau The Maya death god, usually referred to as God 'A'†.

Hunhunapú In the Quiche Creation

Legend as told in the Popul Vuh the son of Xpiyacoc and Xmucane. He and his brother Vukub-Hunapú were induced by a challenge to a ball game to enter Xibalba, the cavern world of the Quiches, where they were murdered by its rulers. However, his two children by a Princess Xquiq, Hunapú† and Xbalanqué†, later avenged their father's death.

Huntin An African tree spirit to whom fowls were occasionally sacrified; associated with the Xhosa†.

Hurakan Together with Gucumatz† one of the chief gods in the Quiche Creation Legend as told in the Popul Vuh. He was a wind god known as 'the Heart of Heaven' and vented the anger of the gods upon the first human beings by causing a deluge and a thick resinous rain which completed their destruction. Alternative spelling Huracan.

Huron Indian Creation Legend In the myth of the Huron North American Indians the two brothers Tsentsa and Tawiscara† (who are the equivalent of Enigorio† and Enigohatgea) who were of virgin birth and the first leaders of the tribe after the Deluge quarrelled and fought. Tsentsa was successful and Tawiscara had to flee. Tsentsa made life possible on earth by defeating the Great Frog which had swallowed all the waters (i.e. the Deluge) and returning them to the rivers and valleys. One of the other Huron deities was Onniont†, the snake deity.

Huruing Wuhti Two mother goddesses in the Hopi† Indian Creation Legend. In fact they appear to have been two Deluge survivors who were the mothers of the ancestors of the tribe and who were assisted in their difficulties by Ragno†, who also occurs in the Pomo† Indian Creation Legend.

Hutameh Third stage of the Islamic hell Daru el-Bawar†, an intense fire for Jews.

Hvergelmir In Nordic myth twelve rivers flowed from the fountain of Hvergelmir in Niflheim† or Hel†. These were: Fimbul, Fjorm, Gjoll, Gunnthra, Hrith, Leiptur, Slith, Svaul, Sylgil, Thulr, Vith, and Ylgr. As, with the exception of Fimbul, these names occur nowhere else in the Eddas, it is presumed that they must represent the oldest geographical memories of the pre-Ice Age era. The twelve rivers are together known as Elivagar.

Hy-Brasil In Celtic myth a mysterious island in the Atlantic thought by some to be the last vestiges of Atlantis to which fled the leaders of the Tuatha de Danann† after their defeat by the Milesians†. Hy-Brasil was shown on maps of the Atlantic even after the discovery of America. Whether this is in any way related to the Nordic Yggdrasil† has not yet been determined.

Hymir A Nordic giant who was the father of Tyr† and the possessor of a magic cauldron. In the Hymiskvida Edda is told the story of the journey of Thor† and Tyr in quest of the cauldron, to bring it to the banquet of Aegir†.

Hyndla The Hyndlu-Ljod Edda poem is contained in the Flatey Book. It tells how Freyja†, mounted on her golden boar, invites the giantess Hyndla to ride on her wolf, and for them both to go to Valhalla. The rest of the poem consists of the genealogical trees of several of the Norwegian dynasties, which are quoted by Freyja or Hyndla as proof of their ancestry. Inserted in the text is the shortened version of the Völuspa.

Hyposouranios One of the giants, child of Fire† in the Phoenician† Creation Legend of Philo Byblos. He was the first to build towns, while his brother, Ousoos† was the first to make garments from skins.

Hyrrokin In Nordic myth a giantess† who was called in by Odin† to assist in the launching of Hringhorn†, the ship of Balder†, which was to be used for his funeral pyre. When she succeeded in doing this single-handed, Thor† was so furious that he tried to kill her.

I

Goddess 'I' Usually presumed to be the Mayan water goddess, represented in the Dresden Codex as holding an inverted earthenware vessel from which water flows. She may possibly be an equivalent of Chalchihuitlicue†, the Aztec water goddess, but lacking her benign character.

Ibe Dji A special idol of the Yoruba† tribes to commemorate the deaths of twin sisters.

Iblis (Eblis) An Islamic name for devil, which comes from *balas*, a wicked person. The term is used nine times in the Koran, and in some cases the term is synonymous with Shaitan†. The name is sometimes applied to Azazel†. He was father of Sut†, and of the Ghaddar by a wife which Allah† had created for him. He was governor of the lowest heaven and of the earth. He was also known as Taus, the peacock angel.

Ictinike In Sioux† myth the son of the sun god who was expelled from heaven by his father for deceit and trickery and who is considered by the Sioux as 'the father of lies'. The stories told of his disputes with the beaver, the flying squirrel, the kingfisher, and the musk-rat, all totems of the Sioux, show that he was always defeated by them, and he was probably a culture hero of some tribe whom the Sioux absorbed in the course of their history.

Idun(a) The story of the Apples of Iduna which preserved the life and health of the Aesir† in Nordic myth may be a reverse side of the stealing of the Apples of the Hesperides by Hercules. They also seem to have formed part of the treasures of the Tuatha Dé Danann†, for whom they were stolen by the sons of Tuirenn. The tale of their theft, as told in the Conversations of Bragi, is as follows: Loki† was kidnapped by Thiassi† and obtained his release by promising to deliver Iduna into the hands of Thiassi. He enticed Iduna into the forest by saying he knew where she could obtain better apples than her own. On entering the forest she was kidnapped by Thiassi. Without their daily supply of apples the Aesir grew old and grey, and it was only when they were at the point of death that they discovered what had become of Iduna. Under threat of punishment Loki was ordered to bring her back and, making use of the feather cloak of Freyja†, he flew to the home of Thiassi and rescued Iduna. He was pursued by Thiassi to the outskirts of Asgard, where he was killed by the Aesir. Iduna, about whom little is known except for her guardianship of the apples, was the daughter of a dwarf, the wife of Bragi†, and one of the Asynjor†.

Ifa In Yoruba mythology the name of an oracle, a man-god, who was sent by god to put the world to rights.

Igigi Babylonian spirits of heaven, as contrasted with the Anunnaku†, or spirits of earth. They may be the stars of the southern heavens.

Ikh The glorified state of existence after death, as visualized by the Egyptians. For further details *see* Egyptian† Religion.

Ikto In Sioux† myth the inventor of human speech and a being whose activities place him midway between the Egyptian Thoth† and the Nordic Loki†.

Il Semitic name for god; similar to El†; to be found in various combinations.

Ilah Moon god of the southern Semites, similar to Ilmaqah.

Ilamatecuhtli Ancient Aztec fertility goddess known as 'the Old Princess'. She was originally linked with Mixcoatl†, the Cichimec god. Her secondary name, Citlalinicue†, 'Star Garment', may link her with the Milky Way. She was the lord of the thirteenth hour of the day.

Illinus Brother of Anu† and Aus† in the Babylonian† Creation Legend of Damascius. May possibly be El† or Elat†.

Illiyun The seventh heaven of the Islamic paradise Dar el-Jannah†, where was kept the register of the good deeds of all Moslems.

Ilmaqah Semitic moon god, predecessor of Allah†, in pre-Islamic pantheon. He had a privileged place in the astral trinity, Imaqah, Sams†, and Atter†, being a god common to Semitism. From him may have been derived certain obvious essentials of Babylonian religion, Mosaic monotheism, and even Islam. In this particular pantheon the moon was masculine and the sun feminine, giving an indication of its great age, although even at that it may well have been preceded by a trinity of mother goddesses. He may be equated to Il† or Ilah†.

Ilmarinen A culture hero of the Kalevala, the Finnish national epic. He was the brother of Väinämöinen†, and the son of a human mother, although born on a hill of charcoal. He was a great smith and craftsman, and was described as a handsome young man.

Ilmatar A heroine of the Kalevala†, the Finnish national epic; daughter of the air, creatrix of the world, and mother of Väinämöinen†.

Ilythyia–Leucothea An Etruscan† fertility goddess.

Imberombera Culture heroine and first ancestress of the Kakadu tribe of Von Arnhem Land.

Imhotep In Egyptian myth the deified minister of King Zozer (Djoser) of the third dynasty. He was a patron of science and medicine and has been identified with Asklepios. In Greek the name is spelt Imouth†. He was one of the Memphis Triad† as the son of Ptah† and Nut†.

Imouth Greek spelling of Imhotep†. Alternative spelling Imouthes.

Imset In Egyptian myth an alternative spelling for Amset†.

In In Japanese myth the Chinese dualistic principles Yang† and Yin†, male and female respectively, became In and Yo†. Details will be found under Koji-Ki†.

Ina A name by which Sina†, the Polynesian moon goddess, was known in Mangaia.

Inari Japanese god of agriculture whose shrines may be recognized by the two foxes which stand before them and who are said to be his messengers. The personality of Uke-mochi†, an earlier mother goddess, has gradually been absorbed into that of Inari.

Inca Creation Legends As the Incas were comparatively late arrivals in Peru, being the last of a whole series of pre-Columbian cultures, their Creation Legends are scanty in the extreme. Several of them are centred on Tiahuanaco†, where there are monolithic structures of great age far outdating the Incan culture. Here it was believed that both men and animals had been created, and the two mother goddesses of the lake, Mama Cocha† and Copacati†, appear to have been connected with this. Later Titicaca became a centre of sun worship to which pilgrimages were made.

In common with many other American races the Incas tell of a time when humanity sought refuge in a cave known as Pacari† from which came the founders of the Inca culture. Another story is that of Ataguju†, from whom descended Guamansuri†, the father of Apocatequil† and Piguerao†. Finally there was the mother goddess Mama Pacha†, from whom originated Pachacamac†, the earth god. Further details will be found under the following headings: Epunamun†, Guarchimines†, Ka-Ata-Killa†, Mama Allpa†, Mama Ocllo Huaca†, Mama Pacha†, Mancocoapac†, Punchau†, Supay†, Thonapa†, Tiahuanaco†, and Viracocha†.

Indech In Celtic myth a king of the Formors† said to be a son of Domnu† who was later killed in battle by Ogma†, a chief of the Tuatha Dé Danaan.

Indra In Vedic myth a god of battle and of rain. He appears to have been a real king, a jolly fair-haired fighting man of the Nordic type, who was deified after death, and whose worship spread at the expense of the older gods. Eventually, he was ousted by the Brahmans in favour of Vishnu†, and sank from the position of a heaven god to that of king of Swarga, the Hindu paradise. His sacred city was Amaravati. His title of Vritrahan†, said to have been acquired by his defeat of Vritra†, may be taken from the name of Verethraghna†, the Zoroastrian god of victory, whose name means the Slayer. In his military campaigns, Indra fought successfully against the Asuras†, the Daityas†, the Danavas†, and the Dasyus†. He is frequently shown mounted on an elephant, named Airavata†.

Infoniwoo God of Generation in the Creation Legend of Taiwan.

Initiation Ceremonies These ceremonies, no matter from what part of the world they originate, have a tendency to resemble each other in outline. There are usually three stages: Katharsis, corresponding to baptism; Paradosis, corresponding to confirmation; and Epopteia, corresponding to ritual death and rebirth. The first two of these still exist in the Christian Church. The third stage, that of rebirth, is the period of meditation and temptation which all the great religious leaders of the past have had to undergo: Buddha sitting under the Bo-tree, Christ spending forty days in the wilderness. In many ceremonies the third stage included passage through a ring of fire, as with Brynhild†, Menglad†, and Skirnir†.

Innana Early Babylonian mother goddess who later became merged in Ishtar†. She was also known as Ninanna†. Both terms appear to have been generally applied to pre-diluvial goddesses.

Invisibility Garments and rings producing invisibility are listed under Treasures†.

Io Abstract supreme being of the Maori and the Polynesian peoples. The fact that Io had receded into the background seems to show that he may have been an early god or culture hero of these races who was already in process of being displaced when they first arrived in the Pacific.

Ioi Sister of Blue Jay† in the Creation Legend of the Chinooks† and participant in many of his adventures.

Iphtimis *See* Nefertum†.

Irin Mage Powerful magician who in the Tupi-Guarani† Creation Legend extinguished with a deluge the conflagration of the world caused by Monan†. Another version of this occurs in connection with Tawanduare† and Arikute†.

Irish Calendar The A.M. or Anno Mundi system of dating frequently found in Irish legends may roughly be equated as follows:

A.M.   I = B.C. 5195
A.M.   195 = B.C. 5000
A.M.   1195 = B.C. 4000

A.M. 2195 = B.C. 3000
A.M. 3195 = B.C. 2000
A.M. 4195 = B.C. 1000
A.M. 5195 = A.D. 1
A.M. 6194 = A.D. 1000

Irmin (Hermin) Culture hero of a west German tribe, the Herminones. He may possibly be equated with Tiwaz†. The mysterious Irminsul, or 'Column of the World', which stood in a sacred grove was destroyed by Charlemagne.

Iroquois Indian Creation Legend In the myths of the Iroquois tribes Athensic†, the ancestress of mankind, fell from heaven into the waters of the Deluge as it was receding and she found herself on dry land which soon became a continent. Later Enigorio† and Enigohatgea, the twin brothers, began to organize life again, and when the Iroquois migrated to the Land of the Stone Giants, their enemies were overcome by the efforts of Hinun†, the thunder god, and his brother the West Wind. One of their later culture heroes was Atatarho†.

In another version of the story the twins are named Tsetsa and Tawiscara†, as in the Huron† Creation Legend.

Irra In Babylonion myth a plague demon who at the instruction of Allatu†, Queen of the Underworld, tormented Ishtar† when she visited it to find Tammuz†.

Ishtanu The Hittite sun god, in Hattic Eshtan†.

Ishtar The Babylonian goddess of fertility. Her cult was first recorded in Erech, but probably started much earlier and spread to the whole of the Middle East, and even to Greece. On the Mediter-

ranean coast she appears a Ashtart†, but
without alteration of her essential
characteristics. She was adopted into the
pantheon of many races, and appears as
the consort of Marduk†, Asshur†,
Tammuz†, and even as Ninlil†, consort
of Enlil†, the storm god. She has also
been identified with Damkina†, wife of
Ea†, in which capacity she is the mother
of Tammuz†. She was sometimes considered to be the daughter of Anu† or of
Sin†, while Frazer equated her with the
Esther of the Old Testament. The story
of her descent into Aralu, the Babylonian Hades, to bring back Tammuz†, is
told on a tablet in the British Museum.
When she arrived at the gates she found
them shut, and threatened to break them
down to free the dead and to devour the
living. On hearing this Allatu†, Queen
of the Underworld, gave orders for her
admittance. After performing the customary rites, which consisted in the re-
moval of part of her clothing and ornaments at each of the Seven Gates, she
arrived naked in the region of those
'whose bread is dust, whose food is
mud, who see not the light, who dwell
in darkness, and who are clothed like
birds in apparel of feathers'. Allatu
mocks her and orders Namtar†, the
plague demon, to smite her with disease
from head to foot. (This is obviously
the description of an initiation ceremony
in one of the early mysteries.) During
her absence from earth, all fertility is
suspended for man and beast. Shamash†,
the sun god, receives the dread news
through Papsukal†. He consults Ea and
Sin, and Ea creates a being called
Ashushu-Namir who is sent to Allatu to
demand the release of Ishtar in the name
of the Great Gods, a demand which
Allatu could not refuse, so Namtar was
ordered to bring Ishtar forth and to

sprinkle her with the Water of Life. She
was then conducted back through the
Seven Gates and her garments and
jewels returned to her. On her coming
back to earth, life resumed its normal
course. Ishtar occurs several times in the
Epic, as befits the importance of her
role as chief of the Igigi†, or spirits of
heaven, and as the enemy of Gilgamesh.

At some stage she absorbed Anunitum
and Nina†. She was the morning manifestation of the star Venus.

Isis Egyptian goddess, daughter of
Geb† and Nut†, sister and wife of
Osiris†, sister of Nephthys† and Set†,
and mother of Horus the Child†. One
of the Ennead†. Although Isis, who was
the prototype of the good wife and
mother, is usually considered in relation
to the myth of the murder of Osiris by
Set, and her struggle to put her son
Horus on the throne, in actual fact she
would appear to have been a goddess in
her own right, and possibly even before
Osiris.

Her magical powers were shown
when Set caused a scorpion to sting her
son Horus, and she managed to avert
any evil result by reciting certain spells.
On another occasion, when Horus and
Set were fighting and had assumed the
forms of huge black bulls, she was sufficiently powerful to slay them both. She
could transform herself into any kind of
creature, and travel through earth, air,
fire, and water with ease.

On one occasion, however, she was
defeated by Horus, who was so infuriated with her for releasing Set after a
battle in which he had been captured
that he cut off her head. Thoth†, however, magically changed it into the head
of a cow and reattached it to her body.
This myth arises from the identification

of Isis with Hathor† in some localities, and also from the fact that she was under the care of Hathor in the swamps of the Delta when rearing Horus.

The lament which Isis and Nephthys were said to have sung after the death of Osiris was the official Egyptian funerary dirge. The worship of Isis spread far and wide, and images of Isis were found in many parts of Europe. With the advent of Christianity these were taken over as 'Black Virgins'. In the same manner there was a Black Aphrodite in Cyprus.

On one occasion Isis desired to know the secret name of Ra†. This she accomplished by collecting his saliva and forming it into a poisonous snake, which caused Ra to become very ill when it bit him. As Ra had not created the snake, as he had the rest of the world, he was unable to remedy the ill. Isis promised to cure him if he told her his secret name, by which she would become all-powerful. The god tried to avoid the issue by telling her his other names, but to no avail, and at the end he had to tell her and 'it passed from his bosom to hers'.

Isis was known by many names, including Aset†, Aust†, Eset† and Hest†.

Isis, Mysteries of Egyptian religious ceremony which became widespread over the Mediterranean area, and which was still being performed in the sixth century A.D. They cover the death and resurrection of Osiris†, and the hiding of his coffin in a tree trunk at Byblos, from which Isis excised him. The best description is in Plutarch's *De Iside et Osiride*.

A similarity to this ritual may be found in the Jewish ceremony of hiding the Passover cake known as Afikoman†

A similarity to this ritual may be found in the Jewish ceremony of hiding the Passover cake known as Afikoman†.

Istar Northern Semitic spelling for Ishtar† as goddess of the evening star (Venus).

Italapas In the Chinook† Creation Legend this name is given to Coyote†, to whom have been attributed a whole succession of good deeds, including the driving of the sea away from the prairie land so that men could settle down, and the laying down of the codes of taboos and hunting laws. The mischievous qualities of Coyote in other myths have in this case been attributed to Blue-Jay†.

Ith A Milesian, the brother of Bile† and the son of Bregon†. When he landed in Ireland at Londonderry he was murdered by the three kings of the Tuatha Dé Danaan†, a deed which was followed by the Milesian invasion. He appears to have been a corn king of the Ivernians and to have come to Britain from the Mediterranean. The name survives in a Cornish cromlech called 'Grugith', or Barrow of Ith, and also in the Cornish parish of St. Teath.

Itum Alternative form of Nefertum†, the human-headed Egyptian god of the Ennead†. *See also* Iphtimis†.

Itzamna In Mayan myth he was the moon god, father of gods and men. He was the god of the west. He was also known as Zamna†. He may be God 'K'†.

Itzlacoliuhque The curved obsidian knife god. An Aztec god who may be identified with Tezcatlipoce†.

Itzli The stone knife god, Aztec god identified with Tezcatlipoca†. He was the lord of the second hour of the night.

Itzpapalotl Aztec agricultural goddess known as 'Obsidian Knife Butterfly'. She seems to have been a minor fire goddess of the Cichimecs.

Iuchar and Iucharba In Celtic myth the brothers of Brian†, the sons of Tuirenn and the murderers of Cian who, as a penalty, had to seek and find what subsequently became the treasures of the Tuatha†.

Iusas In Egyptian mythology the wife of Ra†, also known as Eus-os†, Uert-Hekeu† and Rat†.

Iusaset In Egyptian myth a minor goddess of Heliopolis.

Iweridd In Celtic myth the wife of Llyr† and the mother of Branwen† and Brân†. The word means Ireland and shows that Llyr was of Irish origin.

Ix One of the four Bacabs, the Maya gods of the cardinal points. He represented the west and his colour was black.

Ixazalvoh Maya† goddess of weaving, wife of Kinich Ahau†, the sun god.

Ixbalanqué *See* Xbalanqué.

Ixchel 'The Rainbow', consort of the Mayan Votan†, also known as Ix-kanleom, the spider's web that catches the morning dew.

Ixcuinan 'Queen of cotton', an alternative name for Tlazolteotl†.

Ixtab Maya goddess of the noose or the gallows.

Ixtliton Aztec god of medicine and good health known as 'Little Black Face'. The priests of this god were medicine men or shamans and specialized in the treatment of children with the various medicines which they kept in stock.

Izanagi and Izanami The first human couple encountered in Japanese myth. Looking down from the floating bridge of heaven they stirred up the brine with a jewelled spear and the island of Onogoro arose from the expanse of waters. On it they settled and their children were Amaterasu†, the sun goddess; Tsukiyomi†, the moon god; Susano†, the sea god; and Kagu-Tsuchi, the fire god. After the birth of the latter child Izanami died, and her husband pursued her to Hades, where he found only her suppurating body, from which he fled in horror. This story is taken from the Kojiki, the Japanese Creation Legend.

Iztat Ix A name given to Alaghom Naum†, the goddess of the Tzental tribe of the Mayas†. She was the wife of Patol†.

J

Jacy In the Tupi-Garani† Creation Legend, Jacy, the moon, is the creator of plant life. As the moon under the name of Toruguenket† is the force of evil, it is possible the Jacy was originally some other celestial body, possibly the planet Venus. His fellow creator gods were Guaracy† and Peruda†.

Jagan-natha In Vedic myth a vast idol, without legs, and having only stumps for arms, stated to contain the bones of Krisna†, which stands at Puri in Orissa, India. The term Jagan-natha means 'Lord of the World', and festivals are held in his honour, particularly in Puri, where as many as two hundred thousand pilgrims assemble for the occasion. At the Ratha-yatra held in the month of Asarha, the temple car containing the images of Krisna† and other gods is drawn through the town. In former times many devotees cast themselves beneath its ponderous wheels and were crushed to death. It is from this that the expression 'beneath the wheels of the Juggernaut' is derived.

Jahannam The purgatorial or first stage of the Islamic hell, Daru el-Bawar†. From this word comes the biblical term Gehenna.

Jahi In Persian mythology a demonic female who embodies debauchery.

Jahim The sixth stage of the Islamic hell, Daru el-Bawar†, a hot fire of idolators.

Jamshid In Zoroastrian myth one of the earliest kings, and said to have reigned seven hundred years. He was killed by being sawn asunder by his enemy Zuhak (Zahhak)†. He introduced cultivation of the vine and other useful arts.

Jann In pre-Islamic myth the lowest, or fifth, species of jinn†, who had been transformed downwards for misdemeanours as some animals are transformed from men.

Jannatu el-'Adn The fourth stage in the Islamic paradise Dar el-Jannah†, the Gardens of Perpetual Abode, symbolized by large pearls.

Jannatu el-Firdaus The eighth stage in the Islamic paradise, Dar el-Jannah†, the Gardens of Paradise, symbolized by red gold.

Jannatu el-Khuld The Garden of Eternity, the first stage of Dar el-Jannah†, the Islamic paradise, symbolized by green or yellow coral.

Jannatu el-Ma'wa The fifth stage in the Islamic paradise, Dar el-Jannah†, the Gardens of Refuge.

Jannatu el-Na'im Sixth stage in the Islamic paradise, Dar el-Jannah†, the Gardens of Delight, symbolized by white silver.

Jarnsaxa ('Iron Dirk') In Nordic myth a giantess, the wife of Thor†, who may also have been known as Sif†. She was the mother of Modi† and Magni†, the sons of Thor, who were two of the survivors of Ragnarok†. She was not a member of the Asynjor†, although she was the wife of Thor.

Jerah Alternative Hebrew spelling for Erah†, the Semitic moon god.

Jessis An early Slavonic deity whom later historians have identified with Jupiter.

Jezi-Baba See Baba-Yaga†.

Jikoku One of the Japanese guardians of the cardinal points. He was the guardian of the east.

Jimmu-Tenno Mythical human emperor of Japan who is said to have succeeded the divine dynasty in the seventh century BC. He is probably a culture hero of a pre-Japanese race, as the Japanese themselves cannot claim to have made any contribution to the history of Japan until at least a thousand years later.

Jinn In the pre-Islamic Arabian mythology the jinn were living beings of superhuman kind. They were not pure spirits but were corporeal beings, more like beasts than men, usually represented as hairy or having some animal shape. Their bodies were solid, but they had a mysterious power of disappearing and reappearing, or even of assuming human form. It should be observed that jinn are not recognized as individuals; the Arab says 'the Ghul appeared', not 'a Ghul appeared'; with the advent of Islam, the term jinn became applied to many of the pre-Islamic gods. Four hundred and twenty species of jinn were marshalled before Solomon. The jinn of the Arabian Nights, who have distinct personalities, would appear to be later additions. According to Mohammedan tradition, the prophet assigned the healthy uplands to the believing jinn and the fever-haunted lowlands to the unbelieving.

There were five orders of jinn: the Marid†, the most powerful; the Efrit†; the Shaitan†; the Jinn; and the Jann†. The development of this hierarchy appears to have arisen from the necessity of accommodating several groups of pre-Islamic gods in the pantheon of evil as represented by the jinn. There were also other jinn who fitted more or less into the classification given above. For details consult Azazel†, Dalhan†, Efrit†, Ghaddar†, Ghul†, Hatif†, Iblis†, Jann†, Lilith†, Marid†, Marut†, Nasnas†, Qutrub†, Shaitan†, Shiqq†, Silat†, Sut†, and Taus†. Among the Persians, the jinn were Devas†, Narahs†, and Piris†.

Jizō A Japanese Buddhist god, the protector of children and the consoler of parents. He may originally have been a god of the seas whose temples were found in caves on the seashore, in which case his guardianship of children would date from the advent of Buddhism.

Jom The sun in the Ugarit scripts.

Jord In Nordic myth a giantess, the daughter of Nott†. She was the mother of Thor† and also one of the Asynjor†. She seems to have been originally an earth goddess.

Jormungard In Nordic myth the Midgard† serpent spawned by Loki† and the sister of Fenrir†. There are several stories of the combats between the serpent and Thor†, a wrestling match is mentioned under Skrymir†, and Thor's fishing for the serpent in the sea in Hymiskvida Edda†. Finally Ragnarok† tells how it was slain by Thor.

Jorōjin (**Jurojin**) Japanese god of longevity similar to Fukurokuju†. He is one of the seven divinities of luck, the Shichi Fukujin†.

Jotunn (**Jotnar**) In Nordic myth the giants†. They seem to have been the representatives of some pre-Scandinavian race not necessarily of exceptional size but bigger than the Aesir†, who built the city of Asgard† as a stronghold against them.

The land of the giants was known as Jötunheim and its chief city was Utgard†. It was a snowy region on the outward shores of the deep ocean, known to both the Aesir and the Vanir†. The fact that in the Edda† it says, 'The golden age lasted until the women of Jötunheim corrupted it,' shows that intermarriage must have been fairly common, which is confirmed by the giant women in the Asynjor†.

Jo-Uk In the Shilluk† Creation Legend the great creator, the maker of the Sacred White Cow, which came up out of the Nile. The title of Jo-Uk is still given to Shilluk kings.

Joukahainen A Lapland woman mentioned in the Kalevala, the Finnish national epic, as being pledged to Väinämöinen, wooer of Aino†.

Judi Landing place of the Ark in Kurdish tradition on left bank of Tigris. An alternative spelling is Djudi†. For further information see Babylonian† Creation Legend.

Juichimen In Japanese mythology the Buddhist god of mercy.

Jukurokujin or **Fukurokuju** The Japanese god of luck.

Jupiter Ammon A statue of the Egyptian god Amon†, situated at the oasis of Siwa in Libya, which was reported to have given spoken oracles. Lysander, Hannibal, and Alexander the Great were among those who visited this statue for guidance.

Jurojin Japanese god of longevity. Alternative spelling Jorōjin.

Jurupari Principal deity of the Uapes tribe of the Tupi-Guarani Indians of Brazil. He is essentially a man's god whose worship resembles freemasonry. Women who happened to see any of the symbols of the worship were put to death. The story goes that he was born of a virgin and that when he grew up he was burnt to death by the tribe for having indulged in ritual cannibalism. From his ashes grew the Paxiuba-tree from which the sacred instruments were cut.

K

God 'K' Mayan wind god who may be equated with Ehecatl†, the wind god of the Aztecs.

Ka The Egyptian believed that the body was animated by a vital force, which he pictured as a counterpart of the body, which came into the world with it, passed through life in its company, and accompanied it into the next world. This is called a Ka, and is often spoken of in modern treatises as a 'double', although this designation describes the form of the Ka as represented upon the monuments rather than its real nature. For further details *see* Egyptian† Religion.

Ka-Ata-Killa Pre-Inca† moon goddess worshipped on the shores of Lake Titicaca. The story goes that a race of giants† who were her followers were turned into the Colossi of Tiahuanaco†.

Kabandha In the Ramayana he is the chief demon whom Indra† struck with a thunderbolt and compressed his body into a squat shape.

Kaboi Culture hero of the Karaya† Indians known as Kamu† to the Arawaks†, Tamu† to the Caribs†, Kame† to the Bakairi Caribs, and Zume† to the Paraguayans. After the Deluge he led the ancestors of the tribe from their cave refuge on Tupimare† Mountain to the outer world, being guided by the call of a bird. Other details of the story are given under Tupuya† and Ges Creation Legends, and Anatiwa†.

Kabul Alternative name for Itzamna†, the Maya† moon god. He was also known as Zamna†.

Kaggen In Bushmen† myth a being resembling the Coyote† of North America, mischievous and full of tricks, whose representative on earth is the praying mantis. He is to be identified with Cagn†.

Kagu-Tsuchi Japanese fire god whose birth caused the death of his mother Izanami†. By the time the Koji-Ki† had been written in the eighth century he had already dropped into partial oblivion.

Kahil Early Arabian name for moon; may possibly be connected with Kalkail, the guardian angel of Islam.

Kailasa In Vedic myth the city of Ganesa†, Kubera†, and Siva†, situated on Mount Meru†, the Hindu Olympus.

Kaizuki In Buganda he is the brother of Death, who was unsucessful in his attempt to kill his brother, and so prevent human beings from dying.

Kalevala The Finnish national epic, which resembles the Hero† of Estonia.

It was first put into book form in 1835 by Elias Lonrot. It consists of fifty cantos, called 'runes', and apart from a recital of the adventures of the various participants gives an account of the Creation of the world corresponding to those of the Nordic races. It also includes details of a cosmic disaster affecting the moon, causing high tides and earthquakes in the land of the Finns. The wars in which the heroes were involved were those of the Great Migrations and the period of resettlement. It is possible they may have been the Frost Giants, the enemies of the Aesir†. For further details *see* Aino†, Ilmarinen†, Ilmatar†, Joukahainen†, Kaukomieli†, Kullervo†, Lemminkainen†, Väinämöinen†.

Kali In Vedic myth the wife of Siva†. Kali also appears in the following forms: Ambika†, Anna-Purna†, Bhavani†, Durgha†, Kamakshi†, Kumari†, Sati†, Uma†, Vijaya†. As Kali, the goddess of time, she is usually depicted dancing through space. She has four hands, and her garment is draped with human heads. In one hand she holds a sword; in a second hand a freshly severed human head; the third hand is raised in a gesture of peace; and the fourth hand is grasping for power. At her feet lies the body of her husband, on whom she has trampled in her frenzy. She would appear to be an early war goddess who was absorbed into the Hindu pantheon as the creator or mother of Siva, whom she subsequently married. Her other names are doubtless those of goddesses who have been treated in the same cavalier fashion. Her worship is usually accompanied by sanguinary rites. She was the titular goddess of the thugs. Calcutta, or Kali-ghat, was named after her. The male aspect of Kali was Maha-Kala†.

Kalki In Vedic myth the tenth, and last, avatar of Vishnu† when he will be revealed in the sky riding a white horse. The word means 'Time'. His role resembles that of the Four Horsemen of the Apocalypse.

Kallevipoeg The principal character of the Hero† of Estonia, in which he is a king. In the Kalevala†, the Finnish national epic, he is known as Kullervo† and is a slave.

Kalpa In the Hindu† Creation Legend the Kalpa, or Day of Brahma†, is subdivided as follows:
1 Kalpa = 1,000 Mahayugas = 14 Manvantaras; 1 Manvantara = 71,428 Mahayugas = 857,139,000 divine years; 1 Mahayuga = 4 Yugas = 12,000 divine years; 1 divine year = 360 human years.

The Hindu obsession with big numbers makes these figures very suspect. As mentioned elsewhere, if the 12,000 divine years of the Mahayuga are taken as ordinary years, this would give a date corresponding roughly to that of the beginning of the Hindu calendar in 11,500 BC.

Kalu Babylonian priests ministering to Enmesharra†, a god of the underworld.

Kama In Vedic myth the son of Lakshmi†, and the god of love. He is represented, like Cupid, as a young boy with bow and arrow and wings. His wife was Rati†, the fair-limbed.

Kamakshi In Vedic myth one of the benign aspects of Parvati†, wife of Siva†. The name means 'Wanton-Eyed', and may be that of some early fertility goddess whose personality was merged with that of Parvati.

Kame and Keri In the Creation Legend of the Bakairi Caribs the mystical twin heroes Kame and Keri populated the world with animals which they brought from the hollow trunk of a tree which was later connected with the Milky Way. They believed that the sun and moon were being aimlessly carried about by two birds until the twins seized them by cunning and put them on their present courses. Kame is a rendering of Kamu†, the name given by the Arawak Indians to Zume†.

Kamennaia Baba The Stone Mothers, a name given in south Russia to the numerous monolithic statues of male and female figures carrying drinking horns scattered through this area.

Kamonu In the mythology of the Barotse people of Zambia, he imitated god to such an extent that ultimately god was forced to remove himself to a place where Kamonu could not reach him.

Kamu Name given by the Arawak† Indians to the Zume† of the Paraguayans, the Tamu† of the Arovac Caribs, and the Kaboi† of the Karayas. He was an early culture hero of a similar type to Quetzalcoatl†, and may be the Kame† of the Bakairi† Caribs.

Kan One of the four Bacabs, the Maya gods of the cardinal points. He represented the east and his colour was yellow.

Karaia-I-Te-Ata In the Mangaia† Creation myth the daughter of Miru†, the god of the underworld.

Karaya Indian Creation Legend This is given under Tupuya† and Ges Creation Legends. Their culture heroes were Kaboi†, Kame†, Keri†, and Saracura†.

Karliki According to Russian tradition, when Satan was expelled from heaven some spirits fell into the underworld and, becoming dwarfs†, were given this name; others became the Lychie† of the woods. This explanation seems to be an attempt on the part of Christian missionaries to discount the stories of the old gods of the Slavs.

Karma The doctrine of causation in Buddhist† faith. The assumption is that every living being is the heir to the accumulated effects of his own deeds in former existences, and that until all these activities have been written off as the result of conscious efforts or deeds the wheel of rebirths will continue. This doctrine differs considerably from the Hindu transmigration as it is more in the nature of the carry forward at the closing of an annual balance sheet than the actual transfer of the Atman or soul. The release from this state of bondage is called Nirvana†.

Karshipta The name of the bird, possibly a dove or pigeon, sent out by Yima† after the Flood to convey news of his safety to any survivors.

Kartikeya (**Karttikaya**) In late Vedic myth a god of war, known also as Kumara† and Skanda†. He was said to be the son of Agni† or Siva†. He was the leader of the forces of good against the demon Taraka, whom he defeated with the aid of the weapons fashioned from the rays of the sun as told under Saranyu†.

Karu In the Creation Legend of the

Mundruku tribe of the Tupi-Guarani† Indians a culture hero who created the mountains by blowing feathers about.

Kasyapa In Vedic myth the husband of Vinata† and father of Garuda†. He was one of the seven great Rishis†. Alternatively, he was the husband of Diti† and father of the Daityas† and the Maruts†.

Kathar-Wa-Hasis The Vulcan of the gods of Ugarit, a craftsman and artificer, who fashioned everything from jewellery to palaces. He was domiciled in Egypt, which would indicate that it was from there that technical crafts spread northwards. He made the two clubs, 'Driver' and 'Expeller', used by Baal† to depose Yammt†.

Katkochila In the Creation Legend of the Wintun† Indians he was a god who sent a great fire to burn up the earth in revenge for the theft of his magic flute. Later, however, the fire was put out by a flood.

Kato Indian Creation Legend In an island above the waters lived Tcenes†. He rescued a child, Nagaitco†, who was floating on the branch of a tree, and he grew up to be the first man. One day a woman and a dog came to the island, the three of them sailed away to the mainland to become the ancestors of the tribe.

Kaukomieli A name by which Lemminkainen†, the hero of the Kalevala†, the Finnish national epic, was also known.

Kaustubha In Vedic myth the jewel of Vishnu, which was produced at the Churning of the Ocean in the Kurma† avatar.

Keb The earth in early cosmogony, also referred to as Geb†.

Kedesh A variant of Qedeshet†, a Syrian goddess who was worshipped in Egypt.

Kehtahn A cigarette-shaped reed filled with tobacco and other offerings to the gods, mention of which occurs in Navajo† myth.

Kekui and Kekuit Two of the gods created by Thoth† mentioned in the Egyptian† Creation Legends.

Kelpie In Celtic Scottish myth a god of lakes and rivers reputed to cause travellers to drown. He often takes the shape of a water horse.

Kenet Egyptian goddess of Syriac origin.

Kewawkqu In Algonkian† myth a tribe of powerful magicians who were defeated by Gluskap†.

Khaibit The ancient Egyptians believed man's personality to be made up of a 'Ka'† (or double), a 'Ba'† (or soul), and even of a 'Khaibit' (or shadow), thereby resembling the Ya Chi'o Miao, who believed that man had three souls, one his shadow, one his reflection as seen in water, and one his real self. For further details *see* Egyptian† Religion.

Khasm The modern name for Aesma†, the Zoroastrian Deva† or evil spirit of wrath, to whom was applied the term 'with the terrible spear'.

Khat The physical body of the Egyptian which was preserved by mummification, but which – except in the eyes of the ignorant – did not rise again. It is possible that the original idea of preservation of the body was for the benefit of the Kat and also because they felt that the Sahut or spiritual body was germinated in the physical body. For further details *see* Egyptiant Religion.

Khebieso Ewe god of lightning also known as Sot, linked with Bot.

Khensu Human-headed Egyptian moon god, the third member of the Great Triad of Thebest, declared to be the son of Amon-Rat and Mutt. He was worshipped with great honour at Thebes. He had seven forms, and was known as 'the Traveller'; he may be equated with Khonst and was occasionally confused with Thotht.

Khenti Amentiu In Egyptian myth a title given to Osirist, meaning chief of the inhabitants of Amenti, i.e. the dead.

Khepera Egyptian scarab god, the creator of the universe, who arose from Nut, the primeval watery chaos. The scarab beetle was the emblem of Creation owing to its habit of rolling a ball of dung into which it lays its eggs. One of the eight gods of Hermopolis. Also identified with Rat. Also known as Khoprit or Khepri.

Kherebu Assyrian spirits from whose name comes the biblical cherubimt.

Khnemu (**Khnum**) Ram-headed creator potter-god of the Elephantine Triadt, associated with Maatt, Ptaht, and Thotht in the Creation. Although he was the husband of Satit and Anoukist (or Anquett), he may originally have

been a goddess. He was also known as Khnoumis. He is said to have created the universe; made the cosmic egg, and to have shaped man on his potter's wheel.

Khons Considered to have been the original name of Chronos in Crete. May be equated with Khensut.

Khopri A variant of Kheperat, the Egyptian scarab god.

Khors God of health and hunting in the group of Slavonic gods in Kiev Castle. His image had the form of a stallion. He resembled Freyrt in many ways. The others were Dabogt, Percount, and Stribogt.

Khoser-et-Hasis Marine god of the early Phoenicians. He played a prominent part in the destruction of Baalt by raising the sea and the river against him. One of the marine beasts he enlists for this purpose is the Leviathant of the Bible, while others are the Zabel of the Seat and the Suffete of the Rivert. He was also known as Bn-Ymt.

Khu The shining impalpable and immortal essence which may be likened to an aura. The Khu, like the Kat, could be imprisoned in the tomb, unless special precautions were taken. Usually figured as a crested bird. For further details *see* Egyptiant Religion.

Khuzwane Creator in the mythology of the Lovedu, a Bantu tribe of the Transvaal.

Kibuka The war god of the Bugandans. He was the brother of the great god Mukasat.

Kieva In Celtic myth the wife of Pryderi†.

Kiho Tumu Supreme god of the Tuamotu archipelago in Polynesia. *See* Te Tumu†.

Kingu Babylonian god of the powers of darkness, who was placed by Tiamat† in command of the brood of monsters spawned by Hubur†, and of the Eleven Mighty Helpers, in her fight against the powers of good led by Ea†, who had destroyed her husband Apsu†. Kingu, who is Tammuz†, was the counterpart of Anu†, the sky god. He appears also to have become the second husband of Tiamat. When Tiamat appointed him as her captain, she also gave him the Tablets of Wisdom, or Dup Shimati, saying 'Whatsoever goes forth from thy mouth shall be established.' In spite of this he was deported by Marduk†, who had been chosen as the champion of the new order, and who seized the Tablets of Wisdom and placed them on his own breast. Later, when Marduk created man out of 'blood and bone', Kingu was named by the gods as a sacrifice for this purpose as a punishment for having fought against Marduk. He was seized and, after being fettered, 'they inflicted punishment upon him and let his blood', from which Ea† fashioned mankind for the service of the gods.

Kinich-Ahau The sun god of the Mayas, 'the Lord of the Face of the Sun' who may correspond to Quetzalcoatl† as sun god.

Kintu The first man among the Bugandans.

Kishar The host of earth, one of the second pair of Babylonian gods to arise from the depths of chaos. The other one was Anshar†, the host of heaven.

Kishi Bojin A goddess of Indian origin worshipped in Japan as the protectress of young children.

Kishijoten Japanese goddess of luck, and sister of Bishamon†.

Kissare Name given to Kishar† by Damascius in the Babylonian Creation Legend.

Kitche Manitou In the Creation Legend of the Muskwari† Indians he is stated to have destroyed the world twice, first by a fire and secondly by a deluge.

Klamath Indian Creation Legend This Oregon tribe have a myth of a demon called Kmukamtch† who tried, unsuccessfully, to destroy the world by fire.

Kleesto In Navajo† myth the name of the Great Snake.

Kmukamtch A demon in the Creation Legend of the Klamath† Indians who tried to destroy the earth by fire.

Knpua Generic term for the demigods of Hawaii. One of them referred to in the story of Laieikawi was named 'Eyeball of the Sun', and lived in a place called 'the Shining Heavens' on the borders of Tahiti. The full gods were known as Akua†.

Kobold In Teutonic myth a dwarf who was originally a miner, as it is from this word that we get cobalt. He subsequently degenerated into a German leprechaun, but this transformation appears to be one mainly due to the advent of Christianity.

Kodoyanpe In the Creation Legend of the Maidu† Indians of California the survivors from the Deluge were Kodoyanpe and Coyote†, who created mankind out of wooden images and then quarrelled, Kodoyanpe being forced to flee to the east.

Kohin Culture hero of the Herbert River tribes. He is the same as Koin† of the Macquarie tribes. He is linked with Birral† and Maamba†.

Koin Culture hero of the Lake Macquarie tribes of Australia. He is the same as Kohin†. He is linked with Birral† and Maamba†.

Koji-Ki A Japanese book completed in AD 712 in which is recounted the Japanese Creation Legend. In the beginning In† and Yo†, corresponding to the Chinese Yang† and Yin†, being the male and female principles of Dualism†, lay dormant in the choatic egg, which eventually split into heaven and earth, which latter floated on the surface of the water. The first god to appear was Kuni-Toko-Tachi, from whom proceeded seven generations of divine beings, culminating in Izanagi† and Izanami, the first human pair. At the time when the waters of the Deluge receded and the islands of the Pacific began to appear above the surface, this couple settled on Onogoro. Their children were Amaterasu†, Tsuki-Yomi†, Susano†, and Kagu-Tsuchi†, and from them was descended the royal line of Japan. Although this doctrine was enforced under the impact of militant Shintoism† during the Second World War, in actual fact the relationship between the Japanese ruling family and the aboriginal inhabitants was so slight as to be almost non-existent.

Kola In the Shilluk† Creation Legend the son of the Sacred White Cow and the grandfather of Ukwa†, the ancestor of the Shilluk nation.

Kolpia The wind, husband of Baau† and father of Aion† and Protogonos† in the Phoenician† Creation Legend of Philo Byblos.

Komoku One of the Japanese guardians of the cardinal points. He was the guardian of the south.

Komorkis Moon goddess of the Blackfoot† Indians.

Kompira A Japanese Buddhist deity of obscure origin who has been identified with Susano† and with other Shinto gods. He was a patron of seafarers and may have been brought in by traders from practically any part of the eastern hemisphere.

Ko-no-hana In Japanese mythology the Blossom Princess, who married Ninigi†, the grandson of Amaterasu†.

Korobona Culture heroine of the Warrau tribe of the Arawaks† who, having been seduced by a water demon, produced the first Carib†, a great warrior who slew many Arawaks.

Korraval In Tamil myth the goddess of victory and the wife of Silappadikaram†.

Korrawi The Tamil goddess of battle and victory.

Krimen In the Tupi-Guaranit Creation Legend one of three brothers, the others being Coemt and Hermittent, who escaped from the Deluge by climbing trees or by hiding in caves.

Krimhild In the Nibelungenlied the sister of Gunthert, who married Siegfriedt. In the Volsung Saga she had the name of Grimhildt, and was the mother of Gudrunt, whom she enabled to marry Siegfried, thanks to a magic draught. In the Thidrek Saga she was the sister of Gunnart, who usurps the place of Gudrun and marries Siegfried.

Krisna (**Krishna**) The Krisna of Vedic myth as told in the Māhabhārata would appear to have been a Ksatriya warrior, who fought at the battle of Kurusksetra at the time when the Indo-Germanic peoples were fighting their way towards the great Indian plain. His mystical teaching was received from Ghora Angirasa, as recorded in the Chandogya Upanishad and finally incorporated in the Gita of the Bhagavads. It is possible that the story of his overthrow of the tyrant Kamsa has a factual basis; the remainder of the legends about Krisna are probably myths of earlier heroes which have been incorporated into his story in the process of making him into a god. The Vishnut worship which grew up about Krisna may have been the result of an attempt to foist a sectarian god on the Vedic peoples by identifying Krisna as the eighth avatar of Vishnu. Details as to the manner in which Vasudevat was brought into the picture are given under the relevant entry. The legends of Krisna's boyhood among the cowherds of Brindaban arise from his confusion with Gopala, a cowherd god of the nomadic tribe of Abhiras, who

migrated into India about the first century AD, bringing with them the worship of a boy god and legends of the massacre of the innocents. The name Harit usually applied to Vishnu is sometimes given to Krisna. To the Tamils he was known as Mayon. His twin brother was the fair-haired Bala-Ramat.

Krita In the Hindut Creation Legends the first of the four Yugast of the current Mahayugat, having a length of 4,800 divine years.

Kronos Originally a fertility god before being taken into the Greek pantheon.

Kshathra One of the seven Immortal Holy Ones, the attendants of Ahura Mazdat. Kshathra represented Dominion. He was the genius of metals.

Kuan-Ti In Chinese myth the god of war who, contrary to other gods of his type, was mainly concerned with the averting of conflict and with the protection of people from the horrors of war.

Kuan-Yin The guardian angel of mankind of Chinese Buddhist faith. She is the patron goddess of mothers, the patroness of seamen, and the model of Chinese beauty. She received her name because when about to enter heaven she heard a cry of anguish arising from the earth and, moved by pity, paused before crossing the threshold.

Kubera (**Kuvera**) In Vedic myth a king of the Rakshasas and half-brother to Ravanat, who drove him from Lanka, presumably the capital of Ceylon. Kubera migrated to Mount Kailasa and became regent of the north, having allied himself to the Hindu invaders. He usually travelled in the Pushpaka, his famous aerial chariot.

Kujata In Islamic myth a giant bull, with four thousand eyes, ears, noses, mouths, tongues, and feet, each of which is five hundred years' journey from the other, standing on the fish, Bahamut†. On the back of Kujata is a rock of ruby, on which stands an angel carrying the earth. There is also some resemblance to the Akupera† in Vedic myth.

Kuksu Culture hero who appears in the Creation Legends of the Maidu† Indians, and the Pomo† Indians. To the Maidus, Kuksu was the first man, but to the Pomos he was the elder brother of Marumda† and the god who not only created the world, but also tried twice to destroy it, by fire and by flood.

Kukulcan 'The Feathered Snake whose Path is the Waters'. Archaic great god of the Mayas who at some later date became merged with Quetzalcoatl†, the Aztec culture hero. He invented the calendar and was the god of craftsmen. Representations of him in his robe of a feathered serpent appear at Chichenitza. He is also the Gucumatz† of the Quiches.

Kullervo Fourth hero of the Kalevala, the Finnish national epic, a morose and wicked slave of gigantic strength which he always misuses. His history is a terrible tragedy which has been compared to that of Oedipus. In Estonia he was known as Kallevipoeg.

Kumara In Vedic myth an alternative name for Kartikeya†.

Kumarbi Hurrian chief deity, successor to Anu†, overthrown by Teshub†.

Kumari In Vedic myth one of the repellent aspects of Parvati†, wife of Siva†. The word means 'the Damsel', and from it is derived the name of Cape Comorin, which it has held since the days of Pliny. Kumari was probably an indigenous mother goddess, whose personality was absorbed into that of Parvati.

Kumu-Tonga-I-Te-Po In the Mangaia† Creation myth the daughter of Miru†, the god of the underworld.

Kung-Kung In the Chinese Creation Legend a dragon who caused the Deluge by knocking down the pillars of heaven with its head, thereby showing that in China the Flood was preceded by severe earthquakes.

Another version of the story makes him the commander of the tribesmen of Omei Shan, who, on being defeated in battle, tried to end his life by battering his head against the heavenly bamboo. In consequence he tore a great hole in the canopy of the sky through which the waters of the firmament poured on the earth, causing a flood.

Kurgal A Canaanite term for Adad†, the Babylonian storm god, meaning Great Mountain.

Kurkil The raven creator god of a Mongol tribe of Russian Siberia. The raven flew to earth to create the world and men, and taught them the crafts of civilization.

Kurma In Vedic myth the second, or tortoise, avatar of Vishnu† or Brahma†. This constitutes the second episode of the Deluge story which began in Matsya†. Here the god descended to the bottom of the ocean to recover the treasures of the Vedic tribes which had been lost during the Deluge. As a tortoise he stationed himself at the bottom of the sea and on his back was placed a mountain, around which was coiled Vasuki†. With the gods at one end and the Asuras† at the other they churned up the following precious objects: Airavata†, the elephant of Indra†; Amrita, the ambrosia of the gods; Chandra†, the moon; Dhanvantari†, the physician of the gods; Dhanus, the bow of victory; Kaustubha, the jewel of Vishnu; Lakshmi† (or Sri†), the goddess; Parijata, the Tree of Knowledge; Rambha†, the first of the Apsarases†; Sankha, the horn of victory; Sura†, the goddess of wine; Surabhi†, the cow of plenty; Uccaihsravas†, the first horse; Visha, a poison.

Kvasir In Nordic myth the wisest of gods, whose murder by the dwarfs Fjalar and Galar in Spartheim is told in the Conversations of Bragi, one of the Eddas. After his death his blood was distilled in Odherir, the magic cauldron, and gave wisdom and the art of poetry to the drinker. As *kvass* is the Slavonic word for a fermented drink, the story may relate to the distillation of a highly intoxicating brew of mead, producing effects similar to the Soma† of the Vedic myth.

Kutchis Supernatural beings similar to the Muramura† who are known to the medicine men of the Dieri tribe of Australia.

Kwannon Japanese name for Kuan-Yin† the Buddhist goddess of mercy. She may have been a pre-Buddhist mother goddess, and in Japan she was so popular that she had thirty-three holy places. She is known as Sho, the Wise; Juichimen, Eleven Faced; Senju, Thousand Handed; Bato, Horse-headed; and Nyoirin, Omnipotent.

Kwei Chinese mythological name for the spirits of the dead arising out of the practice of ancestor worship so common in China until the fall of the Manchu dynasty. It is possible that this name may be related to Kwen-Lun, the mountain on which lived Hsi Wang Mu†, the queen of the genii, and her husband, Tung Wang Kung.

Kwoiam Culture hero of Mabuiag in the Torres Straits (New Guinea). He made two crescent-shaped ornaments of turtleshell that glowed when he wore them at night. These became the insignia of two of the clan groups on the island.

Kybele Phrygian queen of nature and fertility, possibly in origin a mountain goddess, who fell in love with Attis†.

L

God 'L' 'The Old Black God' of the Mayans, depicted as an old man with toothless gums with one half of his face covered with black paint. He may be equated with Ekchuah†, the god of travellers.

Lake, River, and Well Priestesses It would seem probable that the goddesses of rivers and wells, such as Tamesis† and Morgan†, evolved from the priestesses of the water sources and springs, the name in every case being that of the first holder of the office. Practically all the holy wells, with their attendant saints, are of exceedingly remote origin, which may also be said of the goddesses of hot springs, such as Sul†. The many tales of sub-aquatic palaces and towns seem to refer to the remains of the villages in the areas now covered by the Irish Sea, the North Sea, and the English Channel, whose submergence is of comparatively recent date. The Celtic Kelpie† is one of the few priests.

Lakhame and Lakhmu In Babylonian myth two of the old gods who first emerged from the womb of Mommu†, the dark primeval ocean. Lakhmu was a monster serpent and was enrolled by Tiamat† in the fight against Marduk†.

In the Babylonian† Creation Legend of Damascius they were the children of Tauthe† and Apsu†.

Lakhe and Lakhus Names given by Da-mascius to Lakhame† and Lakhmu. Alternative spellings are Lahamu and Lahmu.

Lakshmi In Vedic myth the wife of Vishnu†. She was the Hindu goddess of good luck and plenty and the personification of beauty. In order to take her place as the mate of Vishnu she assumed the personalities of the wives of Vishnu in each of his avatars. This, however, may be taken to be a later development of doctrine. Lakshmi was probably an early mother goddess and may even have been the mother of Vishnu. Lakshmi is also known as Sri†. She was the mythological mother of Kama†, the Vedic god of love. She is stated to have risen from the waves at the Churning of the Ocean in the Kurma† avatar.

Lamassu Guardian angel in the Babylonian religion.

Lanka The name of an evil spirit who accompanies Siva† and Devi.

Lara The son of Fintan† who, with his wife Balma†, escaped from the Deluge. The story is told in Celtic† Creation Legends.

Lassar A giant† mentioned in Celtic myth as having fished up out of an Irish lake, a cauldron which had the property of reviving the dead. This cauldron figures in the story of the battle between

Brânt and Matholwcht. It is listed among the treasurest of the Tuatha Dé Danaant.

Laseo Culture hero and sun lord of the Toradjas (Celebest) who came to them from the sea and married one of their women. He had two sons who went to Napu and Luaa where they founded lines of chiefs. The Luaa version is that their rulers are descended from a sky god, Puang Matowat, who married the ancestor of the Raja who is regarded as an incarnate deity.

Laz Prehistoric goddess of Cuthak, the wife of Nergat, the Babylonian god.

Laza Second stage of the Islamic hell, Daru el-Bawart, reserved for Christians.

Lebé In the mythology of the Dogon of Mali, a human being who represented speech, the word, and who became a victim on behalf of his fellow men.

Legba In Benin a trickster spirit who taught men to interpret signs and omens.

Lei Kung In Chinese mythology the Duke of Thunder, an ancient storm deity.

Lemminkainen One of the heroes of the Kalevala, the Finnish national epic. He is a jovial, reckless person, always getting into scrapes from which he escapes either by his own initiative or with the aid of his mother.

Lenapo Indians Details of the Creation Legend of this tribe are given under Tallit and Wallum Olumt.

Leodegrance A name given to Brânt in Celtic myth. It may indicate his position as a sea captain, as in Welsh the word *lodemange* means a pilot.

Leprechaun This word originates from Luchorpant, an early Irish word meaning dwarf†. The word is first mentioned in a story of a man who obtained from a leprechaun instruction how to travel beneath the seas.

Leradh In Nordic myth the tree that stands in the hall of Odint at Asgardt.

Leucetios A thunder god of the continental Celts of whom very little is known apart from his name.

Leviathan A seven-headed sea monster, vanquished by Baalt with the aid of Mott, in the Ugarit stories. The episode is described in terms almost identical with the description of the slaughter of Leviathan by Jahveh in the Old Testament, so there can be no doubt as to the common origin of the two stories.

Li Governor of Fire in Chinese mythology.

Light Child, with Firet and Flamet, of Genost and Genea, in the Phoeniciant Creation Legend of Philo Byblos.

Li-Ki The fifth of the nine authoritative works on Confucianismt. The name means 'Book of Rites' and the text contains rules for life and conduct based on the teachings of Confucius. The forty-six chapters of which it now consists were put together in the second century BC. The preceding work in the series was the Chun-Tsiut; the next work is the first Shu, the Lun-Yut.

Lilith The night devil of Isaiah xxxiv. 14. She was especially feared in Babylonia where a special class of priests, the 'Ashipu', were employed to ward off the harmful effects of witchcraft. The term was originally applied to certain of the jinn of the northern Semites; it was only later that it was applied to the person of Lilith of the Talmud, the first wife of Adam. She may be equated with the ghwl of pre-Islamic myth and with Ninlil†, the Babylonian goddess.

Lissa (Lisa) Chameleon goddess of Benin who married Maou†, (Mawu). They became the parents of the other gods. Sometimes Lissa is a goddess, and Maou a god.

Litavis An early Celtic deity whose name is usually paired with that of Mars Cicolluis.

Lithuanian Creation Legends There are three variants of the Lithuanian Deluge myth, all connected with Pramzimas†, the pre-diluvial culture hero. The first is that he dropped a nutshell from the sky which turned into a ship, in which a man and woman survived the Flood. The second version is that many animals and some humans sought refuge on a mountain to which Pramzimas sent a magic vessel in which all sailed away except an old man and a woman. Those who went away never returned, whilst the couple who remained were the ancestors of the Lithuanians. The third version says that after being saved the old couple were past the age of child-bearing. Pramzimas advised them to jump nine times over the bones of the earth. Each time they did so a couple appeared who became the ancestors of the present

Lithuanians. For further details *see* Bushes†, Menulis†, Perkunas†, and Pramzimas†.

Litur One of the dwarfs† of Nordic myth who was cast alive by Thor† on to the funeral pyre of Balder†.

Ljeschi An alternative spelling for Lychie†, the satyrs and fauns of the Russian forests.

Llawereint 'The Silver Handed', a name given to Ludd†, the British river god. His Irish equivalent, Nuda†, was known as Argetlam†.

Lleu Law Gyffes Early British culture hero who may be considered to be the same as the Irish Lugh†. He was the son of Arianrhod† and Gwydion† and the grandson of Dôn† and Beli†.

The parallel pedigrees of Lleu and Lugh are as follows:

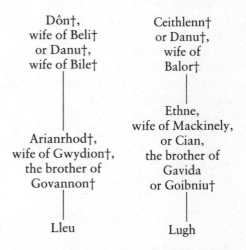

Dôn†, wife of Beli† or Danu†, wife of Bile†	Ceithlenn† or Danu†, wife of Balor†
	Ethne, wife of Mackinely, or Cian,
Arianrhod†, wife of Gwydion†, the brother of Govannon†	the brother of Gavida or Goibniu†
Lleu	Lugh

He was worshipped in Gaul. He was the eponymous founder of Lyons (Lugdunum) when he was known as Lugus†. His festival was Lugnasad.

Llyon Llion In Celtic myth the Lake of Waves, the overflowing of which caused the Deluge, from which Dwyvant† and Dwyvach escaped in the ship built by Nefyed Nav Neviont. The story is given under Celtic† Creation Legends.

Llyr In Celtic myth the father of Brant†, Branwent, and Manannant. To the Irish he was one of the Tuatha Dé Danannt and a hero of a legend concerning the children of his first wife, Aebh, who were turned into swans by his second wife, Aeife, who herself was punished by Borvet. It is certain that, like his son Manannan, he was a great seaman, and as such eventually became a sea god both in Ireland and in Wales.

Lodehur (Lodur) In the Nordic Creation Legends he was associated with Odint and Hoenirt in the creation of the first humans. It is possible that the word may be a variant of Lokit.

Lokapalas In Vedic myth the name given to the regents of the eight quarters of the world. They were Indrat, east; Agnit, south-east; Yamat, south; Suryat, south-west; Varunat, west; Vayut, north-west; Kuberat, north; Somat, north-east.

Lokasenna In the Nordic Eddat this title, meaning 'the Taunt of Loki't, was an alternative name for the Aegisdrekka, or Carousal of Aegirt.

Loki In Nordic myth a culture hero who was one of the Aesirt. He was the husband of Sigynt. Although the stories of his activities in the Eddas describe him as being beautiful, he would appear in fact to have been related to the dwarfs, which is shown by the numerous occa-

sions on which he acted as intermediary between them and the Aesir. The confused stories of these activities may arise from endeavours to fuse his identity with those of Lodehurt, one of the original companions of Odint, and Logi, a fire god mentioned in the Lay of Skrymir. It may have been in this latter capacity that he destroyed the hair of Sift. His role seems to have been that of a malicious Merlint, and the word 'Loki' appears to have had the sense of Magus, certainly when it was applied to the ruler of Utgard in the story of Skrymir. He is also mentioned under Aegirt and Sleipnirt. He was the father of Fenrirt and Helt. He has been compared to Coyotet and Ikto.

Longar In the mythology of the Dinka people of the Sudan, Longar was an ox acquired by the hero Aiwelt, who from then on was known as Aiwel Longar.

Lono The name by which Rongot is known in Hawaii.

Lords of the Day and Night The Aztecs considered that the hours of the day and the night were each ruled over by one or other of the gods who were known as the Lords of the Day and the Lords of the Night. There were thirteen Lords of the Day, one for each hour as follows: 1, Xiuhtecuhtlit; 2, Tlaltecuhtlit; 3, Chalchihuitlicuet; 4, Tonatiuht; 5, Tlazolteotlt; 6, Teoyaomiquit; 7, Xochipillit; 8, Tlaloct; 9, Quetzalcoatlt; 10, Tezcatlipocat; 11, Mictlantecuhtlit; 12, Tlahuizcalpantecuhtlit; 13, Ilamatecuhtlit. There were nine Lords of the Night Hours from sunset to sunrise. They were 1, Xiuhtecuhtlit; 2, Itzlit; 3, Piltzintecuhtlit; 4, Cinteotlt; 5, Mictlancihuatlt; 6, Chalchihuitlicuett;

7, Tlazolteotl†; 8, Tepeyollotl†; 9, Tlaloc†.

Losna Etruscan moon goddess.

Lovar Among the dwarfs† of Nordic myth the Lovar were a small tribe of whom the names of eleven individuals were mentioned: Ai, Alfr, Eikinsjalldi, Fith, Fjalar†, Frosti, Ginnar, Skandar, Skirflir, Virfir, and Yingvi. No further details are available regarding any of these except Alfr, who is supposed to be linked with the group of dwarfs referred to as the Alfar†.

Loz Co-ruler of Meslam†, the Babylonian Hades, with Nergal† and Ninmug†.

Luchorpan *See* Leprechaun.

Luchtaine (**Luchta**) In Celtic myth the 'wood worker' who, with Goibniu† and Credne†, made the weapons needed by the Tuatha Dé Danann† to defeat the Formors†.

Lucifer 'Bringer of Light' – but usually regarded as Satan.

Ludd British name for Nudd†, Nuda†, or Nodens†, a Celtic river god. In the same way as Nuda he had an artificial hand and was accordingly known as Llawereint†, the 'Silver-handed'.

Lugalbanda The Third Divine King of Erech and father of Gilgamesh† by the goddess Ninsun†. He was the legendary hero of several of the adventures now accredited to Gilgamesh. He took part in an expedition to Aratta, a land over the mountains lying to the north-east.

Lugh Lamh Fada The Celtic culture hero son of Cian and Ethne and grandson of Diancecht† who was placed in command of the forces of the Tuatha Dé Danann† in the victorious battle at Mag Tuireadh against the Fomors†. He would appear to be the same as Lleu Law Gyffes†, under which entry are given comparative pedigrees. His sword and his hound – the whelp of the King Ioruaidhe – form part of the treasures of the Tuatha.

Lugnasad The Celtic festival of the first of August, now commemorated by August Bank Holiday. It was held in honour of Lugh† and until recently was known in England as Lammas. A similar festival was also held at Lyons (Lugdunum). In Ireland it was also known as Brontroghain. The other three main festivals were Oimelc†, Samhain†, and Beltaine†.

Lugus A continental form of Lugh†, from which come the names of such towns as Laon, Leyden, and Lyons.

Lu-hsing The Chinese god of salaries.

Lumawig Culture hero of the Boutacs of Luzon, Melanesia, who civilized them and married a woman of the tribe. Their children were all killed. The version Lumauig occurs in the Philippines.

Luminu'ut Culture heroine and ancestress of the Minehassa tribe of the Celebes†. She married To'ar†, priest of the sun god. In some versions he is stated to have been her son.

Lun-Yu The sixth of the nine authoritative works on Confucianism†. The name means 'Analects', and in its twenty chapters records the utterances of

Confucius on political and social themes. No attempt is made to enforce any doctrine by sanctions derived from the unseen or supernatural. This work, which is the first of the Shu, or 'Books', follows the Li-Ki† and precedes the Ta-Hsuch†.

Lyangombe A god chief among the Congo tribes, who is a combination of supreme being and folk hero.

Lychie A Slavonic name given to the partly human forest fauns and satyrs, who were reputed to have green hair. An alternative spelling is Ljeschi†.

M

God 'M' A Mayan god of travellers corresponding to Yiacatecuhtli†, the Aztec god of travelling merchants. He is usually represented as bearing a heavy package on his head and it is possible that he was the black god Ek Ahau†.

Maahes A lion-headed god of Nubian origin worshipped in Egypt.

Maamba Early culture hero of the Herbert River tribes who may be linked with Birral† and Kohin†.

Maat In Egyptian myth a goddess associated with Thoth†, Ptah†, and Khnemu† in the Creation. The word means 'straight', or law and order, and as such gave her an almost unique position in the hierarchy of the gods. As the daughter of Ra†, a lady of heaven, queen of the earth, mistress of the underworld, she sat in the Judgment Hall of Osiris† to judge the dead, wearing in her hair a large upright feather (*maat*) as the symbol of justice (as can be seen in the Anhai papyrus in the British Museum). She it was who ordered the daily course of the sun, and was with Ra when he first appeared from Chaos. Maat is probably one of the first pre-dynastic mother goddesses, and was so enthroned in the hearts of the early Egyptians that no incursion of male gods or of new contestants for that rank could disturb her. Alternative spelling is Mayet†.

Mabon In Welsh myth a great hunter who had a wonderful hound and rode on a steed swift as the waves of the sea. He was released by Arthur† from prison at Gloucester in order to take part in the campaign against Twrch Trwyth. He appears to have been an early Celtic ruler, and his release from prison has only been attributed to Arthur in the process of writing up the Arthurian legends. His name means simply 'the Great Son'.

Macha In Celtic myth no fewer than three war goddesses seem to have been given this name.

Mackinely In Celtic myth the brother of Gavida†, the smith. His wife was Ethne†, and he may be equated with Cian†. Comparative pedigrees are given under Lleu†.

Mac Oc In Celtic myth a name given to Angus† the son of Dagda†. The words mean 'Son of the Young'.

Macuilxochitl Alternative name for Xochipilli†, Aztec god of pleasure. The name means 'Five Flower'. He was the god of dancing and sport.

Macusis Indian Creation Legend This British Guiana tribe say that only one man and one woman survived the Flood and that from them sprang their ancestors. They share this myth with the Tamanaquest†.

Maeldune A legendary Irish traveller skin to Brandan† and Corra†. He is stated to have visited no less than thirty-three islands of which it has only been possible to identify a few.

Mafdet Egyptian lynx goddess.

Magba Title given to the high priest of Shango†, the culture hero and chief deity of the Yoruba† tribe.

Magi A non-Aryan, possibly Turanian, tribe of professional magicians, astrologers, and priests, established in western Persia before the advent of the Iranians, and certainly before that of Zarathustra†. The Wise Men from the East, mentioned in the New Testament, were probably of this tribe, as was Zoroaster†, the Magian. After the development of Mazdaism the Magi held a similar position to that of the Levites, in that they alone had the ritual knowledge necessary to slay the victims, to prepare the sacred Haoma†, and to hold the Barsom (the bunch of fine tamarisk boughs). The words magus and magician constitute a present-day tribute to their legendary powers.

Mag-Mell 'The Field of Happiness' one of the distant places to which fled the leaders of the Tuatha Dé Danann† after their defeat by the Milesians†. Other places were Hy-Brasil† and Tir-nan-Beo†.

Magni In Nordic myth the son of Thor† by Jarnsaxa and brother of Modi†. He survived his father at Ragnarok, and with his brother took

possession of Mjolnir, the hammer of Thor.

Mag-Tuireadh The 'Field of the Towers', a megalithic site near Sligo in Ireland, where stand many cairns, dolmens, and circles which are said to relate to the great battle in which the Fomors† were defeated and Balor† was killed by the Tuatha Dé Danann† under Llugh†. The number of the stones is only exceeded by that at Carnac in Brittany.

Māhabhārata In this colossal epic poem of 220,000 lines is contained the background of Vedic myth. The pre-Brahmanic version of this work may be dated to 500 BC or even earlier, and the eighteen books into which it was eventually assembled may be taken as covering the period of the Great Migration when the Indo-Germanic tribes were advancing southwards into the Indian mainland and driving out or enslaving the aborigines. Naturally, the work has suffered severely from the censorship of the Brahman priests, but in spite of all their efforts it is still possible to conjure up an idea of a series of campaigns which led to the conquest of India. Kings and princes and the generals of the opposing armies have long since been transmuted into gods or demons, Devas† or Asuras†, and on their shoulders have been thrust the characteristics of the gods which the conquerors brought with them, or which they seized as spoils of victory.

Maha-Deva In Vedic myth a title meaning the Great God, applied to Siva†; in the same manner his wife Parvati† is known as Maha-Devi, the Great Goddess.

Maha-Kala In Vedic myth one of the destructive aspects of Siva†. The words mean Great Time, and as such he is the destroyer of all things. The feminine aspect of this is Kala. How Siva and his wife Parvati† became Kala and Kali† is not clear. There would appear to have been a fusion of some early war goddess and her husband with these two.

Maha-Yuga In the Hindu† Creation Legend a name given to an epoch of four Yugas†, totalling 12,000 divine years. One thousand Mahayugas make a Kalpa†, or Day of Brahma†, the period from the beginning to the end of the world.

Mahih-Nah-Tlehey A name meaning 'the Changing Coyote'† employed in the myth of the Navajo† Indians.

Maidu Creation Legend This California† tribe of Indians have several Creation myths. One tells how Talvolte† and Peheipe†, the survivors from the Deluge, were found floating in a canoe by the Creator who, together with Coyote†, is living in an earthly paradise. The Creator produces the first men while Coyote plays the part of the tempter and the spirit of evil.

Another version, which seems to be earlier, tells how Kodoyanpe† and Coyote were the only survivors from the Deluge. After having created mankind from wooden images they quarrelled and Kodoyanpe was forced to fleet to the east. Kuksu†, the first man who appears in the former legend, is known to the Pomo† Indians as a creator god.

Maina In the mythology of the Luyia people of Kenya the son of the ancestor of the people.

Maire (Maira) In the Tupi-Guarani Creation Legend a higher power which caused an inundation from which only those who hid in caves or climbed to the tops of trees were saved. Three survivors, Coem, Hermitten, and Krimen, were the ancestors of some of the tribes.

Maiso The Stone Woman, mother goddess of the Paressi tribe of the Arawaks†, who produced all living beings and all things. This tribe had a legend that neglect of the couvade† had brought disaster on the world.

Maitagarri A lake priestess† of the early Basque† peoples.

Make Make *See* Meke Meke†.

Makila In the Pomo† Indian Creation Legend he and his son Dasan†, leaders of a bird clan, came from the waters and brought civilization with them.

Makonaima In the Arawak† Creation Legends the father of Sigu†, the Arawak Noah. He may be taken to be the same as Aimon Kondi†.

Malek, Mlk, Malik Semitic term meaning king and as such applied to their gods. Later, however, the Jews changed the term to Moloch†, owing to intense religious dislike of their neighbours.

Malsum *See* Maslum†.

Mama Allpa Inca† harvest and earth goddess who was many-breasted like the Diana of Ephesus.

Mama Cocha Inca mother goddess, the mother of all mankind. She was also a goddess of the sea, which supplied fish for the subsistence of the coastal population. At Tiahuanaco she was associated with Copacati as one of the two divinities of this inland sea.

Mamaloi The designation of a priestess among voodoo worshippers of Haiti. Her male counterpart was called Paparloi†.

Mama Nono The earth mother goddess of the now extinct Caribs† of the Antilles. In their Creation Legend the founder of the race created their ancestors by sowing stones into the soil from which sprang men and women.

Mama Ocllo Huaca Sister and wife of Mancocoapac†, the Inca culture hero who taught to women the arts of domestic life.

Mama Pacha Earth mother goddess of Inca legend from whom proceeded Pachacamac†, the universal creative spirit.

Mambo An ancestor, possibly historically authentic, of the Lovedu people.

Mana A term used in Melanesia† to describe the power of magic possessed by some. While the word is frequently used in connection with magical stones it may also describe any form of ghostly activity. The origin of the word dates back to the race which built the megalithic structures scattered all over the Pacific Islands. These persons were known as 'Vue'† and were potent as givers of life, being full of Mana.

Manannán In Celtic myth the son of Llyr†, the sea god of the Celts. He had a self-propelled ship called 'Wave Sweeper,' and a horse called 'Splendid Mane'. His wife, whom he deserted, was Fand. He returned to her after he had appealed to Cú Chulainn† for aid. His magic cauldron was also stolen by Cú Chulainn, which seems to equate him to Mider†. His chariot was one of the treasures of the Tuatha Dé Danann† and under the name of 'the Chariot of Morgan Mywnoawr' was also one of the treasures of Britain. An alternative version is Manawydan†, or Morgan Mywnoawr.

Manawydan A name by which Manannán† was known in Wales. It is probably another version of the Morgan Mywnoawr whose magic chariot was one of the treasures of Britain. While he was at the wars with his brother Brân†, Caswallawn succeeded in getting possession of his kingdom and his power thanks to a cloak of invisibility. He was one of the seven survivors of the battle between Brân and Matholwch†, and he later married Rhiannon†.

Mancocoapac (**Manco Capac**) The founder of the Inca race of Peru. With his sister Mama Ocllo Huaca† he descended in the neighbourhood of Tiahuanaco from the celestial regions. They had been instructed by the Sun and the Moon, their mythological parents, to proceed across country until they found the spot where a golden wedge, which they had brought, would sink into the ground. This happened at Cuzco, the ancient Inca capital, which they founded. Having brought the knowledge of civilized life to the Incas they died leaving a son and daughter. From that time brother and sister marriage was insisted on for the Inca royal family. In an alternative version, with his brothers

Pachacamac† and Viracocha†, he came from Pacari the Cave of Refuge.

Mandan Indians The myths of this tribe are told under Sioux Indian Creation Legends.

Maneros Name by which a corn spirit was known in Egypt.

Mangaia Island Creation Legend. The myth of this Polynesian island is divided into two sections. The first being before the island was submerged beneath the waves, and the second after its reappearance. In the first Vatea† and Papa† ruled Mangaia and had two children, Tangaroa† and Rongo†. Although Tangaroa was the heir his mother managed to dispossess him in favour of his younger brother, and Tangaroa settled in Rarotonga. At some later date the first ruler of the newly emerged island was Rangi†, who called himself the grandson of Rongo, although this relationship is improbable. He made his two brothers, Mokoiro† and Akatauire†, co-rulers of the island with him. For further details *see* Amaite-Rangi†, Angarua†, Apu-Ko-Hai†, Ina†, Karaia-y-te-ata†, Kumu-tongu-i-te-po†, Miru†, Ngaru†, Papa†, Ruange†, Tepotatango†, Tumu-i-te-are-Toka†, Tu-papa†, Vari-ma-te-takere†, and Vatea†.

Mani In Nordic myth a moon god who kidnapped Bil† and her brother Hjuki. The story is so ancient that there is no other reference to this god in Nordic myth.

There was a Lithuanian moon god named Menulis† who may be the same.

Manibozho Hero of the Creation Legend of the Algonkian† Indians. On one occasion he was hunting when a great lake overflowed and submerged the world. From his place of refuge he sent a raven to seek for land, but the bird came back. The second time he sent an otter, and the third time a musk-rat, who reported that the flood had died down. He was known as 'the Great Hare', and in view of the similarity between the word for hare and that for light he was probably a sun god. He subsequently married the musk-rat, becoming the ancestor of the tribe.

Mannheim In Nordic myth that part of Midgard† inhabited by man (i.e. not by dwarfs† or giants†).

Mantchet (Manjet-boat) The morning boat of Ra†, the sun god in Egyptian myth.

Mantus and Mania The guardians of Hades in Etruscan religion.

Manu In Hindu myth the name given to the ruler of the world during a Manvantara, or fourteenth part of a Kalpa. The present Manu, who is the seventh, is Vaivasvata†, who is referred to in the Puranic Deluge story in the Hindu Creation Legend. The original seven Manus were probably the same as the seven Prajapatis† and the seven Rishis†, men of traditional fame, who were promoted to these positions.

Manvantara In the Hindu† Creation Legend a fourteenth part of a Kalpa† ruled over by a Manu†.

Maou (Mawu) In the myth of Benin the creator of all visible things and invisible. He was symbolized by the sun and formed, with his sister Lissa† and their son Gou†, a celestial trinity, adored by the fetish worshippers of Benin. The similarity with Maui†, the name of the sun god in Polynesian myth, should be noted though sometimes Maou is feminine (the moon) and Lissa masculine (the sun).

Mara The tempter of Buddha†.

Marae Generic name of the sacred places of the Polynesian Islands. These are all remnants of a widespread megalithic culture. In some places they took the form of ziggurats†, one at Raiatea, discovered by Captain Cook, having a base 267 feet by 67 feet and being some 50 feet high.

Marco, Prince In Slavonic myth the Serbian hero prince, whose mother was a Veela†. He is popularly supposed to sleep on his horse in a cavern in Mount Urvina. While he sleeps his sword slowly rises from its sheath. From time to time he awakens, and looks to see if the sword is fully visible. When this happens he will ride forth and deliver his country from its foes. Details of his encounter with Raviyoyla† are given under that heading.

Mardoll 'Shining One over the Sea', a name given to Freyja† in Nordic myth.

Marduk Babylonian god of the spring sun, the Bel† of the Old Testament, and head of the Babylonian pantheon. He was the son of El† and Damkina† and was the champion of the gods in their fight against Tiamat†. To this end he was made king of the gods, and given the power that his commands, whatever they might be, would be effected immedi-

ately. After the great battle he defeated Tiamat and her husband, Kingu†, and cut her body into two parts, one of which he made into the dome of heaven and the other into the abode of his father El†. This victory was celebrated at the new year's feast. After arranging heaven and earth he caused Kingu to be sacrificed, and from his blood El created man. Another version says that he decapitated himself and from his own blood man was formed. Marduk had fifty ceremonial names, in a similar manner to the seventy-five praises of Ra† and the ninety-nine names of God mentioned in the Koran. He appears to have been originally a vegetation god, similar to Baal† and Tammuz†. The battle with Tiamat was one stage in the ousting of the mother goddesses. He is equated with Tagtug and with Merodach†.

Marerewana Culture hero of the Arawak Indian Creation Legend†, who at the time of the Great Deluge escaped with his followers in a canoe.

Marid In pre-Islamic myth the most powerful class of jinn†, even more so than the Efrit†, who were the second most powerful jinn, and Shaitan†, who was a third.

Maritchi In Vedic myth a goddess corresponding to Tou Mu†, the Chinese bushel mother.

Marnas God of Gaza, who remained until Christian times, when he was the personal enemy of St Hilarion.

Martummere A name occasionally applied to Nurrendere†, culture hero of the Narrinyeri tribe.

Martu The name by which Adad†, the Babylonian storm god, was worshipped in Canaan, where he was also known as Kurgal, or Great Mountain.

Marumda In the Pomo Indian Creation Legend† he and his brother Kuksu†, having created the world, twice tried to destroy it, first by fire and then by water, being rescued on each occasion by Ragno†, the old mother goddess.

Maruts In Vedic myth the Maruts were the eleven sons of Rudra†, the storm god, and his wife Prisni†, when they had become the companions of Indra†. In another version they were the sons of Diti†, the daughter of Daksha†.

Marwe A folk heroine in the mythology of the Chaga people of Kenya.

Masai Creation Legend As with many of the African tribes, the memories of the Masai do not seem to carry back to a Creation Legend. Their principal deity is Ngai†.

Mashia and Mashiane In the Zoroastrian Creation Legend the children of Gayomart†, the first man. Some accounts say they were born in the shape of trees, in a similar manner to the Nordic Askr†. Alternative spelling Mashya and Mashyane.

Mashongavudzi The chief wife of Mwari†, the great spirit of the Mtawara† tribe of Zimbabwe. To the present day the first wife of the reigning chief takes this name.

Masis Alternative spelling for Amasis†, the name given to Ararat† in Babylonian myth.

Maslum (Malsum) In the Algonkian Creation Legend the evil twin brother of Gluskap† who strove in vain to offset the good deeds of his brother, by whom he was eventually decisively defeated.

Matao-Anu In Polynesian myth 'Cold Space', one of the Multitude of Space†.

Matarisvan (Matariswan) In Vedic myth the messenger of the gods, who brought Agni†, the divine fire, to Bhrigu†, the Rishi†.

Mate-Anu In Polynesian myth 'Space of Cold Death', one of the Multitude of Space†.

Math Hen In Celtic myth the son of Mathonwy, the uncle of Amathaon† and the brother of Danu†.

Matholwch In Celtic myth the King of Ireland who married Branwen† and who was provoked into ill treatment of her by Evnisien. Eventually his brother-in-law Brân† attacked him, and after a great battle he and most of the Irish were killed. His son Gwern was burned to death by Evnisien, and Branwen returned to England with Brân.

Matowelia Culture hero of the Mohave† Indians of Colorado who led them from the 'White Mountain' to their present abode. Later it was believed that the souls of those who had been cremated returned to the White Mountain and those who had not been ritually buried passed the rest of their existence as screech-owls.

Matsya The first avatar of Vishnu†, when in the guise of a fish he intervened to save Manu† Vaivasvata†, the Aryan, from the consequences of the Deluge. Subsequently he destroyed Haya-Griva†, an underwater demon who had stolen the Vedas. A possible earlier version of this story which appears in the Māhabhārata makes the fish an incarnation of Brahma†. The story of Manu follows the familiar pattern of Deluge legends. The main point of interest is its similarity to the Babylonian story of Oannes† the Fish God. It may have been acquired from the Dravidians. The battles with Haya-Griva†, Hiranyaksha†, and his brother Hiranya-Kasipu† may properly belong to this episode. The story is continued in the Kurma† and Varaha† avatars.

Maui Early Polynesian culture hero and sun god. There is a large body of myth about his various adventures, which appear to have begun at a time when the first Polynesians lived in a relatively cold northern climate and to have continued into the period between the first and fifth centuries AD when the Polynesians were beginning to spread in a southeasterly direction from Indonesia. The similarity with Maou†, the name of the sun god in Benin, should be noted. His sister was Sina†, the moon goddess.

Maweja One of the names of the supreme being found among the peoples of the Congo.

Mawu supreme god of the Fon people of Benin.

Maya Alphabetical Gods Owing to the destruction by the Spaniards of the vast majority of the Maya codices and the reluctance of the survivors of the Spanish excesses to assist them in any way it has been a matter of great difficulty to equate the pictured representations of

the gods in the codices with the main deities of spoken myth. In order to get over this Schellhas decided upon an arbitrary naming of the more important gods occurring in the codices with the letters of the alphabet. The series goes from A to I and from K to P. Although other unidentified gods have been found the series was not extended any further.

Maya Creation Legends Owing to the destruction of the entire literature of the Mayas, with the exception of a few codices which no one has been able to interpret successfully, the myths of the Mayas have largely passed into oblivion. Their Creation Legends appear to have resembled those of the Aztecs†, although it is possible that the Popul Vuh† of the Quiches† presents a record having decided similarities with Maya ideas as to their origin. The Tzental† tribe of the Mayas had a mother goddess known as Alaghom Naum†, who was credited with the creation of mind and thought. Further details are available under the following headings: God 'A'†, Alaghom Naum†, God 'B'†, Bacabs†, God 'C'†, Cauac†, Chac†, God 'D'†, God 'E'†, Ekchuah†, God 'F'†, God 'G'†, Ghanan†, God 'H'†, Hunab-ku†, Goddess 'I'†, Itzamna†, Ix†, Ixazalvoh†, Iztat Ix†, God 'K'†, Kabul†, Kan†, Kinich-Ahau†, Kukulcan†, God 'L'†, God 'M'†, Mulac†, God 'N'†, Goddess 'O'†, God 'P'†, Patol†, Tzental Indian Creation Legend†, Yum Kaax†, Zamna†, and Zotzilaha Chimalman†. The note on Maya Alphabetical Gods† should also be consulted.

Mayet *See* Maat†.

Mayon In Tamil myth an ancient equivalent to Krisna†, the Black God.

Medb (Nedhbh) In Celtic myth the wife of Conchobar†, whom she subsequently left for Ailill†. After the death of her husband she was murdered by one of the sons of Conchobar. Her sister Eithne became the second wife of Conchobar.

Medecolin A race of sorcerers whose defeat by Gluskap† is recounted in the myth of the Algonkian† Indians.

Megingjardir Thor's Belt of Power, listed under Treasures†.

Mehen Serpent which protects Ra†, the Egyptian sun god, when voyaging in his celestial boat.

Mehueret Pre-dynastic Egyptian mother goddess, 'the Celestial Cow', who gave birth to the sun and to the Seven Wise Ones in the shape of hawks, who helped in the work of creation. Whether she was separate from Hathor† or Nut†, it is difficult to say. The Judgment Scene of the Book of the Dead takes place at her abode. She is the same as Neith†.

Meke Meke Creator god of Easter Island, or Rapanui, who is probably Tangaroa†, the Polynesian god. He is represented in the petroglyphs of the island as being one of the bird men, and eggs were offered to him at his annual feast. Alternative spelling Make Make.

Melanesian Myth Details of Melanesian myth are given under Celebes† Islands Creation Legends, Lumawig†, Mana†, Tindalo†, and Vue†.

Melili Wife of Benani†, queen and mother of the Babylonian Monsters of the Night enrolled by Tiamat† in her fight against Marduk†. They were placed under the command of Kingu†, the Babylonian god of the powers of darkness. For further details *see* Babylonian† Creation Legend.

Melkart The Canaanite who journeyed to Erytheia (the Red) in the kingdom of Herion, to rob him of his sacred bulls. This adventure of the Pelasgian Hercules recalls that of his classical namesake. He was Baal of Tyre and was said to be the child of Zeus Demaros. The name means 'God of the City'. He was a maritime god, and one of the gods of the Phoenician cosmogony.

Memphis Triad of Gods In Egyptian myth this consisted of Ptah†, Sekhmet†, and Imhotep†. Occasionally Nefertum† replaced one of these.

Memphis Triune God A fusion of Ptah†, Seker†, and Osiris† in Egyptian myth.

Menaka An Apsaras† sent to entice Viswamitra† from his devotions. In the event she was successful, and as a result became the mother of the nymph Sakuntala†.

Mendes The name of the sacred ram Ba Neb Djedet ('The soul of the lord of Djedet') became contracted into Banaded†, which was rendered into Greek as Mendes. The soul of Osiris† was incarnated in him.

Menglad, or Menglod Two names applied to Freyja† in Nordic myth. The first occurs in the epic poem of Svipdag and Menglad, where a hero has to pass a wall of flame to reach his bride, while the second means 'necklace glad', from her ownership of Brisingamen.

The myth of the wall of fire seems to be related to the ritual sacrifices or initiation ceremony to the goddess of fertility in order to ensure a good crop. Similar episodes occur in the tales of Brynhild† and Skirnir†.

Meng-Tsze The ninth of the nine authoritative works on Confucianism†. The work is a record of the life and teaching of the philosopher Meng-Tsze, who lived 150 years after Confucius himself.

Menrva Etruscan goddess of wisdom, lineal ancestor of Minerva the Roman goddess. Like Pallas Athene, she is shown armed and with the aegis on her breast, but in addition she sometimes has wings. She was the third of the Etruscan Triad with Tinia† and Uni†. She seems to have been allied to Nortia†, the goddess of good luck. She wielded thunderbolts at the vernal equinoxes.

Menthu (Mont) Ancient hawk-headed Egyptian war god worshipped at Hermonthis and Karnak, where he was lord of the sky. As a war god he was known as the Bull, this animal being sacred to him. The Menvis Bull† of Ra† – with whom he was sometimes associated as Menthu-Ra – was known as Menuis†. He is probably the same as Munt†.

Menuis In Egyptian myth an alternative name for Merur†, or Merwer, sometimes known as the Bull of Meroe.

Menulis *See* Mani†.

Menuqet Egyptian goddess of Amenti†, the first region of the Place of Reeds.

Menvis (Mnevis) In Egyptian myth alternative name for Menuis†.

Meret The ancient Egyptian goddess of song and happiness.

Merodach Variant of Marduk† in Babylonian myth.

Merlin In Welsh Celtic myth an early culture hero, bard, and magician whose name has become linked with many of the Arthurian legends. His mistress was Viviane† (or Vivien), daughter of Dylan† and Lady of the Lake.

Mert In Egyptian myth the goddesses of the north and south inundations. They appear to be a duplication of Isis† and Nephtys† in that the Book of the Dead† refers to them as Watch Merti†.

Mertseger A snake goddess of the Theban necropolis in Egypt.

Meru In Vedic myth the mountain at the centre of the world, the Hindu Olympus. On its seven spurs are built the cities of the gods, including Swarga†, Kailasa†, Vaikuntha†, and Brahmapura. Beneath it lie the seven circles of Patala†, ruled over by Sesha†.

Merul and Meruil Twin gods of Nubia.

Merur (Merwer) The bull, incarnation of Ra† at Heliopolis, sometimes known as the Bull of Meroe. Also known as Menuis†.

Mesektet-boat The boat in which Ra† made his journey during the hours of darkness.

Meskhenit (Meshkent) Egyptian goddess of birth and child-rearing, equated with Hathor†. In the Book of the Dead she is associated with Renenet†.

Meslam The Babylonian lower world, ruled over by Nergal†, consort Ninmug† (Ereshkigal†), and Loz†, his co-ruler. Alternatively it was known as Aralu† and has some relation to Sekhet Aaru†.

Mestha In Egyptian myth one of the four divine sons of Horus†, the gods of the cardinal points and of the Canopic jars. The others were Duamutef†, Hapy†, and Qebhsneuf†. Mestha was also referred to as Amset†, Imset†, and Mesti†.

Mesti In Egyptian myth the alternative spelling for Mestha†, one of the divine sons of Horus†.

Metztli Aztec moon god sometimes referred to as Tecciztecatl†.

Miach In Celtic myth the physician son of Dianchecht†, the founder of medicine, who, with the aid of his sister Airmid†, made an artificial hand of silver for King Nuda†, a deed for which his father killed him. On his grave healing grasses were said to grow. The story may be that of some divine sacrifice.

Miao Yachio An ancient Chinese tribe that believed that mankind had three souls: the shadow, the reflection in water, and the real self. This doctrine has a distinct resemblance to the Ka†, the Ba†, and the Khaibit† of the ancient Egyptians.

Mictlan The Hades of the Aztecs† ruled over by Mictlantecuhtli† and his wife Mictlancihuatl†. This other world of the Aztecs may well have originated with the caverns of refuge so frequently encountered in the Creation Legends of the American tribes, as, for example, Chicomoztoct†, the Cavern of Seven Chambers, from which the five tribes left by boat from Aztlan†, bringing with them their chief god or leader, Huitzilopochtli†; the Xibalba† of the Popul Vuh†; the Nunne Chaha† of the Creeks†; and the Nine Caverns of the Mixtecs†. It is uncertain whether the name Mictlan was derived from that of its two rulers or vice versa. On the whole the latter alternative seems more probable.

Mictlancihuatl Aztec goddess of death, the wife of Mictlantecuhtli†. She was the lord of the fifth hour of the night.

Mictlantecuhtli Aztec god of the dead who may be equated with God 'A'† of the Mayas. He was the husband of Mictlancihuatl†. He was the lord of the eleventh hour of the day.

Mider (**Midhir**) In Celtic myth the son of Dagda† and king of the Gaelic underworld. He was the husband of Etain and father of Bláthnad†. His magic cauldron, which was stolen from him by Cù Chulainn† with the connivance of his daughter, was one of the treasures of the Tuatha Dé Danann†. He may be equated with Manannán†. His wife Etain eloped with Angus†, the son of Dagda, his stepbrother.

Midgard The region of Nordic myth between Svartheim†, the land of the dwarfs† or elves†, and Jötunheim, the land of the giants†. It contained Mannheim†, the world of men, and rested above the cavernous dwelling of Hel†.

Midgard Serpent Jormungard†, the offspring of Ang(u)rbodi† by Loki†.

Míl, sons of In Celtic myth the Milesians were reported to have come from the Mediterranean, possibly the Iberian Peninsula, their leader having been described as a king of Spain. When they landed their emissary was killed by the Tuatha Dé Danann†, and accordingly a great battle took place at which the Tuatha were defeated. Only the leaders of the Tuatha, however, appear to have fled; the people remained as producers of milk and corn for the Milesians.

Mimi A name given by the aborigines of Australia to the artists of the numerous cave paintings of running human figures, which they say are no longer within their capacity to draw. The difference between the work of the mimis and that of the native of today is so great that it must obviously have been the work of an earlier culture which has since migrated or died out.

Mimir In Nordic myth a giant, the brother of Bolthorn† and the uncle of Odin†. He was the guardian of the well of wisdom hidden under Yggdrasill. One day Odin came to ask for a draught of this water, but was obliged to leave one of his eyes behind as a pledge for it. Practically he was one of the Aesir† and was invariably consulted by Odin in any matter of serious import. He occurs in the Völundar Kvida and in the stories of the Nibelungenlied. The name may have been that of the chief of a tribe of artificers.

Min Egyptian god of virility and generation; also known as Amsu†. He was worshipped at Koptos, where he was the god of the eastern desert. The statues of him which have been found are ornamented with shells and swordfish from the Red Sea. He may have been the god of some maritime or eastern people reaching Egypt by this route.

Minnetaree Indians Creation Legend The myths of this tribe are told under Sioux† Creation Legends.

Miru (Milu) In the Mangaia Creation myth the god of the underworld, which was a place of incineration – not punishment.

Mist The name of one of the Valkyries†, meaning 'fog'.

Mithra Mithra, or Mitra, first appears as a god in the Vedic Hymns, where he is mentioned some hundred and seventy times. He would appear to have been a human being who became elevated to divine rank after his death, which occurred before the Aryans reached India. In the Rig-Veda he was one of the twelve Adityas†. With the development of the Hindu religion into Brahmanism the figure of Mitra gradually vanished.

The Persians, however, made him one of the Ameshas† as the 'genius of Heavenly Light'. He was the chief of a heavenly host of Ahura, whom he led against the evil forces of the Devas†. In the reform of the Mazdean religion arranged by Zoroaster, Mithra was reduced in status from the rank of Amesha to that of Yazata†, where he stood between the opposing forces of good and evil, always willing to assist in the saving of souls.

The worship of Mithra is always associated with the killing of bulls. It was introduced into the Roman world from Cappadocia. By the time of Xerxes I, it had spread into Greece, and by that of Pompey the Great it had reached Rome. It was an ascetic religion of truth, purity, and right for men only – women worshipped Kybele†. The doctrine and mysteries became slightly modified in their passage from Persia to Rome, and included a form of baptism. The great power was Zervan Akarana†, or Aeon. It was a Dualistic religion with good and evil equally balanced and its background was the purification of character by chastity and continence. Had it not been for the appearance of Christianity Mithraism would perhaps now be the religion of Europe.

Mixcoatl Stellar god of the Aztecs, originally a hunting god of the Otomi tribe, and sometimes known as Camaxtli†. He was the father of Quetzalcoatl† by Xochiquetzal†, and of Huitzilopochtli† by Coatlicue†. He was the son of Cihuacoatl†, and may possibly be equated with God 'C'†. He was also linked with Ilamatecuhtli†.

Mixtec Indian Creation Legend In the myths of this tribe it is told how the Wind of the Nine Serpents, manifested as a bird, and the Wind of the Nine Caverns (Gucumatz†), manifested as a winged serpent, caused the waters of the Deluge to subside, and land appeared. The fact that the Nine Caverns are mentioned shows that this tribe took refuge at the time of the Deluge in a cave rather than on a mountain top.

Mjolnir The Crusher, the hammer of Thor†, which may also have been a thunderbolt. To use it Thor had to wear iron gloves and a belt to increase his strength. Up to Christian times weddings were hallowed by the hammer of Thor, while marriage at a blacksmith's forge at Gretna Green only ceased a year or so ago.

Mnevis Bull *See* Menvis.

Moccus Epithet of a Gaulish Mercury.

Modi In Nordic myth one of the sons of Thor† by Jarnsaxa and brother of Magni†. At Ragnarok they both survived their father.

Moelo In the mythology of the Bushongo people of the Congo, Moelo and Woto† were the first pair of twins born to Bomazi†, who appeared from the sky and married their mother.

Mohave Indian Creation Legend In the myth of this Colorado tribe it is told how Matowelia† led them from the 'White Mountain', where they had taken refuge at the time of Deluge, to their present abode.

Mokoiro In the myth of Mangaia† Island he was the brother of Rangi†, the husband of Angarua† and co-ruler of the island.

Moloch In the Semitic countries Malek†, or Melek, was, and still is, the common term for king, and as such was applied to their gods. The Jews, however, from religious dislike, inserted the vowels of *bosheth*, meaning 'shameful thing', and this addition to Mlk produced Moloch. The Moloch of the Old Testament may have been the Baal-(H)Ammon of Carthage, who is represented as an old man with ram's horns, holding a scythe, and to whom small children were sacrified until after Roman times.

Mommu (Mummu) On the Babylonian Creation Legend tablets Mommu was the chamberlain of Apsu† and Tiamat†.

Monan Creator god in the Tupi-Guarani† Creation Legend who decided to destroy mankind by fire because of their evil conduct. The blaze was put out by a deluge caused by Irin Mage† or, in another version, by Tawenduare† and Arikute†.

Moombi The female creator in the mythology of the Kikuyu people.

Morgan The Morgan la Fée of the Arthurian legends who took Arthur† away to be healed and who induced Merlin† to abandon the world would appear to have been a lake or river priestess healer who was the same as the Irish Murigen.

Morgan Mywnoawr In Celtic myth the possessor of a chariot which would take the user wherever he wanted to go. This vehicle, which was one of the treasures† of Britain, would appear to have belonged to Manannán†, who was known in Wales as Manawydan†, an alternative rendering of Mywnoawr.

Mormo Name given to certain beings, 'the Hairy Ghosts', by the Australian aborigines.

Morrigu (Morríghan) Great goddess of the Celts, may possibly have been a moon goddess of some pre-Celtic race. She was to be seen hovering over the field of battle as a carrion or hoodie crow, still hated by the Celts. Associated with her were the war goddesses Badb†, Fea, Macha†, and Nemon.

Mot The god of death, and son of the gods of the Ugarit tablets, hero of the combats with Aleion, An(th)at†, and Baal†.

Moymis In the Babylonian† Creation Legend the daughter of Tauthe† and Apsu†, sometimes confused with Mommu†.

Moyna Among the Dogon of Upper Volta the man who invented the bull-roarer.

Mtawara Creation Legend This Zimbabwean tribe have a great spirit named Mwari† who had two wives, the first named Mashongavudzi† of Gosa, and the second who is 'the Rain Goddess'. Up to the present time the first wife of the reigning chief is named Mashongavudzi and is *ex-officio* a paramount chief of the tribe and sacrifices are still made to the rain goddess when there is a drought.

Mujaji Among the Lovedu of the Transvaal, the rain queen.

Mukasa In Buganda the great god, whose brother was Kibuka†, the god of war.

Mulac One of the four Bacabs, the Maya gods of the cardinal points. He represented the north and his colour was white.

Mullaghmart, Earl Gerald of In Celtic myth a nobleman who sleeps with his knights in a cellar under the castle in Kildare. For details of similar stories *see* Sleeping Prince†.

Mullo The chief of an early Celtic clan having an ass totem.

Mulopo Among the Congolese, one of the names for a supreme being.

Multitude of Space In Polynesian myth these are four storm gods: Matao-Anu†, Mate-Anu†, Whakarere-Anu†, Whakatoro-Anu†, who were descended from Rangit. They appear to be memories of the spreading of the antarctic ice cap.

Muma Padura In Slavonic† myth kindly wood sprite of the Rumanian forests, who helped to rescue lost children.

Mungan-Ngana Culture hero of the Kurnei tribe of Australia. He taught them how to make nets, implements, canoes, and weapons. His adopted son Tundun† was the ancestor of the tribe. He is of similar type to Baiame†, Bun-Jil†, Daramulum†, Nurelli†, and Nurrundere†.

Muninn ('Memory') In Nordic myth one of the raven messengers of Odin† the other being Huginn†.

Munt Alternative name for Menthu†, the Egyptian hawk-headed god. He was also known as Bukhe†.

Muraian The turtle man, a culture hero of the myth of the Kakadu, a tribe of Arnhem Land.

Muramura Culture heroes claimed as ancestors by several Australian tribes whom they found as half-formed human beings. The Urabunna, Kuynai, and other southern tribes tell that the Muramura came from the north and introduced stone knives for circumcision. They are now said to inhabit trees and to be visible only to medicine men. The Dieri tribe believe that their medicine men not only communicate with the Muramura but also with other supernatural beings known as Kutchis.

Murias In Celtic myth the city of the west, now sunken beneath the seas; one of the four cities from which came the Tuatha Dé Danann†. From here came Undry†, the cauldron of Dagda†, described as 'a hollow filled with water and fading light', one of the treasures of the Tuatha†, and possibly the origin of the Grail. The other cities were Gorias†, Falias†, and Finias†. In Wales, Murias was known as Morvo, and in France as Morois.

Murigen Irish lake goddess, possibly the same as Morgan†, the subject of a legend of a minor deluge, and who was afterwards changed into a salmon. This story may be related to that of Finn† catching the Salmon of Knowledge from the Boann†.

Murugan Chief god of the ancient Tamils.

Musa In the mythology of the Songhay of the Upper Niger, a spirit who travels and hunts, and generally brought to mankind the useful arts.

Muskwari Indian Creation Legend This tribe of North American Indians has a myth that Kitche Manitou† destroyed the world on two occasions, first by fire and then by deluge.

Muspel The fire giants of Nordic myth who were ruled over by Surt† and whose invasion of Asgard, resulting in the defeat of the Aesir†, is told in Ragnarok and in the High German poem *Muspilli*.

Mut Early Egyptian goddess and consort of Amon Ra†; depicted as a vulture, or with a vulture head-dress.

She was mother of the gods, the world

mother. With Khensu† and Amon† she completed the divine triad at Thebes.

Muyscaya Indian Creation Legend In the myths of the Muyscayas and the Chibchas† light, which existed before all things, was brought to earth in a casket known as Chimini-Pagus† and two blackbirds distributed the shining matter in their breaks. The Flood was caused by the moon goddess Chia†, or Hunthaca†, who flooded the land so that only a few survivors escaped by reaching the mountain tops. The earth being at the time without a moon she was transformed into our present-day Luna as a punishment. The survivors, under the leadership of their culture heroes Bochica†, Nemquetcha†, and Sua†, set to work to organize life anew.

Mwambu The Luyia of Kenya take him to be the first man.

Mwari The great spirit of the Mtawara† tribe of Zimbabwe. He had two wives, the first named Mashongavudzi† and the second known as 'the Rain Goddess', both of whom came from Gosa.

Myrddin Original name of the Celtic hero who later became known as Merlin†. He was also known as Emrys†.

N

God 'N' The Maya god of the end of the year, and the five intercalary days.

Nabu Babylonian god of wisdom; son of Marduk† and husband of Tashmetu†, the Nebo† of the Old Testament. In Babylonian myth Nabu occupies a position similar to that of Thoth†, being the scribe and messenger of the gods, the god of wisdom and justice, and the guardian of the Dup Shimati, or Tablets of Wisdom. His temple was at Borsippa, the site of the ziggurat known as the Tower of Babel.

Naga When the Hindus arrived in India they battled with chiefs of Naga (i.e. Asura†) descent, who had the Serpent Banner and the title of 'Supreme Lord of Bhagavati,' thus claiming descent from the Naga Rajas of Patala. The word *naga* is the Indian name for the cobra, but this would appear to have arisen following on the serpent worship of the pre-Hindu races. In the Vishnu Purana mention is made of a certain Ahi Naga, one of the royal family of Ajudha.

Nagaitco In the Kato† Indian Creation Legend the ancestor of the tribe who, as a child, was discovered by Teenes† floating on the waters of the Deluge clinging to the branch of a tree. Later a woman and a dog came to the island and the three of them sailed away to the mainland.

Naglfar In Nordic myth the ship of the Frost Giants†, captained by Hrim or Ymir†. The nails which held it together were said to be those of dead men. It was larger than Skidbladnir†, the ship of Freyr†, but smaller than Hringhorni†, the ship of Balder†. Naglfar is mentioned as the first husband of Nott† from which it may be presumed that he was a dwarf† and the builder of the ship.

Nahar Sun goddess in the Ugarit scripts.

Nakshatras Daughters of Daksha† who married the moon.

Nambi The daughter of the king of heaven in Bugandan mythology who married Kintu†, the first man.

Namtar Plague demon of Aralu, the Babylonian Hades. On the orders of Allatu† he smites Ishtar† when she descends into Hades in search of Tammuz†. Later, however, on the orders of the gods, he sprinkled Ishtar with the waters of life and cured her.

Nanâ Sumerian goddess of Erech from ancient times. Her statue was removed in 2220 BC and recaptured by Asshurbanipal 1,850 years later.

Nana Buluku Among the Fon of

Benin, the primordial mother who created the world.

Nanautzin The shabby and despised god who sacrificed himself by throwing himself into a fire so that the sun should continue to light the world. He is an aspect of the flayed Aztec god Xipé Totec†.

Nancomala In the Guayamit Creation myth he waded into the waters as the Great Deluge receded and there encountered Rutbe†, the water maiden, who later became the mother of twins, the Sun and the Moon, who were the ancestors of the human race.

Nandi In Vedic myth the Snow-White Bull of Siva†. Nandi was the calf of Surabhi†, the Cow of Plenty.

Nandini The cow of plenty belonging to Vasishtha†, one of the Rishist†, and in common with Nandi†, a calf of Surabhi†.

Nanna In Nordic myth the daughter of Nef the wife of Balder†, who died of anguish at his death and whose body was burnt on the same funeral pyre. She was one of the Asynjor† and the mother of Forseti†. Her magic ring was left to Fulla†.

Nanna(r) Moon god of Ur, the centre of this worship. As the word *ur* means light, it is possible that the city grew up around a shrine. Also equated with Sin†.

Nantosuleta A protective Gallic goddess.

Nantosvelta Possibly a variant of Nantosuleta†, with the emphasis on water or springs.

Naoise The elopement of Naoise with Deirdre†, and their subsequent deaths at the hand of Conchobar†, is one of the most tragic love tales of Celtic myth.

Napi Culture hero and founder of the tribe of Blackfoot Indians.

Narahs In Zoroastrian myth a species of being similar to the jinn† of Islam.

Narasinha The man lion, the fourth avatar† of Vishnu† in which he slays the demon Hiranya-Kasipu†, who held the world in thrall. In common with the first three avatars this appears to relate to some pre-Vedic disaster legend.

Narayana In the Hindu Creation Legend the name given to the primeval egg which floated on the waters, from which sprang Brahma†. An alternative name was Hiranya-Garbha†.

Narbrooi Spirit of the woodland mists of Papua New Guinea, who took away the souls of the sick and only returned them on the receipt of suitable gifts.

Narru A name of Enlil†, one of the chief gods of the Sumerian pantheon, who became merged with Marduk† in time.

Nasnas In pre-Islamic myth a form of jinn† living in the Yemen and the Hadramut, having one leg, one arm, and half a head. In the Hadramut they were eaten. A species having wings like bats lived on an island in the Sea of China. They were said to be the offspring of Shiqq† and human beings.

Nata and Nena Hero and heroine of an Aztec† Creation Legend who were commanded by Tezcatlipoca† to build a ship to save themselves from the deluge which occurred in the year Ce-calli.

Natchez Indian Creation Legend The creator of the first men and the ancestors of the Natchez tribe was named Thoume† Kene Kimte Cacounche. After this the men became bored with life and so the creator gave them tobacco, but even this proved inadequate so at last he created women.

Naunet The Egyptian underworld sky, which the sun crosses during the night.

Navajo Indian Creation Legend The process of the breaking down of the myth of this Indian tribe has resulted in all but the bare details of the Creation Legend having been obscured by later myths. In it Ahsonnutli†, their creator god, made both heaven and earth and placed men at each of the cardinal points to uphold the sky. Other aspects of Navajo myth will be found under Begochiddy†, Coyote†, Dontso†, Hashje-Altye†, Hogahn†, Kehtahn†, Kleesto†, Mahih-Mah-Tlehey†, and Sontso†.

Ndengei A serpent deity of Fiji.

Nebhet Alternative name for Nephthys in Egyptian myth.

Nebo Name given in the Old Testament to Nabu†, the Babylonian god of wisdom.

Nefertum Human-headed Egyptian god of the Ennead†, god of the setting sun at Heliopolis, a form of Ra†. He was

the son of Sekhmet† and Ptah†, and sometimes formed part of the Memphis Triad of Gods†. He was symbolized by a lotus.

Nefyed Nav Nevion The builder of the ship in which Dwyvan† and his wife Dwyvach escaped from the deluge which was the first of the Three Awful Events in Britain mentioned in the Triads. The story is given under Celtic† Creation Legends. Nefyed appears to be the same as Nemed†, who is said to have colonized Ireland after the deluge. An alternative spelling is Nevyd†.

Nehalennia A sea goddess of the Belgae or Frisians who is known by several inscriptions.

Neith Egyptian war goddess of Sais, possibly of Libyan origin. May be equated with Pallas Athene, the Heavenly Virgin Mother. She was a virgin goddess, self-begotten, and, according to the priests of Sais, the mother of Ra†, and was of sufficient importance to form a triad with Osiris† and Horus†. She became prominent in the twenty-sixth dynasty but later tended to become confused with Hathor† and Isis†. Net† is an alternative spelling.

Nekhebit Great crowned goddess of Upper Egypt, represented as a vulture or a serpent. Her sister Uadjit† occupied a similar position in Lower Egypt.

Nekhen In Egyptian myth the goddess of law.

Nemed (Nemhedh) In Celtic myth the founder of the third dynasty of Ireland after the Deluge who succeeded that of Partholon†.

Nemon 'The Venomous', a Celtic war goddess subordinate to Morrigu†. At Bath she was known as Nemontana.

Nemquetcha Culture hero of the Muyscayas, who may be Bochica† in that the fourfold division of the tribe is attributed to him. On the other hand he may equally well have been as associate of Bochica. His wife was Hunthaca, who subsequently became a moon goddess, and is sometimes confused with Chia†. Alternative spelling Nemterequeteba.

Nemu Demigods of the Kai tribe of New Guinea who inhabited the world before the present race, whom they created. They were stronger and more powerful than the black and white men who followed them. They discovered edible fruits, agriculture, and house building. They made bananas ripen gradually instead of in bunches as before and prevented houses from moving about. At first it was always day, but they told the sun to go down in the evening to give time for sleep. When they died they became blocks of stone or animals. At the end they were all destroyed by a great flood.

Nephthys The daughter of Nut† and Ra†, sister and wife of Set†, sister of Isis† and Osiris†, and mother of Anubis† by Osiris, a member of the Ennead†. The lament which she uttered together with Isis after the death of Orisis gave them the title of the Weeping Sisters.

While she has been overshadowed by her sister Isis, there is no doubt that she also was a great magician in her own right, and that she knew the words of power used to raise the dead; because of this she was considered as a protector of the dead in the Book of the Dead and in the great body of Egyptian myth.

It seems fairly certain that, as with Isis, she was one of the mother goddesses of early pre-dynastic Egypt, and that their being linked together as members of the family group with Osiris, Set†, and Horus† came at a later date when, perhaps, their ranks and titles were those of the priestess queens of early Egypt.

She was also known as Nebhet†.

Nergal Babylonian deity, lord of the lower world and the dead; husband of Ninmug† (or Ereshkigal†), queen of the lower world. He had his chief cult at Cutch (possibly Tel Ibrahim). His temple was named E-Meslam, or House of Meslam (the lower world). Nergal was also known as Meslamtea (he who rises from Meslam) in his capacity as a solar god. His cult seems to date back to pre-historic times.

Nerthus (**Hertha**) A Teutonic fertility goddess, mentioned by Tacitus, who participated in the biannual fertility festivals and whose temple was in a sacred grove on a Baltic island, possibly Zealand. Although she corresponds to Jord†, her ritual – particularly the fact that both the goddess and her chariot had to be washed in a sacred lake by slaves who were subsequently drowned – recalls the worship of Svantovit† on the island of Rügen. In later times she became the male god Njord† in Norway and Sweden.

Nerrivik Alternative name for Sedna† in Eskimo mythology.

Nessa In Celtic myth the mother by Fathach of Conchobar† who obtained for him the throne of Ulster from her lover Fergus†.

Nesshoue River god of Benin.

Net In Egyptian myth an alternative spelling of Neith†.

Neter Early Egyptian name for God. Brugsch defined it as being 'the active power which produces and creates things in regular recurrence; which bestows new life upon them and gives back to them their youthful vigour'. This idea was later supplanted by the Heliopolis Company of Gods headed by Ra†. The hieroglyph for Neter was an ox head let into a wooden handle.

Nevyd An alternative spelling for Nefyed†, hero of a Celtic† Creation Legend.

Ngai Chief deity of the Masai tribes of East Africa.

Ngani-Vatu A giant man-eating bird, recorded in Fijian myth. It is akin to the Poua-Kai† of the Maori legends and the Roc† of the Arabian Nights. Other relevant myths are given under Polynesia†.

Ngaru In the myth of Mangaia† Island a culture hero who defeated Miru†, the god of the underworld, by causing a deluge which put out the hot fires on which he had intended to cook him. He also defeated Amaite-Rangi†. He defeated Tumu-I-Te-Are-Toka†, the sea monster.

Ngunza Hero of the Mbundu people of Angola who tries to avenge his brother by overcoming Death itself.

Ngurunderi Alternative form of Nurrundere† and the same as Baiame†.

Nibelungenlied The various stories based on the theft of the treasure of the Nibelungs are so interwoven into Nordic, Teutonic, and Anglo-Saxon myth that it would appear probable that there may have once been an actual treasure, the loot of many campaigns, at one time in the ownership of the Aesir†, which brought with it the legacy of murder, treason, and betrayal which accompanied all such hoards before the institution of bankers' strong-rooms. That the great heroic tragedies of the past should have been linked up with the existence of such a treasure is a legitimate device, but in practice the adventures of Sigurd† and Brynhild† should be considered separately from the treasure. A comparative table of characters in the various stories is given below: Alberich†, Andvari†, Brunhild, Brynhild†, Fafnir†, Gudrun†, Gunnar†, Gunther†, Gutrune†, Hagen†, Högni†, Krimhild†, Regin†, Siegfried†, Sigelinde, Siegmund, Sigmund†, Sigurd†, Tarnkappe†. Details of the stories are given under Beowulf†, Thidrek Saga†, Ring Cycle†, Volsung Cycle†.

Nichant In the Creation Legend of the Gros-Ventre† Indians he was the god who destroyed the world by fire and water.

Nick The 'Old Nick' of popular English fable would appear to be a male variant of the Teutonic Nixe†. The lake, river, and well priestesses† of Europe being female, he is in all probability a fairly recent development. The Nickard mentioned by Aubrey as stealing children may be of the same origin.

Nicor Alternative spelling for Nick† or Nixe†.

Nidim Early name for Ea† in Babylonian myth.

Niflheim The description in Nordic myth of Niflheim as a place of mist, cold, and darkness seems to have been based on the experience of hunters, or raiding parties, who were caught by winter in the frozen wastes of the Arctic. Here was to be found Hvergelmir†, the fountain.

Nikkal Sumerian sun goddess and bride of Yarih†. Yarih sent Hirihbi†, a Sumerian king, to Baal†, with the offer of 10,000 shekels of gold for her hand. She is Ningal† in her lunar aspect.

Nina In Babylonian myth daughter of Ea† and sister of Ningirsu†, from whose temple at Nina, now Nineveh, she gave oracles. Her sign was 'the House of the Fish', from which it seems she may have been a marine goddess akin to Oannes†. Later she was merged with Ishtar†. Her cult was linked with those of Enki† and Ningirsu.

Ninanna Alternative name for Innana†, an early Babylonian mother goddess.

Ninella Alternative name for Damkina†, the pre-diluvial Babylonian mother goddess.

Nina Stahu Cave of refuge from which the ancestors of the Blackfoot† Indians emerged into the world.

Nine Worlds In Nordic myth, the universe was divided into nine sections as listed below:

1. Ljosalfaheim, the heaven of the righteous, separated by Vidblainn from
2. Muspellheim, the home of the flame spirits, separated by Andlang from
3. Godheim, the dwelling of the Aesir†.
4. Vanaheim, the dwelling of the Vanir†.
5. Mannheim, the abode of mankind.
6. Svartalfheim, the cavern world where dwell the elves.
7. Jötunheim, the land of the giants.
8. Helheim, the region of death.
9. Niflheim, the lowest region in which dwelt also Nastrond.

It is interesting to note that the Aesir insisted on retaining their social status vis-à-vis the Vanir, even although the two races had fused into one.

Ningal Early sun goddess and wife of Sin†, the Babylonian moon god, and mother of Shamash†. *See also* Nikkal†.

Ningirsu Babylonian god of irrigation, consort of Baba or Bau†. His cult was linked with those of Enki† and Nina†. In one of his forms he is lion-headed, supported by two lions, on the backs of which his claws rest. He originated in the earliest times in Lagash and is to be equated with Ninib†.

Ninib God of the summer sun in Babylonian mythology, akin to Nergal†, god of war and of the Kingdom of the Dead, and the enemy of Marduk†, the spring sun and god of vegetation, who dies and sinks into the underworld with the advent of summer. Ninib had a temple at Calah, mentioned in Genesis x. 11 as having been built by Asshur†. He was also a god of storm and of fertility. He had two consorts, Gula† and Baba or Baut. In Girsu, Ninib was known as Ningirsu†. It was here that the festival of his marriage to the goddess Baut was held. Ninib is also called Enurta†.

Ninigi In Japanese myth grandson of Amaterasu†. He ascended to the throne on the abdication of Onamuji, the son of Susano†. He brought with him to the throne the three symbols of Japanese imperial power, the jewel, the mirror, and the sword. The commander-in-chief of the armed forces with which he compelled his predecessor to abdicate was named Saruto-Hiko.

Ninkharsag (Ninhursag) Lady of the Great Mountain, a title given to Ninlil†.

Ninlil Consort of Enlil†, the Babylonian goddess of grain; also Ninkharsagt or Lady of the Great Mountain.

Ninmug Consort of Nergal† and Queen of Aralu†, the lower world. Also known as Ereshkigal† or Allatu†.

Ninsun A minor goddess of Erech, mother of Gilgamesh† by Lugalbanda†.

Ninurta Probably to be identified with Ningirsu†.

Nirrita In Vedic myth a god of death, usually depicted as riding pick-a-back on a man. He is sometimes considered to be one of the Rudras†. His feminine aspect was Nirriti†.

Nirriti A Vedic goddess of destruction and death, whose personality has become merged with certain of the aspects of Parvati†, the wife of Siva†, in

particular Durgha†. Her masculine aspect was Nirrita†.

Nirvana In Buddhism† the state of release from the bondage of Karma† and rebirth where desire and lust have ceased to have power and no renewal of existence will take place after death. To gain Nirvana was the goal which the Buddha set before his followers as a supreme end to their efforts and longings. The northern school of Buddhist teaching has interpreted Nirvana to mean an actual paradise of existence after death attained as the reward of a saintly life on earth.

Nisaba 'Goddess of Wisdom', the Sumerian goddess of the scribal profession.

Nithud (Nithad) In the Völundar Kvida the King of Troy, and the father of Bodvild†, who was seduced by Völund.

Nixe In Teutonic myth the priestesses of the lakes, rivers, and wellst were known by this name. Wormius thought that the 'Wasser Nixe' fabled to have been seen as late as 1615 may have been the Nickard of Aubrey, which used to steal children. The Grisly Waterman of Spenser's *Faerie Queen* would appear to have been of this family. Another kindred was Nantosuleta†, as was also 'Old Nick'.

Nizir Chaldean name for the landing place of the Babylonian Ark. Further details will be found under Babylonian† Creation Legends.

Njord In Nordic myth he was a giant who was one of the Vanir† and at the conclusion of the war with the Aesir† was sent to them as a hostage. There he married the giantess Skadi†, the daughter of Thiassi†, and became the father of Freyr† and Freyja†. It is possible that he is a masculine form derived from Nerthus (Hertha)†, the earth mother goddess.

Noatun The zodiacal† house of Njord†.

Nodens (Nodons) A river god of the Severn estuary who seems to have displaced Tamesis.

Nootka Sound Indians The chief god of this tribe was Quahootze†.

Nordic Creation Legends The story of Ragnarok†, although given in the form of a prophecy, appears to be that of some great natural disaster as seen by early man in northern latitudes. Apart from this, the world is assumed to have started with a vast ocean of chaos, with mist and cold to the north, and fire or volcanoes to the south. Ymir†, the giant, was killed by the sons of Bor†, and from his body the world was created. From his blood came the great flood. Among the survivors were Bergelmir† and his wife, who escaped in Naglfar†; Askr† and Embla†, who escaped in a canoe and were rescued by the sons of Bor, who escaped by some other means. There is also a story of the lowering of the strand lines around the northern coasts, told under Skrymir†, and of a lunar disaster, told under Bil†. The story of the repopulation of the world is given under Rig†.

Norns The Nordic fates: Urd†, (Fate or Destiny): Verdandi†, (Being); Skuld†, (Necessity). Some were said to be descended from the Aesir†, some from the giants, and some from the dwarfs or

elves, being described in the Prose Eddas as the daughters of Davalin. In fact they would appear to have been a college of sibyls at Asgard†, with which the Valkyries† may have been associated. They may originally have been the guardians of the sacred fountain at the foot of Yggdrasill.

Nortia Etruscan goddess of fortune.

Nott ('Night') In Nordic myth a giantess and the mother of Dag (day). Her horse was Hrimfaxi ('frost-mane').

Novena A form of Geasa†, or couvade†, peculiar to the Irish Celts. It consisted in a whole tribe, after the birth of a royal child, being subjected to twelve days' seclusion.

Ntlakapamuk Indians Creation Legend This tribe of Thompson River has a legend that at some remote period in the time of their forefathers there was a great fire which consumed the whole world and that subsequently the waters of the earth arose in a deluge and put out the flames.

Nuda (Nuadha) King of the Tuatha Dé Danann† whose sword from Finias was one of the treasures of the Tuatha. He lost his hand in battle with the Firbolgs†. Because of this infirmity he was deposed and replaced by Bress†, son of King Elthan† the Fomor†. However, Dian Cécht† fitted him with a silver artificial hand and he regained his throne afterwards, being known as Argetlam†. He may be considered to be the same as Ludd†, who also lost his hand.

Nudd In Britain Nuda†, the Celtic culture hero, was known sometimes by this name instead of Ludd†.

Nudimmud Also Nidim†. Early name for Ea† in Babylonian myth.

Nu-kua In Chinese mythology the creator goddess, sometimes taken to embody both male and female elements within herself.

Nuliajuk Alternative name for Sedna† in Eskimo mythology.

Numitarom (**Num Torum**) Culture hero of the Voguls, a Slavonic tribe of the northern Urals.

Nu(n) Egyptian god of the primeval watery chaos out of which the world was created. From Nu rose Khepera†, the first form of the sun god.

Nunne Chaha The great mountain in the Creek† Creation Legend which emerged from the waters after the Deluge and on which Esaugetuh Emissee† resided, and from the mud of which the first men were created. In the myth of the Choctaw† Indians the survivors emerged from the cave on this mountain. This cave was the home of Esaugetuh Emissee.

Nurelli Culture hero of the Wiimbaio tribe of Australia. After creating the land he brought law and order to them. He had two wives, each of whom carried two spears. He eventually ascended into the sky from Lake Victoria and became a constellation. He is of a similar type to Baiame†, Bun-Jil†, Daramulun†, Nurrundere†, and Mungan Ngana†.

Nurrundere In Australian myth culture hero and later supreme being. He made all things on earth, initiated death rites and ceremonies as now used, and later ascended to the sky. He was also known as Martummere†. Once in order to punish his wicked wives and their families he caused a deluge. He is of a similar type to Baiame†, Bun-Jil†, Daramulun†, Nurelli, and Mungan-Ngana.

Nusku Assyrian fire god, best known by a series of eight tablets in the British Museum, in which he is referred to as the offspring of Anu†, offspring of Shamash†, first-born of Enlil†, etc. His symbol was a lamp. He was also known as the son of Sin†, the moon god, and was sometimes equated with Nabu† and Gibil†.

Nut Mother goddess of Egypt. Sister of Shu† and Tefnut†, sister and wife of Geb† and mother of Osiris†, Haroeris†, Set†, Isis†, and Nephthys†. One of the original Heliopolis Company of Gods. At first she personified the day sky and the night sky. She is usually represented with her hands and her feet on the earth, the curve of her body being the arch of the sky or, perhaps, the Milky Way, and her limbs the four pillars of the firmament. In the very beginning the sun is said to have raised her up to support the sky, but another story has it that she gave birth to the sun, who passed along her back or across her body on his journey. Legend has it that the birthdays of her five children were the five intercalary days (*see* Osiris). She played an important part in the underworld, where she provided fresh air for the dead. She is also equated with the Celestial Cow, later supplanted by Shu†, to whom a calf was born every morning to be sent across the sky. There are several versions of the story.

Nyame The supreme being in the mythology of the Akan in southern Ghana, and also of the Ashanti.

Nyankopon Another personification of Nyame†, specifically as sun and king.

Nyikango Founder of the Shilluk royal dynasty.

Nzambi Among the tribes of the Congo, one of the names of the supreme being.

O

Goddess 'O' An elderly mother goddess of the Mayas, possible a goddess of the home, or of fate.

Oannes In Babylonian myth the god of wisdom, said to be the father of Semiramis†. Berosus considered Oannes, who was half man and half fish, to have brought culture to mankind, which may indicate an early conquest of Babylonia by a sea-going people. Later he was equated with Ea†. *See also* Matsya†.

Oa Rove Marai Culture hero of the Makeo people of Papua New Guinea†.

Obatalla Yoruba† heaven god in opposition to Odudua†, the earth goddess.

Odherir The magic cauldron of Nordic myth. It was originally one of three belonging to Suttung†, the giant†, the others being Bodn and Son, and in it was brewed the intoxicating mead of the Aesir†. It was first used when the peace treaty between the Aesir and the Vanir† was implemented by both sides spitting into the cauldron. When Kvasir†, who was in charge of the cauldron, was murdered by Fjalar† and Galar†, his blood was mixed with the honey mead and fermented to give an intoxicating liquor which gave wisdom, the knowledge of runes and charms, and the gift of poetry in a similar manner to the Soma† of the Persians and the Vedas. The story of how Odin† stole the secret of its manufacture is told under Gunnlauth† and of the subsequent theft of the cauldron by Thor† under Aegir†, Bragi†, and Hymir†. It was also known as Eldhrimir†.

Odin In Nordic myth the elder son of Thor† by the giantess Besla† (though elsewhere Thor is his son). He was one of the slayers of Ymir† and with his two brothers Vili† and Ve† participated in the Nordic Creation myth. As leader of the Aesir† he gradually displaced Thor, who was the representative of the peasantry, while Odin was the hero of the warriors. His title of 'Allfather' was probably a move to confirm him in this position. Odin was a god of the dead, of cunning, of poetry, and, on occasion, of wisdom. He had originally been chief of a raven clan. He was not renowned for prowess in battle unless backed up by Thor and Tyr†, but was the inventor of tactics. In Ragnarok he died in conflict with Fenrir†. In some measure he resembled Thoth†, the Egyptian god of learning; the story of his 'catching up runes' after having hung for nine days on a gallows-tree pierced with a spear, may relate to some form of initiation ceremony in the same way as his pledging one of his eyes to Mimir† for a draught of wisdom from Odherir, the magic cauldron. His throne, Hlithskjalf; his two ravens, Hugin† and Munin†; his horse, Sleipnir†; his sword, Gungnir; his ring, Draupnir were favourite subjects of northern folklore. Like Haroun Al Rashid, Odin delighted to mix with his people in disguise. Snorri, in the Prose Edda and in Ynglingasaga, postulated the existence of Odin as an historical personage, an assumption which seems to have in it a distinct element of probability, although it should be observed that the various king-lists built up on this basis are probably wildly optimistic. It seems fairly certain that Odin was the chief of one of the most powerful groups of early Scandinavian settlers. He is the Woden† of the Teutons.

Odinic Trinity The Trinity of Nordic myth, consisting of the High, the Equally High, and the Third, referred to in the second chapter of the Prose Edda†; their names were Har, Janfar, and Thridi, in ascending degree of importance.

Odomankoma In Ashanti mythology the creator of the universe.

Odudua Earth goddess of the Yoruba people, the mother of Aganju and of Yemaja. Her husband was Orishako.

Oenghus See Angus†.

Og The giant King of Bashan, from whose name we may have acquired the word 'ogre'. The name is frequently paired as Gog Magog†, when Magog was the Moon Goddess and Gog or Og her spouse or son.

Ogham Alphabet This alphabet, which was said to have been devised by Ogma†, was originally intended for incised inscriptions on stone and other hard materials. It consisted only of straight lines of various lengths and slope, which made it easy to carve.

Ogma (Oghma) In Celtic myth a chief of the Tuatha Dé Danann†, the son of Dagda†, who is also known as Cermait, the Celtic god of literature, who is said to have invented the Ogham alphabet. He married Etan, the daughter of Dian–Cécht†, and had several children, including Caipre† and Tuirenn. He killed Indech, the Fomor† chieftain, in battle and was said to have captured the Sword of Tethra, later to be included in the treasures of the Tuatha. In Gaul he was known as Ogmios. In Britain he has been equated with Gwydion†. He may have been the son of a moon goddess.

Ogun In Yoruba myth the god of iron.

Ogyrvan A magic cauldron† mentioned in Celtic myth and listed in the treasures† of Britain.

Ohrmazd See Ahura Mazda†.

Oimelc The Celtic festival of the beginning of February which was known in Ireland as Earrach. The other festivals were Beltaine†, Lugnasad†, and Samhain†.

Oisin See Ossian†.

Ojin In Japanese mythology the son of the Empress Jingo, who was deified as Hachiman†.

Okelim Fabulous creatures sent by El† to fight Baal†, according to the Ugarit texts. Sometimes known as Auqim†. Further details will be found under

Phoenician† Creation Legend.

Oko In Yoruba† myth a child of Aganju† and Yemaja†.

Okonorote Hero of the Creation Legend of the Warrau tribe of the Arawaks†.

Olle In the Creation myth of the Tuleyone† Indians humanity was saved from the great fire caused by the evil spirit Sahte† by Olle, who caused a great flood and extinguished the flames. All the world was submerged except for one mountain top on which the survivors gathered. In some versions Olle is referred to as Coyote†.

Olokun Poseidonian god of the Yorubas. He was god of wealth, as well as the sea.

Olorun Chief of the Yoruba pantheon, Lord and Supreme One, Chief of the Upper Beyond, and Ruler of Heaven. He is not worshipped, neither is he considered in any way, but leads an entirely inactive mythological existence. He was born from Olokun†, the mighty ocean of the sky.

Olwen In Celtic myth she was the May Queen, the daughter of the May tree, or the Hawthorn, or the White Thorn. She may be equated with Blodeuwedd†.

She was the daughter of Ysbadadden, a King of the Giants, whose life would come to an end on her marriage. In consequence he places every possible obstacle in the way of the prospective bridegroom, but in the end he fails.

Omacatl The Aztec† god of festivity and joy; the name means 'Two Reeds'. At the festival of the god reproductions of his bones were made out of maize paste and ritually eaten. The god was also said to visit unfaithful adherents with severe internal pain and cramps.

Omecihuatl Aztec creator goddess, wife of Ometecuhtli†.

Ometecuhtli Aztec creator god, the lord of duality. His wife was Omecihuatl†. It may be assumed that in common with most cases of paired deities of opposite sexes the father god is a later addition and may have started off as the son or lover of the mother goddess.

Ometeotl In Aztec religion the one god above all. To some extent he is the same as Ometecuhtli† and Tloque Nahuaque†.

Omicle (**Omichle**) Progenitor by Potos (Pothos)† of all things, in the Phoenician Creation Legend of Damascius. Their offspring were Aër and Aura.

Omumborombonga Name given to a tree which the Damara† tribe of South Africa believed to be the progenitor of men and cattle.

Onamuji A Japanese earth god, the son of Susano†. In order that her grandson Ninigi† could come to the throne Amaterasu† sent Futsunushi† and Takemikadzuchi† to force the abdication of Onamuji. In this they were only partially successful as Ninigi had to bring an earmy with him to enforce his demands.

Oni Generic name applied to the powers of evil in Japanese myth.

Onniont The snake deity of the Hurons†. He carried on his head a horn which pierced mountains and rocks.

Warriors of the tribe endeavoured to carry portions of this for luck and even consumed fragments in water to give them courage.

Ono The name given to Rongo† in the Marquesas Islands.

Onouris Alternative name for Anhur† in Egyptian myth.

Oonawieh Unggi 'The Oldest Wind', a wind god of the Cherokee† Indians.

Oossood Serbian Veela† who pronounces on the destinies of newly born children on the seventh night after their birth, and who is perceived only by the mother.

Opet Name under which the hippopotamus goddess Taueret† was worshipped at Thebes in Egyptian myth.

Ophois Alternative name for Upuaut† in Egyptian myth.

Opochtli An Aztec† god of fishing and bird snaring, dating back to the Tenochtitlan period, who, at a later date, appears to have been merged with Huitzilopochtli†.

Orgelmir A name sometimes given to Ymir†, the Nordic giant†.

Orinoco Indians The culture hero of the Orinoco Indians is Amalivaca†.

Orishako Yoruba† god of agriculture; the friend and comrade of Shango† and consort of Odudua†.

Orisha Nla The Yoruba chief god, subordinate to Olorun†.

Orko The Basque thunder god, Orkeguna being Thursday in the Basque language. There was also an alpine thunder giant with a similar name.

Ormazd In Zoroastrian myth an alternative name for Ahura Mazda†.

Oro The great war god of the Polynesian peoples. The name may possibly be derived from Orongo† or Rongo†. In Tahiti the king by virtue of his coronation ceremony became an incarnate god. This was shown by his wearing the sacred girdle, and by the position of his throne in the temple. His houses became the Ao-Roa or clouds of heaven, his canoe became Anuanua, the rainbow, and when he travelled he was never described as journeying but only as flying. He was also the Marai of Opoa in Raiatea, where he originated.

Orongo In Polynesian myth the alternative spelling for Rongo†.

Orunjan In Yoruba† myth he was the son of Aganju† and Yemaja†. He was the god of the midday sun.

Orunmila The name means 'Heaven knows Salvation', denoting the Yoruba god who acted as a mediator and go-between.

Orwandil Name of a giant who was defeated in battle by Thor, who threw one of his toes into the sky, where it became a star.

Ose-Shango The amulet of Shango†, the thunder god and first king of the Yoruba† tribe of Nigeria. It was his badge of authority and is frequently referred to in legend.

Oshalla In Yoruba† myth a secondary god, the son of the sun and husband of the earth goddess.

Osiris The story of the life and death of Osiris, the Egyptian god of the dead, and chief member of the Ennead†, is, probably, the most important contribution which the ancient Egyptians made to the general body of religious myth. Osiris was the son of Nut† and Ra† or of Nut and Geb†, the brother and husband of Isis†, and the brother of Nephthys† and Set†. Before the birth of Osiris, Ra was so infuriated at the faithlessness of Nut that he decreed that her children should not be born in any month of the year. Thoth†, however, gambled with the moon for a seventy-second part of the day and eventually won five days, which were added to the Egyptian lunar year of 360 days, thus enabling not only Osiris but his four brothers and sisters to be born out of any month. The addition of these days, known as the Epact, to the year in connection with the birth of Osiris, shows that it was at this time that the adjustment of the calendar took place.

Later, when Osiris had grown up and married Isis, he was known as a wise and beneficent ruler, who spread civilization throughout Egypt and the surrounding countries. This aroused the hatred of his brother Set, who plotted his murder. This was accomplished by secretly obtaining the measurements of Osiris, and making a special coffer to fit him. On the occasion of a banquet he offered to present the coffer to whomsoever it fitted. On Osiris taking his turn, the lid was slammed down and sealed, and the coffer thrown into the Nile. The waters of the river carried it as far as Byblos, a town in the papyrus swamps of the Delta. It came to rest by a tamarisk-tree, which grew around the coffer, enclosing it.

After a long search Isis obtained possession of the coffer, but during her absence it was discovered by Set, who cut the body of Osiris into fourteen pieces which he scattered in the marshes. Isis recovered the pieces and reassembled them, and by the aid of Thoth brought Osiris to life again for sufficient time for him to beget the infant Horus†. Alternative versions say that the fourteen pieces were buried where they were found, or that they were reassembled and made into a mummy. After this – in all the stories – Osiris became ruler of the kingdom of the dead, Amenti, the Land of the West.

When he came of age, Horus claimed the throne of Egypt, but this was opposed by Set on the grounds that he was illegitimate, owing to the method of his conception. Ra favoured Set, who was a sun and sky god, and the trial was reduced to a succession of combats between Horus and Set, in which, by the aid of magic, they both assumed the forms of wild beasts of various kinds. In one episode, where they were both black bulls goring each other, Isis killed them both.

The council of the gods, however, failed to come to any decision, and Osiris sent a letter pointing out that he was the creator of the barley, on which both gods and men lived, and that for this reason his son should be declared the winner. This also brought no result, so finally Osiris resorted to threats and told the council that he would send savage messengers to fetch the whole Ennead to the nether world unless they declared in favour of Horus. To this they finally agreed. Other aspects of the conflict are given under Horus, Isis and Set.

In the myth of Osiris we seem to have the history of a king of pre-dynastic Egypt, interwoven with the ritual sacrifice of a barley god, and a conflict between two priest kings of Upper and Lower Egypt, perhaps for temporal gain or connected with the driving out of the older sun and sky religion of Set by the newer one represented by Osiris. It has been authoritatively stated that 'The evidence of Osiris as the source of vegetable life, as far as the Old Kingdom is concerned, must be admitted to be very scanty and indecisive, and is completely out-weighed by the evidence testifying as to his kingly character.'

Frazer attributes a lunar origin to Osiris, as did Plutarch. This factor might well explain the violence of the fight with Set.

Over a period of several thousands of years the original conception of Osiris as a harsh god of the nether world was gradually modified to a point where the myth of his resurrection by Isis became the basis for the faith of the average Egyptian for a life beyond the grave.

The linking of Osiris with Nephthys as the father of Anubis† may be a late development.

Osiris was called by many names, of which the following are the best known: Andjeti†, Asari†, Asārtaiti† and Wennofer†.

Ossian (Osian) An Irish heroic poet, the son of Finn†.

Otos Reason, in the Phoenician† Creation Legend of Damascius, child of Aër† and Aura†.

Oulomus In the Phoenician Creation Legend† of Mochus he was engendered by Ether† and Aër†, and himself produced Chousorus†. From him sprang the primeval egg†, which when broken gave rise to Ouranos† and Gea†.

Ouranos This would appear to be a Semitic rendering of Uranus†, dating back to the period when efforts were being made to explain Semitic myth in Greek terms.

In the Phoenician Creation Legend† of Philo Byblos he was the child of Elioun† and Berouth†, the husband of Gea, and the father of Baitulos†, Dagon†, Zeus Damaros† and Pontus†, El† and Ashtart†.

In the Phoenician Creation Legend of Mochus, Ouranos and Gea were the two halves of the primeval egg†.

Both of the versions fit in with the classical myth of Ouranos, the sky god, father of the Titans, including Cronos† (the father of Zeus), the Cyclopes, and the Hecatoncheires. He was emasculated by Cronos, and from the drops of his blood falling into the sea sprang the Gigantes and from the foam Aphrodite.

Ousoos Giant son of Fire† in Phoenician† Creation Legend of Philo Byblos, and the first to make garments from skins; at enmity with his brother Hyposouranios†, who was the first to build cities. This enmity would appear to be founded on the traditional dislike of the pastoral tribes for the first town dwellers although analogies have been traced with the dispute between Aleion† and Baal†.

Oya Mother goddess of the Yoruba tribe of Nigera.

Oynyena Maria In Slavonic myth 'Fiery Mary', who was the counsellor and assistant of Peroun†, the thunder god. She may have been a fire goddess who later became submerged by the new thunder god.

P

God 'P' A Mayan god represented as having the fingers of a frog and a blue background representing water. He was an agricultural deity and may correspond to one of the children of Tlaloc†.

Pa In Chinese mythology the goddess of drought.

Pacari In one of the versions of the Inca† Creation Legend this was the cave from whence issued the four brothers and sisters who founded the four religions of Peru. The first brother was Pachacamac†, the second was unnamed but was the founder of a sytem of worship associated with stone cairns, the third was Viracocha†, and the fourth was Mancoccapac†.

In the other version it was Apocatequil† and his brother Pigueirao† who cut their way out of the cave with the assistance of Ataguchu†.

Pachacamac In Inca myth one of the four brothers who issued from Pacari, the cave of Refuge. His brothers were Viracocha† and Mancocoapact†; the third was unnamed. As, however, Mama Pacha† was the name of the earth mother, it is probable that Pachacamac was an offspring of the original mother goddess.

Pachamama *See* Mama Pacha†.

Paikea In Polynesian myth the god of the sea monsters, the child of Rangi† and Papa†. The name is also that of a whale and of the hero of a famous story of swimming.

Pàmola In Algonkian† myth an evil spirit of the night who was conquered by their culture hero Gluskap†.

Panchamukhi-Maruti In Vedic myth a name under which Siva† was worshipped in western India. Here he was the Hindu Hercules, and his name was invoked every time a weight was lifted.

Pan-ku (Phan-ku) In the Chinese Creation Legend a giant who evolved from the Yang and the Yin, from whose body the earth and the solar system was composed. The Taoists represent him as a shaggy primeval being armed with a huge hammer with which he breaks up rocks.

Papa Great mother of the gods in the myth of Mangaia Island. She was the wife of Rangi† and the mother of Tangaroa† and Rongo†. It was her hatred for Tangaroa which led her to arrange for his displacement by his younger brother, Rongo.

Paparloi The designation of a priest among the voodoo worshippers of Haiti. His female counterpart was called Mamaloi†.

Papsukal In Babylonian myth a messen-

ger of the gods who brings to Shamash†
the news of the imprisonment of Ishtar†
in Aralu.

Parasu-Rama The sixth avatar of
Vishnu†, when as 'Rama with the Axe'
he fought and defeated the followers of
Indra†, the Kshatriyas, after twenty-one
battles. This story appears to have been
invented in order to assist in the displacement of Indra by Vishnu.

Parijata In Vedic myth the Tree of
Knowledge, produced at the Churning
of the Ocean† in the Kurma† avatar.

Parikas In Zoroastrian myth an alternative name for Peri†.

Partholon In Celtic myth the son of
Sera, who arrived in Ireland with
twenty-four married pairs in his train.
After some time, when they had reached
the total of five thousand, the majority
of them were wiped out by epidemic.
This was the second dynasty of ancient
Ireland.

Parvati In Vedic myth the wife of Siva† ,
in her aspect as a mountain goddess.
The fantastic complications of nomencla-
ture, caused by the desire of the Brahmans to symbolize all manifestation of
goddesses as being wives of Siva, have
led to all kinds of historical personalities
being merged into this one entity. Other
names under which she is known are:
Anna-Purna†, 'Full of Food'; Bhavani†;
Durga†; Kali†, 'the Black One';
Kamakshi†, 'the Wanton-Eyed';
Kumari†, 'the Damsel'; Sati†; Uma†,
'the Light of Wisdom'; Vijaya†, 'the
Victorious'; Vindhyavasini†, 'the
Bloody'. Parvati was the mother of
Ganesa†.

Patagonian Indians One of the gods of
this tribe named Settaboth† became immortalized as the Setebos† of Shakespeare.

Patala In Vedic myth the lowest region
of the underworld, inhabited by
Asuras† and their associates. It may
have been the name of a town or a
country inhabited by snake-worshippers
conquered by the invading Hindus; this
opinion is supported by the Nagas†
claiming descent from the Naga Rajas
of Patala.

Patol Husband of Alaghom Naum† or
Iztat Ix† in the myth of the Tzental†
Indian and Mayan tribe.

Pawnee Indian Creation Legend This
tribe of Caddoan Indians of North
America have a myth that at the time of
the Deluge their ancestors took refuge
in a cave and that after the period of
trial had finished an old man who carried a pipe, fire, and a drum, together
with his wife, who had maize and pump-
kin seeds, were the first to return to
the outer world. Their chief deity was
Atius-Tirawa†, and it was he who had
ordered the destruction of the world by
fire which was put out by the Deluge.

Peheipe Early culture hero who appears
in the Maidu† Indian Creation Legend.

Peiroun The hero of a Taiwanese Creation Legend. He was warned that when
the faces of the idols Awun and Infoniwoo in a nearby temple turned red in
colour there would be a deluge. One
day this happened and he hurriedly
boarded a ship just in time to see the
island of Maurigasma, of which he was
ruler, vanish beneath the waves.

Pele In Polynesian myth the fire goddess of Hawaii. There is a deluge legend associated with Pele, who is said to have poured out the seas around the Hawaiian mainland until all but the highest summits were submerged. Later, however, the water receded to its present level. In the West Indies the volcano of Martinique is named Pele, which may indicate a common origin.

Penard'un In Celtic myth the first wife of Llyr† and the mother of Evnisien†.

Perchta Fertility goddess, the Bride of the Sun, of Slavonic origin, whose feast was celebrated by the wearing of masks, those of beauty for the spring and summer, and those without beauty for autumn and winter. *See also* Bercht†.

Peredur A knight mentioned on several occasions in Welsh myth. He was educated by one of the nine witches of Gloucester, which would show his royal blood. He occurs in the story of Olwen and in various episodes of the Grail†, stories where his name has become Percival. A dubious etymological derivation of the name makes it come from *per*, meaning a cup; and *dur*, meaning seeker.

Peri In Zoroastrian myth a name given both to the female demons associated with Ahriman† and to the good and kindly sprites of later days. They seem to have been pre-Zoroastrian river and forest goddesses, although in one of the Ysahts they are referred to as meteors.

Perkunas The Lithuanian thunder god, possibly an alternative spelling of Peroun†.

Peroun (**Perun**) The Slavonic thunder god, who gave his name to Thursday (*Perendan*), in the same manner as Thor† gave it to the northern races and Orko to the Basques. He drove across the sky in a fiery chariot launching shafts of lightning. He was also lord of the harvest, and, as such, may be equated with Perkunas†. At Novgorod a fire of oak wood was always kept burning in front of his effigy; the penalty for letting it out was death. He may have been brought as Thor by Scandinavian traders to the cities of Novgorod and Kiev. In the tenth century treaties between the Slavs and the Byzantines were sworn in the name of Peroun. He was one of the Kiev group of gods, the others being Da-bog†, Khors†, and Stribog†. He was also equated with Trojanu.

Peruda One of the three creator gods in the Tupi Guarani† Creation Legend, the others being Guaracy† and Jacy†. He was the god of generation concerned with human reproduction.

Pet Egyptian term for Amenti†.

Phoenician Creation Legends There are four main versions of the creation legend of the Phoenicians:

(*a*) That of Sanchuniathon (eleventh century BC) as reported by Philo Byblos (AD 42–117): In the beginning there were Aër† and Chaos†, from whom proceeded Wind† and Desire† (Potos†), who produced Mot in the shape of an egg†. In this were formed creatures which remained motionless and dormant until the egg opened, when from it were projected the sun, the moon, and the stars. Later under the influence of Light†, the waters were separated from the sky.

The creation of man was not less complicated. From Kolpia† (the wind†) and his wife Baau† issued Aion† (life) and Protogonos† (first-born). Their children were Genos† (race) and Genea, who were the first to worship the sun. Their descendants were Light†, Fire†, and Flame†, who discovered the use of fire. From Fire issued the giants, of whom Hyposouranios† was the first to build towns, while Ousoos† was the inventor of garments made from skins.

The first gods were Elioun† and Berouth†, whose children were Ouranos† (the sky) and Gea (the earth). From this pair sprang El†, Dagon†, Atlas†, Zeus Demaros† (father of Melkart†), Ashtart†, Baitulos†, etc. El later revolted against Ouranos with the aid of his brothers and sisters, a story which recalls the classical revolt of the Titans against Uranus with the aid of Gea.

(b) That of Damascius (AD 480). Before all, there existed Chronos† (time), Potos† (desire), and Omicle† (mother of all). From the union of the two latter came Aër and Aura†, who in their turn produced Otos† (reason).

(c) That of Mochus, reported by Athenaeus (second century AD). The first principles were Ether† and Aër†, who engendered Oulomos†, who himself produced, first Chousoros†, and then the egg†, which when broken up gave rise to Ouranos† and Gea†.

(d) That of the Ugarit texts, discovered shortly before the Second World War. Although these cannot properly be described as Creation Legends, the portions dealing with cosmological origins not being available, nevertheless they form a parallel to the Sanchuniathon story, having been written about the same time, and having the advantage of

not being distorted to meet the demands of Hellenistic abstract thought: El, the supreme god, lived in the Sad-El† (Field of God) with Asheratian† (the Asher of the Sea), who seems to have been the same as Elat† and may in actual fact have been the mother goddess who preceded El.

In perpetual conflict with El is Baal† (the lord), maintaining the principle of Dualism† which is found throughout this area. The offensive in his conflict is not taken by Baal the younger and more vigorous god, but by El, who sets against his opponent various fabulous creatures including the Auqim†, or Okelim†, which have huge horns and resemble Baal in appearance. Baal, who is attended by Ben Dagon†, is sometimes victorious and sometimes defeated, in which latter case he is sacrificed.

A similar, possibly later, conflict takes place between Mot†, the son of the gods (i.e. of El), and Aleion†, the son of Baal. At some stage in these combats Mot kills Aleion, and the world of nature suffers. Anthat†, the sister of Aleion, goes to Mot and demands the restoration of her brother to life, but failing to secure this she carries out the sentence of death passed by the gods and cuts him in half with a sickle.

Other portions of the story show Baal taking the place of his dead son and eventually killing Mot, while in yet another the eventual victory is given to Aleion. There are other conflicts between Mot and Leviathan†, who is the giant sea beast of the Bible.

These combats, which seem to have been an annual event and to have involved the death of one of the parties, may have replaced the sacrifice of the agricultural god by armed combat between the representatives of two religious groups, in which the loser was the victim of the sacrifice.

The story presents certain points of similarity with those that came later and doubtless it will be possible, in time, to disentangle all the threads. A possible point of contact is the similarity between Aleion and Tammuz†.

Phoenix Name by which the sacred Bennu† bird in Egyptian myth is best known. There is a kinship here with Roc†, the enormous bird of the Arabian Nights.

Piguerao A name meaning 'White Bird' given by the Incas to the twin brother of Apocatequil†. Because of the veneration shown to these brothers, twins were regarded by the Incas as sacred and as protected by the lightning wielded by Apocatequil. He was the son of Guamansuri†.

Pilan (Pillan) Disaster god of the Araucanian Indians. He appears to have been a thunder god who had become abstract in the course of years and as such was only consulted in moments of great urgency.

Piltzintecuhtli A name by which Tonatiuh†, the Aztec sun god, was occasionally known. It means 'the Young Prince'. The possibility of his having been an independent personage is shown by mention of him as the companion of Xochiquetzal†. He was the lord of the third hour of the night.

Pinon In the Creation Legend of the Uapes†, a branch of the Tupi-Guarani† Indians, he was the son of Temioua† and was born girdled with a star serpent, and subsequently became the constellation Orion. His sister, born with seven stars, became the Pleiades.

Ping-i *See* Ho Po†.

Piris In Zoroastrian myth a being similar to the Arab jinn†.

Pishashas In Vedic myth malignant woodland spirits, who disliked travellers, and especially pregnant women.

Pisky Cornish name for brownie†. The word may have been originally spelt pixy.

Polynesian Creation Legends The Creation myths of the Polynesians show a marked similarity to those of Mangaia† Island, which should be consulted. Cognate information will also be found under Akua†, Ao-Kahiwahiwa†, Ao-Kanapanapa†, Ao-Nui†, Ao-Pakakina†, Ao-Pakarea†, Ao-Potango†, Ao-Pouri†, Ao-Roa†, Ao-Takawe†, Ao-Toto†, Ao-Whekere†, Ao-Whetuma†, Apu-Hau†, Apu-Matangi†, Avaiki†, Hawaika†, Hina†, Io†, Kiho Tumu†, Knpua†, Marae†, Matao-Anu†, Mate-Anu†, Maui†, Multitude of Space†, Oro†, Orongo†, Paikea†, Pele†, Sina†, Tawhaki†, Tawhiri†, Waitiri†, Whakarere-Anu†, Whakatoro-Anu†, Where-Ao†. Other myths are given under Easter† Island, Gilbert† Islands, Ngani-Vatu†, Poua-Kai†, Society† Islands, Tahitian† Creation Legend, Vaotere†.

Pomo Indian Creation Legend In the myth of this tribe of California Indians it is told that Marumda† lived in the north and decided one day to create the world and called in his elder brother Kuksu† for assistance. After they had done so they were dissatisfied and decided to destroy it with a deluge, but this proved so disastrous that they themselves had to be rescued by Ragnot, the Old Mother. Again they tried to destroy the world, this time by fire, and again they had to be rescued. Finally they created man, and the ancestors of the tribe built a ceremonial dance house and they taught the people to dance, then, having done this, they left mankind to its own devices.

Another version tells how Dasant and his father Makilat came from the waste of waters and brought civilization to mankind.

Pontus The Sea, one of the children of Ouranost and Get in the Phoenician cosmogony, also a son of Gaea in the classic myth. In actual fact this would appear to be a Greek name given by Damascius to a Phoenician god. He was brother to Atlast, Baitulost, Dagont, and Zeus Demarost.

Pooka A pre-Celtic god, possibly of the dwarfst, who was eventually degraded until he became a goblin, the Puck of English literature.

Popul Vuh The Creation Legend of the Quiche Indians was fortunate in having escaped the destructive efforts of the Spanish conquerors. It may be said to be a reflection of the myths, not only of the Mayas, but to some extent of the Aztecs, and is of considerable assistance in arriving at an interpretation of certain of these. The name means 'The Book of Written Leaves', and it is divided into three parts. The first part deals with the creation of pre-diluvial man, his destruction by the wrath of the gods, by flood and by fire. There is also a section in this part dealing with war of the gods against the giants but this seems to have got out of place as the personages concerned, Hunapút and Xbalanquet, are only born in the middle of part two.

Some of the stories about Blue-Jayt resemble those in the Popul Vuh.

Part two tells the story of the death of Hunhunapú and Vukub-Hanapút at the hands of the rulers of Xibalbat, the Cavern World of the Quichest, and the avenging of these deaths by Hunapút and Xbalanquet. The third part deals with the arising of present-day man and his origin in Tulan-Zuivat. In common with the myths of many of the American tribes the Popul Vuh is vitally concerned with caverns, and it would seem that at some remote period of natural disaster the ancestors of these races were forced to live in caves as places of refuge for several generations. The adventures of the brothers in Xibalba appear to relate to initiation ceremonies carried out in these places. Other references mentioned are Camazotzt, Chimalmatt, Gucumatzt, Hunapút, Huncamet, Hunhunapút, Hurakant, Tohilt, Tulan-Zulvat, Votant, Vukub-Caquixt, Vukubcamet, Vukub-Hanapút, Xbalanquét, Xibalbat, Xmucanet and Xpiyacoc, and Xquiqt.

Porenutius In Slavonic myth an alternative name for Porevitt, the four-headed Slavonic god of the island of Rügen, quoted by Saxo Grammaticus, who says that he had four faces to the cardinal points and one on his chest. He is in measure akin to Rugievitt, Svantovitt, and Triglavt.

Porevit An alternative name for Porenutiust, the four-headed god of the island of Rügen.

Poshaiyankaya Culture hero of the Zuñis who after the Deluge cut a way out of the caves in which they had taken refuge and enabled them to reach the earth again. Alternative spelling Poshaiyangkyo.

Potos (Pothos) Father by Omiclet of Aër and Aura; the name Potos means Desire. One of the three founders of the Phoenician Creation Legend of Damascius.

Poua-Kai A giant man-eating bird, recorded in Maori legends. It is akin to the Ngani-Vatut of the Fijians and the Roc† of the Arabian Nights. Other relevant myths are given under Polynesia†.

Prajapatis. In Vedic myth the mind-created children of Brahma†. For practical purposes they may be considered to be the same as the Rishis†. The name Prajapati, meaning a Supreme Being, is applied to Brahma, Savitri†, and even to Soma†. The original seven Prajapatis were probably the same as the seven Manus† and the seven Rishis†, men of traditional fame, who were promoted to these positions. The name Prajapati is occasionally given to Brahma himself, as the greatest of them all.

Pramzimas Lithuanian pre-diluvial culture hero. The story goes that when the Flood came he threw a nutshell into the waters in which two survivors managed to escape. Other versions are given in Lithuanian† Creation Legends.

Pranas In the Upanishads, the Rudras† are described as the ten Pranas, or senses (vital breaths), i.e. the five Jnanendriyas and the five Karmendriyas, and Manas (the heart) as the eleventh.

Prisni In Vedic myth the wife of Rudra† and mother of the Rudras or the Maruts†.

Prithivi In Vedic myth one of the personifications of the earth.

Protogonos Meaning 'First-born', child of Baaut† and Kolpia† and brother of Aion†, in the Phoenician† Creation Legend of Philo Byblos.

Pryderi In Celtic myth the son of Pywll† and Rhiannon† who was kidnapped at birth and brought up by Teyrnon Twrv Bliant†. He was called Gwrit – 'he of the golden hair.' He married Kicva and was one of the seven survivors of the fight between Brân† and Matholwch†.

Ptah The human-headed smith-creator god of Memphis; the Greeks identified him with Hephaistos. He is also found as a Triune god with Osiris† and Seker†, and at some early stage absorbed Tenen†, a pre-dynastic creator god. He was the architect of the universe who made the egg of the sun and carried out the work of creation, together with Khnemu†, at the command of Thoth†; in this work he was assisted by Maat†.

Puang Matowa Sky god of the Toradja tribe of the Celebes† tribes who married the ancestor of their Raja, who is regarded as an incarnate deity. He may be one of the sons of Laseo†.

Puck In Britain a mildly malevolent evil spirit who appears in the mythology not only of northern Germany, but also Scandinavia. In Norway he is known as Pukje, and along the Baltic Pukis.

Puhsien Name under which the Vedic

sun god, Pushan†, was introduced into China, about AD 300.

Pulug The thunder god of the Andaman Islands in the Indian Ocean. He appears to be the same as the Peroun† of the Slavs.

Punchau An Inca† sun god sometimes called Punchau Inca, usually depicted as a warrior armed with darts. He is probably the same as Epunamun†, the war god of the Araucanian Indians.

Pun-Gel In Australian myth an alternative form of Bun-Gil† used in Victoria and the Murray River. The word means 'Eagle Hawk.'

Purusha In Vedic myth the male half of Brahma† as opposed to Satarupa†, the female half. Purusha has also been described as a primeval giant from whose dead body the world was created. The confusion between Purusha and Viraj† may have arisen from the desire to compress two opposing personalities into a relatively small framework. An alternative name for the male half of Brahma is Skambha†.

Pushan In Vedic myth the sun; the guardian and preserver of cattle; the companion of travellers and guide of the soul in the lower world. About AD 300 he was introduced into Chinese myth under the name of Puhsien†. It is said that at the behest of Siva† his teeth were knocked out by Vira-bhadra†, for which reason he is always shown as toothless.

Pushpaka In Vedic myth an aerial chariot, in which Kubera† usually travelled. In the Ramayana† it is told how it was stolen by Ravana† and later recovered by Rama†, who brought back his bride in it.

Pwyll In Celtic myth the husband of Rhiannon† and the father of Pryderi†. When he went to war on Havgan he changed places with Arawn†.

Q

Qadesh Variant for Qedeshet†, the Syrian goddess worshipped in ancient Egypt and identified with one of the forms of Hathor†.

Qat (**Quat**) Melanesian creator god who was also something of a trickster.

Qebhsneuf One of the four divine sons of Horus†; guardian of the west; Canopic protector of the intestines. The name means 'Pleaser of his Brethren'. The other three were Amset†, Duamutef†, and Hapy†.

Qedeshet (**Qedeshat**) A Syrian goddess worshipped in Egypt identified with one of the forms of Hathor† or of Ashtart†. She was represented as standing naked on a walking lion, holding a mirror and lotus blossoms in her left hand, and two serpents in her right. Later pictures show her wearing the head-dress of Hathor. In the eighteenth and nineteenth dynasties she is called 'Lady of Heaven, Mistress of all the Gods, Eye of Ra, who has none like her'. She was prayed to for life and health, and was sometimes associated with Amsu† and Reshpu†. Also known as Kedesh and Qodshu†.

Qodshu Variant for Qedeshet† in Egyptian myth.

Quahootze War god of the Nootka†

Indians, to whom the following prayer was addressed by braves on the eve of battle: 'Great Quahootze, let me live, not be sick, find the enemy, not fear him, find him asleep, and kill a great many of him.'

Quamta Supreme being of the Xhosa. His worship is accompanied by the raising of mounds of stones to which each passer-by adds one.

Quetzalcoatl A culture hero of the Toltecs, who was absorbed into the Aztec pantheon. He appears to have been a representative of a race on a higher cultural plane than the Toltecs, who brought many arts and crafts, and who was eventually driven away by a local dignitary, who may have been Tezcatlipoca†. He left, promising to return, and when the Spaniards landed it was thought that this was the second coming. He may originally have been a priest of the sun, but later became the feathered serpent, the Aztec god of learning and of priestly functions, and the god Ehecatl† of Cholula. He was the lord of the ninth hour of the day. He is similar to Gucumatz† of the Popul Vuh, the Kamu of the Arawaks, and many other missionaries of culture, a fact which might indicate an early wave of foreign culture in what are now the Latin American states. He was sometimes called Tlapallan†.

Quiche Creation Legend Details of this are given under Popul-Vuh†.

Qutrub Male jinn† of the Ghul† in pre-Islamic myth.

R

Ra The first appearance of this Egyptian sun god is as the grandson of Ra† and son of Nut† over whose arched back he travelled each day, dying at dusk as an old man, and being reborn at dawn. At a later stage in religious development he superseded his grandmother and was depicted as sailing the skies in his celestial boat by day, and as combating the powers of evil in the Tuat by night. He is also associated with an early catastrophe legend in which he was a ruler who sent forth Hathor† and Sekhmet† to destroy his rebellious subjects, but after they had partially done so and were wading in their blood, he repented and caused the goddesses to become intoxicated and cease from slaughter; he then withdrew to the Tuat, or Fields of Peace.

Although he is a typical sun god, the above legend would indicate that he had been linked with an earthly ruler in whose reign occured a cosmic disaster followed by a flood. Whether his worship or that of Hathor was originally accompanied by blood sacrifices cannot be said, but there appears to be no record of this in dynastic times. The boat and the nightly combat with the powers of darkness are among the attributes of typical solar gods. There is also a sun god of the same name in the Pacific Islands. Ra was one of the Ennead† in the Heliopolis company of gods, and as such the father of Osiris†, Isis†, Set†, and Nephthys† by Nut. The Morning Boat of Ra was called Mantchet or Manjet†, and the Evening Boat was Mesektet†.

Atmu†, a local god of Heliopolis, was merged with Ra-Tem†.

More information in connection with Ra† will be found under Af†, Hu†, Neith†, and Saa†.

Rabisu A Mesopotamian demon who appears in nightmares.

Ragnarok The Doom of the Gods in Nordic myth. The story as told in the Völuspa† and also in the Prose Edda† is assumed to have been a prophecy, but it would rather appear to be a faint memory of some great natural catastrophe of the past in which the majority of the Aesir† were destroyed. It began with seven Fimbul winters, i.e. with a severe frost, piercing winds, and no warmth from the sun; these were followed by a period when 'Brethren were each other's bane, an axe age, a sword age, a storm age, a wolf age, ere earth met its doom', which reads like the onset of an ice age. The sun is obscured by the wolf Fenrir†, the earth trembles, the sea rushes over the earth, and on it floats the ship Nagalfar† bearing the last of the frost giants with Hrim† or possibly Bergelmir† as their pilot.

Surt† leads the Host of Muspel† against the Aesir†, breaking down the Bifrost† Bridge. Heimdall† sounds Gjallar†, Odin† rides to the well of Mimir† for advice, Yggdrasil† shakes,

and the Aesir arm for battle, led by
Odin brandishing Gungnir†, his magic
sword. Odin is killed by Fenrir, Thor†
fights Jormungard†, the Midgard† serpent, Freyr† stands against Surt† and is
killed for lack of his sword; Garm† the
moon hell-hound breaks loose and kills
and is killed by Tyr†, while Thor, although victorious over the serpent, dies
from its venom. Vidar† kills Fenrir,
Loki† and Heimdall kill each other. Then
Surt darts flame over the world, most of
which is consumed. The only survivors
are Vidar and Vali† and the two sons of
Thor, Modi† and Magni†. A Balder†
and a Hodur† are also mentioned as
survivors but these are probably titles
and not proper names.

Men appear again on the earth, the
sun has a daughter – which may possibly
mean a new body in the solar system –
a new golden age begins, and the dragon
of darkness is banished.

The story appears to be that of some
great natural disaster as seen by early
man in the northern latitudes. The battle
may have been the last despairing struggles of tribes, or even races, fighting for
safety and existence. It combines a plan-
etary myth with both deluge and fire
myths, and belongs to the great Creation
myths of the world.

Ragno Old mother goddess who occurs
in the Pomo Indian Creation Legend†,
where she rescues Kuksu† and his brother
Marumda† from the consequences of
their own stupidities. She also occurs in
the Hopi† Indian Creation Legend in
connection with the two Huruing†
Wuhti sisters.

Rahab A sea serpent, who is referred to
in the Old Testament as a harlot.

Raiden Japanese thunder god who is
usually depicted as a red demon with
two claws on each foot and carrying a
drum. There are other thunder beings
associated with or derived from Raiden,
such as his son Raitaro; Raicho, the
thunder bird; Kaminari, the thunder
woman; and Raiju, the thunder animal;
and also Fujin†.

Raini In the Creation Legend of the
Mundruku tribe of the Tupi-Guarani†
Indians a god of this name formed the
world by placing it in the shape of a flat
stone on the head of another god.

Raj The paradise of the western Slavs
in contradiction to Svarog†, used by the
eastern Slavs. It was the eastern home
of the sun beyond the ocean where children play among the trees and gather
golden fruit. The story recalls that of
the Hesperides. Raj is akin to Bouyan†.

Rakshasas In Vedic myth representatives of the powers of evil similar to the
Asuras†. In the Ramayana† they are
stated to be led by Ravana†, the King of
Ceylon. Rakshasas are identical with the
Yakshas†. The name Rakshasa was used
for a form of marriage 'with a girl carried off as a prize in war'.

Rama-Chandra The seventh avatar of
Vishnu†, when he became the hero of
the Ramayana and destroyed the demon
Ravana†. This appears to be yet another
attempt to bring the Kshatriyas, the followers of Indra†, into the orbit of
Vishnu.

The name Chandra being that of the
moon may mean that Rama-Chandra was
related to a moon-worshipping family.

Ramayana The epic poem of the war
between the Aryam invaders of India

and the rulers of Ceylon, told in a fashion resembling that of the *Iliad*. It appears to have been composed in its earliest form about 1000 B C by Valmik†, about whom little is known. The scenes are set at a considerably later date to those of the Māhabhārata†. The 96,000 lines of this work are divided into seven books telling the story of Rama†, of his wife Sita† and of their various misadventures culminating in the kidnapping of Sita by Ravana†, the King of Ceylon, and of her rescue by Rama with the aid of Hanuman†, the general of the Monkey-King. The religious character of the work appears to be an afterthought.

Rambha In Vedic myth the greatest of the Apsarases†, who was produced at the Churning of the Ocean in the Kurma† avatar.

Ramman Babylonian deity equated with Adad† as god of storm. Was associated with the Deluge when 'the whirlwind of Ramman mounted up in the heavens and light was turned into darkness'. Was also the Rimmon† of the Old Testament. Hammurabi, King of Assyria, invoked him as follows: 'May he overwhelm the Land like a Flood: may he turn it into heaps and ruins, and may he blast it with a bolt of destruction.'

Ran Wife of Aegir†, the Scandinavian sea king. She had a palace to which she was later said to take drowned sailors. Here she had nine daughters, which would indicate possibly the presence of a college of priestesses.

Rangi The sky god of the Polynesians.

Rapithwin Lord of the Noonday Heat in Persian mythology.

Rashnu In Zoroastrian myth co-judge with Mithra† and Sraosha† of the soul after death. One of the Yazatas†.

Rat Female counterpart of Ra†, also called Eus-os†, Iusas† and Uert-Hekeu†.

Ratatösk In Nordic myth the squirrel that runs up and down Yggdrasil† to breed discord between the eagle at the top and the demon Nidhogg at the bottom.

Rata Grandson of Tahaki†, sailor and adventurer, who determined to rescue his mother, Tahiti Tokerau†.

Ra-Tem In Egyptian myth a variant of Atmu†.

Rati In Vedic myth the wife of Kama†, the god of love. She was known as 'the Fair-limbed', and was the daughter of Daksha†.

Rat-Tanit Mother of Harpokrates† by an Egyptian Horus† god. She was also known as Tanit(h)†.

Ravana An important character in the Ramayana. He was King of Ceylon and leader of the Rakshasas† who kidnapped Sita†, the wife of Rama†, thus precipitating the war between Ceylon and India, during which he was defeated and killed. His kingship had originally been shared with his half-brother Kubera†, whom he drove from the throne, seizing Pushpaka, his brother's aerial chariot. His capital city was Lanka, built by Visvakarma†.

Ravi In Vedic myth one of the twelve Adityas†, or guardians of the months of the year.

Raviyoyla In Serbian myth a Veela†
who accidentally wounded the blood
brother of Prince Marco† and was
nearly slain in consequence; however,
she knew the healing properties of every
flower and berry and was able to heal
not only her victim but also herself.

Regin In the Volsung Cycle the tutor of
Sigurd† (Siegfried†), subsequently killed
by him. In the Thidrek Saga he is a
dragon who is killed by Siegfried†.

Ren In Egyptian† religion term applied
to the 'name' of an Egyptian without
which he could have no future life.
Gods, kings, and great nobles had
several degrees of names, of which the
most secret – which gave power over
them – were never divulged. *See* the
story of Isis† and Ra†.

Renenet Egyptian goddess of birth and
child-bearing; the Harvest in the Book
of the Dead, where she is associated
with Meskhenit†.
   Alternative rendering Ernutit†.

Renpet The Egyptian goddess of
springtide and youth, 'Mistress of Eternity'.

Reret A form of Taueret†, the Egyptian
hippopotamus goddess.

Resheph Variant of Reshput†, a Syrian
god of lightning worshipped in ancient
Egypt.

Reshpu Syrian god of lightning and
thunderbolt worshipped in Egypt, depicted as a warrior with shield and spear
in his left hand and a club in his right.
Above his forehead projects a gazelle,
presumably a symbol of his sovereignty

over the desert. He is described as 'Great
God, Lord of Eternity, Prince of Everlast-
ingness, Lord of Twofold Strength
among the Company of Gods', all titles
borrowed from other gods.

Rhiannon In Celtic myth the daughter
of Heyfeydd the Old, and wife of
Pwyll†, prince of Dyved. At the birth of
her son the child was stolen and she was
suspected of murdering it and had to do
penance for seven years for this. This
child, however, had fallen into the hands
of Teyrnon Twry Bliant†, who brought
it up. Discovering that the boy resembled his father, Teyrnon brought him
back and the child was named Pryderi†,
the Welsh word for anxiety. Later, after
the death of her husband, she married
Manawydan†.

Ribhus In Vedic myth the three great
artificer brothers, who were trained by
Tvashtri†. The excellence of their handi-
work is said to have obtained for them
the gift of immortality.

Rig In the Edda†, Rigsthula, or 'Dis-
course of Rig', tells of the repopulation
of the world by Heimdall† after some
disaster, and how he fathers the three
classes of men: the thralls or serfs; the
karls (churls) or freemen; and the jarls
or earls. This story is also referred to in
Nordic† Creation Legends.

Rimmon The Old Testament variant
for Rammant† the Babylonian god of
storm.

Rind Nordic goddess whom Odin†
forced to bear a son, Vali†.

Ring Cycle Richard Wagner turned the
Nibelungenlied† into a series of four

operas under this name. They were: Rhinegold, Valkyrie, Siegfried†, Twilight of the Gods, covering the whole story from the looting of the Treasure by the Aesir† to the death of Siegfried, and the suicide of Brynhild†. It is largely thanks to the great popularity of these works that the tragic story of Siegfried and Brynhild has become well known.

Rishis *See* Prajapatis†.

Roc Enormous bird of the Arabian Nights, which was strong enough to carry Sindbad the Sailor. The words Roc or Rukh are related to the Persian names for the Bird of Immortality – Akra†, Samru†, and Sinurqh† – which would indicate a kinship with Anqa†, the giant Turkish bird; the Bennu†, the Egyptian phoenix; the Ngani-Vatu† of the Fijians; the Poua-Kai† of the Maoris; and Zu†, the Babylonian storm bird. There was also Ganu or Garuda† the vehicle of Vishnu.

Rongo His name means sound or noise, and the Mangaians represent him with a triton shell. He is known as Lono† in the Hawaiian Islands, where he is a god of agriculture, and in the Marquesas he is Ono†.

Roua, or **Ra** In the Society Islands myth the father of the stars by Taonoui†. His son was Fati†, known otherwise as Fadu†.

Rübezahl In Teutonic myth he was a giant who lived in Silesia.

Rudra In early Vedic myth the storm god, who was accompanied by his eleven sons, the Rudras. At a later stage he became partially merged with Siva†, and his eleven children became the Maruts†, the supporters of Indra†. Still later, in the Upanishads, they became the ten vital breaths – Pranas† – the five Jnanendriyas, the five Karmendriyas, together with Manas as the eleventh. Owing to his association with Siva, the name Hara† was occasionally applied to him. His wife was named Prisni†. The story of Siva's fight with Daksha† was originally told of Rudra and his wife Ambika†, or Uma†.

Rugievit A seven-faced Slavonic god of the island of Rügen in the Baltic. He is akin to Porevit†, Svantovit†, and Triglav†.

Rustum The Persian Hercules whose adventures are described in the Shah Nameh of Firdusi. The wars described in this work belong to the period when the Persians were battling against the Indians on the east, the Caucasians on the north, and the Semites on the west.

Rustum occupies a place akin to that of Arthur, in that he seems to have been an actual person around whose name have been gathered the mighty deeds of a host of others.

Rutbe Culture heroine of the Guaymi† Indians of Costa Rica. Mother by Nancomala† of the ancestors of the human race.

Ryugin In Japanese mythology the dragon king of the sea.

S

Saa In Egyptian myth the child of Ra†, sits in the sun boat of the Creator and also at the judgment of the dead, sometimes included in the Ennead†.

Sac and Fox Indian Creation Legend The myth of this North American Indian tribe tells how two powerful Manitous felt themselves to have been insulted by the tribal ancestor Wisaka†. They attacked him by raging and roaring over the earth, then one of them set the world on fire while the other followed this up with a great rain which put out the fire and flooded the earth. Wisaka sought refuge on a hill top, then as the waters rose he climbed to the top of the highest tree, from which he was eventually rescued by a canoe.

Sad-El Field of God, residence of El†, a Semitic term for the Elysian Fields, which can be equated to the Sekhet-Aaru† of Egyptian myth.

Saehrimnir The boar eaten by the heroes in Valahalla, which renewed itself each day.

Safekh-Aubi Alternative name for Sesheta† in Egyptian myth.

Saga In Nordic myth a giantess, second of the Asynjor†. The name may have originally meant a seeress. Her zodiacal house was Sokkvabekk, which may be linked with the falling or sinking waters caused by Thor's† draining of the seas at his banquet with Skrymir†.

Sagbata Smallpox god of the Benin fetish worshippers. He resembles Shankpanna† of the Yoruba† peoples.

Sahar (Shahar) Moon god of the north and south Semites.

Sahsnot (Saxnot) An old Saxon name for the Teutonic god Tiwaz†; the word means sword-bearer and may be related to Jarnsaxa, the giant wife of Thor†. An alternative spelling is Seaxneat†.

Sahte In the Creation myth of the Tuleyone† Indians an evil spirit of this name set the world on fire. Humanity was saved by Coyote†, who caused a great flood to extinguish the flames and who submerged all the world with waters with the exception of one mountain top on which the survivors gathered. In some versions the name of Coyote† is given as Olle†.

Sahu The spirit body which germinated from the Khat† and is assumed by the dead on attaining the Elysian Fields. Further details will be found under Egyptian† Religion and the Book of the Dead†.

Sa'ir Fourth state of the Islamic hell, Daru el-Bawa†, a flaming fire for the Sabians.

Sakhmis *See* Sekhmet†.

Sakuntala Daughter of Viswamitra† by the nymph Menaka†. The story of King Dushyanta's love for her and their marriage, separation and subsequent reunion is the subject of a famous play.

Sakyamuni Name given by the Chinese to Buddha†.

Salem Venus, the Evening Star, in the Ugarit texts. Name appears to be preserved in 'Jerusalem'. He was the son of El†.

Salinan Indian Creation Legend This California tribe have a myth that after the Deluge, when all mankind had been drowned, a diving bird fetched mud from the bottom of the waters and the eagle god fashioned this into men who were the ancestors of the tribe.

Samas (Shamash) Sun god of the Babylonians.

Sambara In Vedic myth one of the Asuras†, who was defeated in battle by Indra†.

Samhain The Celtic festival of the autumn equinox held at the beginning of November, which was the start of the Celtic year. In Cornwall it was known as Allantide† or apple time, a name related to Avalon†. In Ireland it was also known as Geimredh. The other three festivals were Lugnasad†, Beltaine†, and Oimelc†.

Samkhat Babylonian goddess of joy. When Ishtar† descended into Hades to rescue Tammuz† she was advised to allow Samkhat to enter his liver as a sign of his liberation.

Sammuramat Alternative spelling for Semiramis†, queen of ancient Babylon.

Samru In Persian myth alternative name for Sinurqh†, the bird of immortality.

Sams (Shams) Sun goddess of southern Arabia, but a god in the north.

Sangarios River god of Phrygia. His daughter was impregnated by the fruit of the almond tree and gave birth to Attis†.

Sanjna *See* Saranyu†.

Sankha In Vedic myth the chank-shell horn of victory, produced at the Churning of the Ocean† in the Kurma† avatar.

S(a)oshyant In the Zoroastrian Creation Legend the third and final Saviour.

Sapas (Shapash) A name for the sun in the Ugarit texts.

Saqar Fifth stage of the Islamic hell, Daru el-Bawar†, a scorching fire for the Magi†.

Saracura In the Creation Legends of the Karaya† Indians and the Ges† Indians she was the water hen who saved the ancestors of the tribes from the deluge brought about by Anatiwa†, by bringing earth to the hill-top on which they had sought refuge as fast as the fish sent by Anatiwa nibbled it away. The name given to the hill-top was Tupimare†.

Saranyu In Vedic myth the wife of Surya† or Vivasvat†. She was the daughter of Tvashtri† and the mother of Yama† and Yami and later of the

Asvins†. She is said to have left her husband, the sun, as she could not stand the brightness of his rays. To enable her to return, the sun gave up some of his rays, and from them was fashioned the disk of Vishnu†, the trident of Siva†, and the weapons of Kartikeya† and Kubera†. In the Puranic version she is called Sanjna†.

Sarasvati (Saraswati) In Vedic myth the consort of Brahma†. She was originally a river goddess of a stream in the Brahmvartta region. In some manner her personality has become merged with that of Vach†, goddess of speech.

Sarpanitu Wife of the Babylonian chief god Marduk†.

Saruto-Hiko In Japanese myth the commander-in-chief of the armed forces of Ninigi†, the grandson of Amaterasu†, the sun goddess.

Sasabonsum The husband of Srahman†, the forest dryad. He was a demon of the African forest who devoured travellers.

Satarupa In Vedic myth the female half of Brahma†, as opposed to Purusha†, the male half.

Satet Variant for Sati† in Egyptian myth.

Sati *1.* In Egyptian myth the first wife of Khnemu (Khnum†) and goddess of the Cataracts. Sister goddess to Anquet (Anuket†), Khnum's second wife. Her name means 'She who runs like an arrow'.
 2. In Vedic myth the daughter of Daksha†, also known as Uma†, who,

indignant at the treatment meted out to her father by Siva†, her husband, cast herself onto the sacrificial fire and was burnt to death. This story seems to link with some early account of Rudra† rather than with the adventures of Siva and his wife.

Satyavrata In Vedic myth King of Dravidia, who aided Vishnu† in his fight against Haya-Griva†.

Savitri In Vedic myth one of the twelve Adityas†, or guardians of the months of the year. He appears to be the same as Surya†, the sun, and may be one of the numerous sun gods absorbed at one time or another into the Vedic Pantheon. Also an alternative for Satarupa†.

Sawoye In the mythology of the Chaga of Kenya, a man with an ugly skin disease which disappears when he marries Marwe†, the heroine, and they live happily ever after.

Scáthach In Celtic mythology one of the goddesses who taught the art of war to young heroes. Her name means 'The Shadowy One'.

Schala Wife of Adad†, the Assyrian and Babylonian storm god.

Scorpion Man Babylonian mythological being; guardian of Mount Mashu; one of the allies of Tiamat† in her war against Ea† and Marduk†. He also appears in the Gilgamesh† Epic.

Seaxneat The Sword-bearer, or Companion of the Sword, title given by the Saxons to Tiwaz†, the Teutonic god, sword-dances in whose honour Tacitus reported. An alternative spelling was Sahsnot†.

Seb One of the names for Geb†, the Egyptian earth god.

Sebek In Egyptian myth a crocodile god of the Fayoum; an ancient crocodile totem who appears to have preceded both Ra† – with whom he became Sebekra – and Set†, with whom he was frequently identified. He was also known by the Greek name of Souchos†.

Sedna The Eskimo goddess of food, who lives in the sea. When her taboos are not observed she calls up a storm, or prevents seals, whales, and polar bears from leaving their homes. She derives her power over these water-beasts from their being sections of her fingers which were cut off by her father. Alternative name is Arnaknagsak†.

Segomo A war god of the continental Celts.

Seker 'The Closer of the Day', in Egyptian myth a hawk-headed god of the underworld, associated with Osiris† and Ptah† as a triune god at Memphis. His realm was dark and filled with evil spirits and horrible reptiles, only lighted up when Ra passed through every night on his journey. He is sometimes shown as a mummified hawk borne in the sacred barque of Ra†. The Greek variant for Seker was Soucharis†.

Sekhem The vital force of the individual in Egyptian† religion, which could, under certain conditions, follow him to heaven.

Sekhet-Aaru In Egyptian myth the second region of Amenti†, the Place of Reeds, where dwell the souls who are nine cubits high, under the rule of Ra

Heru Khuti, centre of the kingdom of Osiris, enclosed by walls made of the fabric of heaven. Aaru was sometimes spelt Aalu, and as such has some resemblance to Aralu†, the Babylonian Hades. Can be equated with the Semitic Sad-El†.

Sekhet-Hetep A portion of Amenti†, by which name the Kingdom of the Dead of Osiris† was known in Egyptian myth. It was rich in material blessings, and was a place where the dead lived in companionship with the gods. Originally Sekhet-Hetep was situated in the Delta, but later, with the development of religious thought, was moved to the stars.

Sekhet Tchant Field of Zoan of Psalm lxxviii. Tanis (Tanta), a town in the Nile Delta, is thought by some authorities to be Tchant. Can be equated with Amenti† in Egyptian myth.

Sekhmet Early lioness-headed Egyptian fire goddess, consort of Ptah† and mother of Nefertum† and Imhotep†. She was the 'Lady of the West' and one of the Memphis Triad†. When Hathor† was ordered by Ra† to destroy mankind, Sekhmet assisted her. She became known as 'the Eye of Ra' and later was sometimes identified with Hathor.

Sela In the mythology of the Luyia of Kenya, the name of the first woman.

Selkit (Selket) Human-headed Egyptian scorpion goddess, cognate with Isis†. She was also known as Selquet†.

Selquet Variant of Selkit† in Egyptian myth.

Seminole Indians The Creation Legend of this tribe is given under Creek† Indian Creation Legend.

Semiramis Queen of Babylon and wife of Ninus, King of Assyria. Daughter of Atargatis†, the Syrian fish goddess, by Oannes†, the Babylonian god of wisdom, who, after birth, was fed by the doves of Ishtar† until she was found by Simmos, the loyal shepherd who brought her up and saw her married to Menon, one of the generals of Ninus. Later, on the death of Menon, she married Ninus, and, as his widow and regent for her son, conquered the eastern world. Also known as Sammuramat†.

Semketet Morning boat of the Egyptian sun god Ra†.

Sengen Japanese goddess of Mount Fuji Yama who was also known as Ko-No-Hana-Saku-a-Hime, 'the Princess who makes the flowers of the trees to blossom'. She may be connected with Fuchi†.

Sept Egyptian name for Sirius, the dog-star. A deity of the first order and intimately allied to Thoth†, since the heliacal rising of this star determined the beginning of the year, of which Thoth gave his name to the first month.

Sequana In Celtic myth the goddess of the River Seine whose source has revealed *ex voto* offerings.

Serapis Greek name for the sacred bull of the Serapeum at Sakkarah, near Memphis, where sixty-four mummified bulls were found in 1851. Osiris† was believed to be incarnate in the dead Apis Bull, although sometimes Ptah† took the place of Osiris. An alternative spelling is Asar-Hap (Usar-Hapi)†. The temple of Serapis at Alexandria was described by Rufinus as being one of the greatest wonders of antiquity, towering above the city on a foundation one hundred steps high.

Serim In pre-Islamic myth hairy beings, or jinn†, of the northern Semites, frequenters of the waste lands referred to in Lev. xvii. 7. There may be some link with Lilith†, the night devil of Isaiah xxxiv. 14.

Serket-hetu Another name for the goddess Selkit† or Selket.

Serpent Myths There are many serpent myths in the East, and without exception they belong to the earliest times, being older, possibly, than the mother goddesses. The Old Testament reference to the serpent as the devil appears to be a relic of the effort to stamp out this pre-diluvial religion. *See also* Azhi Dahaka†, Naga†, Shipwrecked Sailor†, Uadjit†, and Yamilka†.

Sesha In Vedic myth a thousand-headed serpent god who issued from the mouth of Bala-Rama† shortly before his death. He was chief of the Nagas†, the clan of the snake worshippers, and ruler of Patala. To him also is attributed the story of the holding back of the waters until overcome by Indra†, for which reason he has been equated with Vritra†. He was also referred to as Ananta†. Vasuki†, another Naga ruler, seems to have been a kinsman of Sesha.

Sesheta (Seshat) Egyptian goddess of literature, also known as Safekh-Aubi†.

Sessrumnir The zodiacal† house of Freyja†.

Sessymir In Nordic myth a name given to the 'Hall of Many Seats' where the Einherjar†, the dead in battle, congregated, half of them being apportioned to Odin† and the other half to Freyja†.

Set In the myth of Osiris†, Set is the child of Nut† and Gea† or Nut and Ra†, the brother and husband of Nephthys†, the brother of Isis† and Osiris, and the uncle of Horus†. He appears to have been a pre-dynastic ruler of a tribe having an animal similar to a pig as its totem, and worshipping a sky and sun god. Associated with him was the Divine King, who was ritually slain, possibly by fire. His position as a sun god is shown by the fact that in the stories of his legal dispute with Horus for the throne Ra always took his part, while on several occasions Isis also did so, even against Horus. That Set was the ruler of Upper Egypt is seen from the final judgment of Thoth†, who awarded Upper Egypt to Set and Lower Egypt to Horus.

The application of the principle of Dualism, however, caused his original position as a sky and sun god to be forgotten, and for him to degenerate into the chief of the powers of evil, as manifested in the serpent, Apep†. In spite of the defeat of this early religion by new ideas from the settled Nile Valley to the north, the cult of Set existed as late as the nineteenth dynasty, when its followers were known as Typhonians and were said to be identified by the redness of their hair.

While the main story of the conflict is given under Horus, Isis, and Osiris, some additional light is given by the division of the stars between Set and Horus, Set taking all the circumpolar stars, i.e. those which never set, and Horus those which rise and set like the sun. To watch over Set, the four sons of Horus, Amset†, Duamutef†, Hapy†, and Qebhsneuf†, were given places in the Great Wain or Chariot of the Gods, in the constellation of the Great Bear.

Set was also a chief god of the Hyksos, which explains why – after their departure – he was degraded to the position of lord of the powers of evil, and had his name erased from many monuments.

Setebos The evil spirit of this name of Shakespeare originated in Settaboth†, a god worshipped by the Patagonians and reported by Francis Drake.

Sethlans The artificer of the Etruscans akin to the Greek Hephaistos and Roman Vulcan.

Settaboth One of the gods of the Patagonian Indians who became immortalized by Shakespeare under the name of Setebos†.

Seven Sleepers, The A Christian variant of the Sleeping Prince motif, the participants being persecuted Christians who stayed for two hundred years in a cave at Ephesus.

Seyon One of the chief gods of the Tamils of India.

Shadows To the Celts, the Teutons, and the Slavs the shadow appears to have corresponded to the Ka† or Ba† of Egyptian religion. The English term 'shade' for a ghost arises from this. In the Tyrol a feast of the shadows was held every spring to celebrate the final defeat of winter. The peasants assume the masks of the shadows who seek to protect winter from the invasion of spring.

Shahar Alternative spelling for Sahar†.

Shaitan Islamic name for devil. Also applied to the third species of jinn. He, together with Iblis†, was created from a smokeless fire. The name is a Semitic word meaning adversary, and is sometimes applied to Azazel†. From this word comes the modern Satan.

Shamash The sun god of Babylon and Assyria.

Shango The thunder god and the fourth king of the Yoruba tribe. His amulet is called Ose-Shango.

Shang-Ti (Shang-Di) He was the Chinese supreme ancestor, whether human or totemistic is not clear. He may have originally been a vegetation god, perhaps the spirit of rice, and he appears to have had a chthonic character, for human sacrifices continued to be offered up to him long after he had risen to be lord of Tien†, or Heaven.

Shankpanna Yoruba† god of smallpox, the son of Aganju† and Yemaja†.

Shawnee Indian Creation Legend These North American Indians have a myth that after the Deluge only one old woman survived and that she kneaded shapes out of clay which were given life by the Great Spirit. This is how the Redskins came into being and why they revere the old grandmother as ancestress.

She Chinese god of the earth or the soil, also known as Thu†.

Shen Egyptian symbol of eternal life for mankind, carried at the annual festival of Osiris† at the rising of the Nile, and usually laid at the feet of the dead. It is similar to the Ankh†.

Shen-nung Early Chinese emperor (2700 BC) who taught agriculture to his people and was afterwards raised to the rank of god. He resembles Hou-Chi†. His wife became the goddess of silk culture.

Shen Yi Chinese sun god, the divine archer. He represents the male principle or *yang*, whilst his wife, Heng-o†, the moon goddess, represents the female principle *yin*.

Shesmu Headsman of Osiris†, who cut off the heads of the wicked in Egyptian myth. For further details *see* the Book of the Dead†.

Shichi Fukujin The seven Japanese divinities of luck: Benten†, Bishamon†, Daikoku†, Ebisu†, Fukurokuju†, Hotei†, and Jorojin†. This pantheon of one goddess and six gods, which originated in the seventeenth century, appears to have been a means of securing a niche for popular divinities, many of non-Buddhist origin, who could not be accommodated within the official framework of Buddhism.

Shi-King The third of the nine authoritative works on Confucianism†. The name means 'Book of Odes', and the 305 lyrics contained within it were selected by Confucius from a collection of 3,000 covering a period of at least a thousand years up to 775 BC. The odes give details as to the beliefs and rituals of the early Chinese. The preceding work is the Shu-King†; the following work is the Chun-Tsiu†.

Shilluk Creation Legend This Sudanese tribe has a story that in the beginning there was a great creator named Jo-Uk† who caused the Nile to give birth to a sacred white cow, who in turn gave birth to a son named Kola†. The grandson of Kola, Ukwa†, took as wives two river priestesses, and was the ancestor of the race. The present kings still take the title of Jo-Uk.

Shimegi The Hurrian sun god.

Shinto Creation Legend Details of such Creation Legends as are furnished by Shintoism are given under Koji-Ki†. Their paucity may possibly be due to the necessity of casting off the myths and legends brought from the mainland by the original Japanese emigrants in order to provide support for the doctrine of the direct descent of the Mikado from Izanagi† and Izanami. As the position of the Japanese militarists became affected by the western world, more and more absurdities were introduced into official Shintoism in order to bolster up the military clique. This process reached its apex in the Second World War and has since fallen off considerably. For further details *see* Aizen Myoo†. Amaterasu†, Amida†, Benten†, Bimbo-Gami†, Binzuku†, Bishamon†, Daikoku†, Dainichi†, Ebisu†, Emma-ō†, Fuchi†, Fudo†, Fujin†, Fukurokuju†, Futsunushi†, Hotei†, In†, Inari†, Jikoku†, Jimmu-Tenno†, Jizō†, Jorōjin†, Kagu-Tsuchi†, Kishi Bojin†, Komoku†, Kompira†, Ninigi†, Onamuji†, Oni†, Qwannon, Raiden†, Saruto-Hiko†, Sengen†, Shichi Fukujin†, Shi-Tenno†, Shoden†, Susano, Taishaku†, Takemikadzuchi†, Tamon†, Temmangu†, Tengus†, Tenjin†, Tsukiyomi, Uke-mochi†, Yabune†, Yatagarasu†, Yo†, Yōmi†, and Zocho†. The number of gods evolved under a polytheistic system such as Shintoism ran into hundreds, and it is impossible to consider more than a few of the more important.

Shipwrecked Sailor In this story of an Egyptian sailor cast on an island ruled by a serpent king there is a relic of a disaster myth. The serpent tells that he used to dwell on the island with his brethren until 'a star fell and these came into the fire which fell with it'. The mysterious island may perhaps be Calypso's Isle mentioned by Homer nearly three thousand years later. This papyrus, which is in the Leningrad Museum, has been translated many times. For further details *see* Yamilka†.

Shiqq In pre-Islamic myth a form of jinn†, resembling half a human being divided longitudinally. They were the parents of the Nasnas† by mating with human beings.

Shi-Tenno The four Japanese guardians of the cardinal points. They are Bishamon† or Tamon†, guardian of the north; Komoku, guardian of the west; Zocho†, guardian of the south; and Jikoku, guardian of the east.

Shoden Name by which Ganesa†, the Vedic god of wisdom, was known in Japan.

Shoney A British Celtic sea deity, to whom sacrifices were offered until late in the nineteenth century by fisherfolk in Ireland and in the Isle of Lewis.

Shoshonean Indian Creation Legend This tribe of North American Indians have a myth that at the time of some great disaster they sought refuge in a great cave called the Sipaput, from which they safely emerged to people the world. They have a vague belief in a sky father and an earth mother which has almost faded into obscurity. This is also the myth of the Comanche Indians†.

Shou-lao Chinese god of long life.

Shu-King The second of the nine authoritative works on Confucianism†. The title means 'The Book of History', and the work consists of a collection of documents covering the history of China from about 2350 BC to 624 BC shortly before the birth of Confucius himself, to whom is attributed the selection and arrangement of the documents. The tone of the book concerns the moral duty of the rulers. The preceding work is the Yih-King†; the following work is the Shi-King†.

Shu In Egyptian myth human-headed god of the air, one of the four children of Ra†. Part of the Heliopolis stage of Egyptian religious thought represented him as having thrust himself between Seb†, the earth, on which he planted his feet, and Nut†, the sky, which he raised on high to become the heavens, or possibly the Milky Way: an Egyptian variant of the Atlas motif. At Sebennytus he formed a dual god with Anhur†. He was a member of the Ennead†.

Sia Indian Creation Legend In the myth of this New Mexico tribe everything began with the spider weaving a web on which Sus'sistinnako†, the creator, played an accompaniment to his songs. As he sang men appeared and then light, and afterwards the Utset† sisters, the first women, one of whom was the mother of the Indians and the other of the other races. From them arose various ancestors of the clan totems, Eagle, Coyote, Bear, etc.

Sida (Sido) Culture hero and fertility god of the Torres Islanders. He originated in New Guinea, and instructed the islanders in language, stocked the reefs with coral shell, and introduced plants useful to man. Connected with his worship there is a cult dance, part of the movements of which serve to explain life after death.

Sidhe In Celtic myth the hill people of ancient Ireland, the word being related to the Celtic name for a hill or mound. The assumption that they were the spirits of the dead appears to have crept into legend at a comparatively recent date. When the Tuatha Dé Danann† were defeated by the Milesians† some of them stayed behind and to each of them Dagda†, who remained behind as their ruler, assigned a barrow or hill on which they appear to have buried their dead, a fact which may be the origin of the assumption that they were ghosts.

Siegfried The hero of the various versions of the story of the treasure of the Nibelungs. In the Nibelungenlied, after having awakened Brynhild†, he weds Krimhild† and aids Gunther† (Gunnar†) to marry Brynhild. For so doing he is murdered by Hagen†.

In the Volsung Cycle, Siegfried is known as Sigurd†, and after having awakened Brynhild, the Valkyrie†, is persuaded to marry Gudrun† thanks to a magic draught administered by Krimhild.

In the Thidrek Saga he is betrothed to Brynhild but for reasons of policy marries Grimhild (Krimhild). In this case also he is murdered when the deception is discovered.

Sien-Tsan Wife of Shen-Nung†, an early Chinese emperor who taught his people agriculture. It is possible that her personality may have become merged with that of some earlier mother goddess. She was the goddess of silk culture.

Sif ('Kindred') In Nordic myth a giantess, the wife of Thor† and one of the Asynjor†. Grimm suggests she is the same as the Anglo-Saxon Sib and the Teutonic Sippia. For her the dwarfs made a wig of golden hair after her own had been burnt off by Loki†.

Sigmund, Sigemund, Siegmund The father of Siegfried† by his sister Sieglinde in the various stories dealing with the treasure of the Nibelungs. In Beowulf† he appears as a dragon slayer.

Sigu In the Arawak† Creation Legends the son of Makonaima† who ruled over the beasts of the earth. When the Deluge came he placed those animals which could not climb in a cave, the entrance of which he sealed. He himself climbed into the branches of a high tree where he remained until the flood was over.

Siguna (**Sigyn**) In Nordic myth the wife of Loki† She was one of the Asynjor† and she may be the Sin of the Prose Edda, the guardian of truth, resembling the Egyptian Maat†. Her name is sometimes rendered Signy.

Sigurd Scandinavian form of Siegfried†.

Sila or **Silap Inna** Supreme being in Eskimo mythology.

Silappadikaram In Tamil myth the name by which Bala-Rama†, the fair-haired brother of Krisna†, was known. He was the husband of Korraval†, the goddess of victory.

Silat In pre-Islamic myth the jinn† of lightning. A she-demon of this name was ancestress of the tribe of Amr-b-Yarbu. The silat lived in forests, and made men dance, which indicates her electrical origin. An island in the China Sea is reported to be inhabited by them, or possibly by Shaitans†, the offspring of human beings and jinn, who eat men.

Siltim In Zoroastrian† myth a malignant demon of the forests.

Silvanus Guardian of forests and god of fields, in Celtic mythology assimilated to a north-British deity Cocidius†.

Sin Babylonian moon god. The fact that the Babylonian calendar was lunar explained his dominant position. He was also a Pre-Islamic chief god of the Hadramut in southern Arabia.

Sina Polynesian moon goddess and sister of the sun god Maui†. In some places she was known as Hina†. In Mangaia she was known as Ina†.

Sindbad the Sailor The seven voyages of Sindbad, as told in the Arabian Nights, have much in common with those of such travellers as Brandan†, Corra†, and Maeldune†, and it would seem that in certain respects they were drawing upon common sources. It is obvious that they all relate to times before the compass was known, which would be quite a while before the present era in the Indian and Chinese seas, and well before 1200 in Europe.

Sinfjotli A Nordic culture hero who is mentioned as a comrade of Sigmund† in the Eriksmal, and who also occurs in Beowulf†. In the Volsung Cycle† he is the son of Sigurd†.

Sinurqh (Simurqh) In Persian myth the bird of immortality. Alternative names are Akra and Samru†.

Sioux Indian Creation Legends The myths of this North American Indian tribe tell how at some period their ancestors lived in a cave with a subterranean lake and that eventually after the period of disaster was over the ancestors of the tribe made their way to the surface and there set up their homes. One of the earliest culture heroes was Ikto†, who is credited with the invention of human speech. Later myths tell of the adventures of Haokah† and Ictinike†. The Mandan† and Minnetaree† Indian Creation Legends are included in the Sioux.

Sipapu A vast cavern in which the ancestors of the Shoshonean Indians took refuge at the time of some great disaster and from which they subsequently emerged to people the world.

Sirat The bridge, sharper than the sword, spanning Daru el-Bawar†, the Islamic hell. The idea was borrowed from the Jews and the Persians; the latter called it Chinvat Peretu†, meaning 'the Bridge of the Gatherer'.

Siriadic Columns According to Manetho, the Egyptian historian, Thoth†, the first Hermes, set up in the

Siriadic land two columns, before the Deluge, on which were inscribed the history of things past. Josephus says that one was of brick and one of stone to permit survival in case of fire or flood. He also says they were put up by Seth (? Set†). Further information can be found under Egyptian† Creation Legends.

Sirona A goddess of the continental Celts, either a stellar deity, or a goddess of springs and wells. She was also known as Dirona†.

Sirrush A mysterious animal depicted on the walls of the famous Ishtar Gate at Babylon, which is thought by some modern investigators to have been a dinosaur. It has scales, a long neck, and four legs, of which the rear two are clawed. Should this assumption be correct, it presupposes both the survival of this animal until recent times, and also a detailed historical memory on the part of the Babylonians of the time of Nebuchadnezzar.

Sit Alternative spelling for Set† in Egyptian myth.

Sita In Vedic myth, as told in the Ramayana†, Sita was the wife of Rama†. She was kidnapped by Ravana†, King of Ceylon, a deed which precipitated a war between Ceylon and India.

Siton A name given to Dagon†, the Phoenician god.

Siva (Shiva) The male generative force of Vedic religion. A god of reproduction, whose symbol is the Linga or Phallus, in the same manner that the Yoni was the symbol of his wife Paravati†. In the course of time Siva has assumed the personalities of other gods, benign and terrible, although this later aspect was mainly linked with Durgha† and Kali†, both manifestations of Parvati. Generally he is figured as a white or silver-coloured man, sometimes with as many as five heads, each of which has a third eye in the forehead. As a deity he was frequently in competition with Vishnu†. His dwelling was at Kailasa, and he was usually mounted on Nandi†, the sacred bull. His two sons were Ganesa† and Kartikeya†. Other names by which Siva is known include Bhadra Vira, Hara†, Maha-Deva†, Maha-Kala†, Pancha-mukhi-Maruti, Somanatha†, and Visweswara†. He was the creator of the monster Vira-bhadra†, which cut off the head of Daksha†.

Si Wang Mu *See* Hsi Wang Mu†.

Sjofna Nordic goddess of love, seventh of the Asynjor†.

Skadi In Nordic myth a giantess who was the daughter of Thiassi† and loved the snow-covered mountains, over which she raced on snowshoes. She was one of the Asynjor†; the wife of Njord†.

Skaldskaparmal, Skaldatal A treatise on skaldic poetry and life of skalds included in the Prose Edda†. It has no mythological value.

Skambha In Vedic myth a term applied to Purusha†, as the male half of Brahma†. Skambha has been described as a vast embodied being co-extensive with the universe.

Skan The sky god and creator of the world in the mythology of the Sioux Indians.

Skanda In Vedic myth an alternative name for Kartikeya†.

Skidbladnir In Nordic myth the ship of Freyr† which was built for him by the sons of Ivaldi, the dwarfs†, and which was said to be capable of being folded up. It was smaller than Naglfar†, the ship of the giants, and Hringhorn†, the ship of Balder†.

Skiold A son of Odin with whom Gefjon† lived after she had ploughed the island of Zealand from Sweden.

Skirnir Freyr's† emissary in his wooing of the giantess Gerd†.

Skrymir A king of the giants in Nordic myth. In the Prose Edda it is told how Thor†, accompanied by Loki† and Thialfi†, after various misadventures arrived at Utgard to visit King Skrymir, who had the title of Utgard-Loki, which may be taken to mean the Magus of Utgard. Thor and his companions undergo a whole series of mystifications culminating in a series of matches at the giants' castle, when Loki is defeated at eating, Thialfi at running, and Thor himself had failed to empty a drinking horn in three draughts, to lift more than one leg of a cat from the floor, and to win a wrestling match with an old woman. The following day on their departure Skrymir explains that Loki was defeated by Logi – meaning fire; Thialfi by thought; that the drinking horn was connected with the sea, and that Thor's prodigious draughts had lowered the sea levels around the northern coasts – a matter which is referred to in Nordic Creation Legends; that the cat was the Midgard Serpent†, the lifting of whose leg had caused vast earthquakes all over the world; while the old woman was Ellit, or old age, with whom no one could struggle. When Thor in a fury at having been deceived turned round to strike the giant, everything disappeared.

Skuld In Nordic myth she was one of the Nornst whose function it was to hold the future in her hands. However, she sometimes left her sisters Urdt and Verdandit to ride with the Valkyriest.

Slavonic Creation Legends It has been said that 'of all the Aryans, the Slavs were the race that remained nearest their original home, and were thus the last to enter history', nevertheless, the fact remains that with the exception of a few Slavonic gods, traces of which have been found outside Russia, there is but little to recall the glorious mythic past of the Slav peoples. They had an island paradise, Bouyant, on which was Alatuirt, the magic stone, and Zaryat, the beautiful priestess. The Slavs had Vilast, or sibyls; vampirest and werewolvest; a series of multi-headed gods: Pornutiust, Rugievitt, and Svantovitt. A remnant of the dualistic system persisted in Bielbogt and Czarnobogt, the white and black gods. The four great pre-Christian gods were Da-Bogt, Khorst, Perount, and Stribogt, whose statues stood in the castle at Kiev. There was a fertility goddess, Perchtat, whose feast was celebrated as late as 1941, as was the Feast of Shadowst. The Slav heaven, Svarogt, resembled the Vedic Swargat. The southern Slavs, having withstood the onslaught of Islam, had their Byess, Djint, Dyavot, and Syent, all due to Arab influence. Their name for God was Bogt, which came from the Sanskrit Bhagat. The fact remains that the impact of Christianity on an almost com-

pletely illiterate population, resulted in the destruction of the majority of the old myths and their substitution by emasculated versions for the converted. Further details are given under Buelunt, Czarnobogt, Da-Bogt, Dajdbogt, Dazh-Bogt, Kamennaia Babat, Karlikit, Ljeschit, Lychiet, Marcot, Muma Padurat, Oynyena Mariat, Porenutiust, Porevitt, Raviyoylat, Stoymirt, Svantovitt, Swietowitt, Triglavt, Trojanut, Velest, Vlkodlakst, Volost, Volusut, Vookodlakst, and Wenceslast.

Sleeping Princes The story of a prince and his retinue who sleep in a cavern awaiting the clarion call to serve their country is a common feature of European myth. The prevalance of these stories is doubtless linked with the early custom whereby on the death of a ruler the principal members of his court were killed and buried with him in order that he should have his retinue in the other world.

Instances of this are given under Alfatint, Barbarossat, Ercildounet, Marcot, Mullaghmartt, The Seven Sleeperst, Stoymirt, and Wenceslast.

Sleipnir In Nordic myth the horse of Odint, chief of the Aesirt. This magnificent animal, which had formerly been the foal of Lokit, was lent to Hermodt after the death of Baldert so that he should ride to Helt to intercede for his return.

So God of lightning of the Ewe peoples, also known as Khebieso.

Society Islands In the Society Islands myth, Rouat was the Father of the Stars, Taonouit was the Mother of the Stars.

Their son was Fati†, known otherwise as Fadu. This myth differs from other Polynesian† stories.

Sokkvabekk The zodiacal† house of Saga†.

Solarljod 'The Song of the Sun', a Christian explanation ascribed to Saemund and included in the Poetic Edda†.

Sol A personification of the sun in Nordic mythology. She was the sister of Mani†.

Soma In Hindu myth an intoxicating liquor consumed by the Vedic priests in order to induce a state of ecstasy. Agni†, the divine fire, was the spirit of Soma†, and the effect of pouring libations on the altar fires was to enable the god to combat the forces of darkness and to maintain the order of light. In some versions Soma is an actual being, but this is a later variation similar to that by which Kvasir† came into being in order to explain the origin of the Nordic Kvas. Eventually Soma became identified with the water of life, and as such linked with the moon. It is identical with the Haoma† of the Zoroastrian faith. Amrita of the Churning of the Ocean may be an earlier name for Soma.

Somanatha In Vedic myth a title meaning 'Lord of the Moon', under which Siva† was worshipped in Gujarat.

Sontso In Navajo† myth a name given to Big Star.

Soucharis Greek name for Seker†, the god of Memphis, in Egyptian myth.

Souchos Greek name for Sebek†, the Egyptian crocodile god.

Spenta Mainyu One of the Seven Ameshast† or aspects of god, seen as spirits, in Zoroastrianism.

Srahman A silk cotton tree dryad of Africa, who taught travellers the secrets of the forests and the art of using herbs. She was the wife of Sasabonsum†, who is associated with the Xhosa†.

Sraosha In Zoroastrian myth the Angel of Obedience and Sacrifice. He is the angel who takes the souls of the dead to paradise, and was the valiant supporter of Ahura Mazda† in his fights with the demons.

Sri In Vedic myth the name by which Lakshmi†, the wife of Vishnu†, is sometimes known. She rose from the waves like Venus, at the Churning of the Ocean in the Kurma† avatar.

Starkad In Nordic mythology one of Odin's† heroes who once witnessed an assembly of the gods, held in a forest, before the killing of King Vikar.

Stones Sacred and magic stones are listed under Treasures†.

Stoymir In Slavonic myth he is a knight who sleeps with his companions in a cavern in Mount Blanik in Bohemia. He is sometimes confused with King Wenceslas†. For details of similar stories *see* Sleeping Princes†.

Stribog A Slavonic god whose statue stood at Kiev with those of Dazh-Bog†, Khors†, and Peroun†.

Sua Culture hero of the Muyscayas† akin to Bochica† and Nemquetcha†.

Sucellos A Gallic god of the Celts, who may have been a fertility god, but who also seems to have been a god of the dead.

Suffete of the River Phoenician river beast which aided Khoser† in his fight against Baal†.

Suku-na-biko A dwarf god in Japan renowned for his courage. He is also connected with hot springs and healing.

Sul(la) A very early goddess of hot springs, worshipped at Bath (Aquae Sulis).

Sumars Blot The spring sacrifices on summer's day (14th April and days following) in honour of the Aesir†, especially Freyr†, soliciting of them 'a good season, and peace'.

Summanus In Etruscan myth one of the great gods who hurled thunderbolts by night and, as such, received more honour from the Romans than Jupiter himself.

Sun Houtzu In Chinese Buddhist myth the monkey fairy or god who is taken to represent human nature. He is the hero of many stories, mainly told in the Hsi-Yu-Chi.

Supay In Inca† myth the ruler of the subterranean world. His empire was similar to the Mictlan† of the Aztecs†.

Sura In Vedic myth the goddess of wine, produced at the Churning of the Ocean in the Kurma† avatar.

Surabhi In Vedic myth the Cow of Plenty, produced at the Churning of the Ocean in the Kurma† avatar. Her calves were Nandi†, the Snow-White Bull of Siva†, and Nandini†.

Surid A pre-diluvial ruler of Egypt, who is stated by Masoudi (AD 1000) to have built the two great pyramids, and to have caused the priests to deposit in them written accounts of their wisdom and science, and records of the stars, their cycles and chronicles, both of the past and for the future. This Arabic version of an early catastrophe myth is to be found in the Akbar Ezjeman collection at Oxford. This story recalls the Siriadic Columns†.

Surt In the Nordic story of Ragnarok Surt is the leader of the Muspel† who rode over the Bridge of Bifrost to capture Asgard, defeat the Aesir†, and consume Valhalla with fire. He may be considered as one of the giants.

Surya In Vedic myth the sun god, one of the twelve Adityas†, or guardians of the months of the year. As a god he ranked with Agni† and Indra†. Mythologically he was the son of Aditya† or of Dyaush-Pitir or of Ushas†. His wife was Saranyu†, or Ushas. His chariot was drawn by seven mares.

Susano Japanese sea and storm god. His name may be translated as 'Impetuous' or may possibly derive from the town of Susa where he had a shrine. He was the son of Izanagi† and Izanami and the brother of Amaterasu†, the sun goddess, by whom he begat eight children. He was also a moon god and there is a myth of his having driven his sister, the sun, into 'the cave of the heavens', leaving the world for some considerable period in darkness. This story, which is of much earlier origin than either Susano or Amaterasu, is probably a memory of some early cosmic disaster of great magnitude. He has also been identified with Kompira.

Sus'sistinnako The creator in the Sia† Indian Creation Legend. He created mankind by singing and accompanying himself by using a spider's web as a harp.

Sut(ekh) *1.* A Hyksos god worshipped in Egypt in the fifteenth and sixteenth dynasties, and identified with Set†.
2. Son of Iblis†, a jinn, who suggests lies.

The identification of this early, Semitic god with the powers of darkness may have occurred in the first place after the expulsion of the Hyksos, and in the second with the adherence to Islam.

Suttung In Nordic myth a giant, the son of the Gilling†, who, together with his wife, was murdered by the dwarfs Fjalar and Galar when they were drunk on the blood of Kvasir†. In revenge Suttung took the dwarfs out to sea to drown them, but eventually spared their lives in exchange for the secret of the fermented beverage which his daughter Gunnlauth† prepared in Odherir. Later Odin† secured the secret of the drink, which was known as Suttung's Mead, by the seduction of Gunnlauth, and although pursued to the very gates of Asgard, he escaped with the secret. The story is told in the Conversations of Bragi.

Suwa An early Arabian sun goddess. An idol of this name is mentioned in the Koran (Sura lxxi. 22).

Svadilfari A stallion who helped one of the giants to build the wall around Asgard, the home of the gods, but who was lured away by Loki† in the form of a mare. The resulting colt was Sleipnir†, Odin's† eight-legged steed.

Svald A dwarf in Nordic mythology who was the father of Idun(a)†.

Svantovit A Slavonic god of the island of Rügen in the Baltic. Saxo Grammaticus states that he had four heads on four necks with a bow in the left hand and a drinking horn in the right. Close by, in the sanctuary, were a bridle and saddle destined for the white horse of the god which the priest alone had the right to mount. No one but the priest could enter the sanctuary and, as with the Parsees, he had to hold his breath while sweeping it out. At the annual festival the quantity and condition of the wine which had been poured into the drinking horn at the previous festival was taken as an augury for the next harvest. From this it is assumed that on this occasion the sanctuary was open to all. An alternative spelling is Swietowit†.

Svarog A Slavonic term for heaven usually employed in relation to Dabog†. The western Slavs used the word Raj†. Svarog appears to have come from the same source as the Swarga of the Vedic religions, and originally been a fire and sun god.

Svartheim In Nordic myth the home of the dark elves† or the dwarfs†.

Svava One of the Valkyries†, the protector of the hero Helgi†.

Swarga In Vedic myth the heaven of

Indra† with its stately city of Amaravati, built by Visvakarma†, the architect of the gods. It is situated on the eastern spur of Mount Meru†. Swarga may be related to the Slavonic paradise Svarog†.

Swastikas These gammadions, whether right-handed or left-handed, are magical sun tokens, dating back to the cave drawings of palaeolithic times.

Swietowit Alternative spelling for Svantovit†, the Slavonic god.

Syen In southern Slavonic myth guardian spirits of the home. They can enter the body of men, dogs, snakes, or even hens. They are cognate with the Djin†, Dyavo†, etc.

Syr The name of one of the Asynjor† in Nordic myth. It was also one of the names of Freyja†.

Syria Dea Name given by Lucian to Ashtart†, the Syrian goddess who is also known as Astarte†.

T

Ta'aroa Creator god of Polynesia, also found as Tangaloa† and Tangaroa†.

Tagtug Sumerian pre-diluvial culture hero who was raised to the rank of a god. He would appear to be linked with Uttu†, the sun god, and might, therefore, be equated with Ziudsuddu†. He may be equated with Marduk†, the Babylonian god of the spring sun.

Tahaki Hero, sometimes a demi-god, of Polynesia, grandfather of Rata†, and father of Tahiti Tokerau†.

Tahitian Creation Legend One couple survived the Deluge by climbing to the top of Pitohito, the highest mountain in Tahiti. After the flood subsided they had two children, a son and a daughter, from whom sprang all the inhabitants. This myth may be pre-Polynesian.

Tahiti Tokerau She was abducted by Puna, who stole her eyes to make lights and then buried her head downwards in the sand. He used her feet to hold up his wife's baskets. Eventually Rata† rescued his mother and killed Puna.

Ta-Hsuch The seventh of the nine authoritative works on Confucianism†. The name means 'Great Learning'. It is in fact chap. xxxix of the Li-Ki†, considered as an independent ethical treatise. It is accompanied by a commentary by Tsang Tsan, a disciple of the master.

This work follows the Lun-Yu† and precedes the Chung-Yung†.

Taishaku Name by which Indra†, the Vedic god, was known in Japan.

Takemikadzuchi Japanese thunder god. As his name is frequently written in Chinese characters he may be an importation from the mainland. Together with Futsunushi† he forced Onamuji† to resign in order that Ninigi† could come to the throne.

Taliesin In Celtic myth the son to whom Ceridwen gave birth after having swallowed Gwion. The entire process of transformation which preceded this seems to be an early initiation ritual for a chief bard. Although Taliesin is mentioned in the Mabinogion very little is known about him and it is quite possible that the name may have belonged to several chief bards or druids. He was said to have been involved in the Battle of the Trees and to have been one of the seven survivors from the great battle between Brân† and Matholwch†.

Talli Culture hero of the Lenape† Indians who after the Deluge led the tribe to the Snake Land, which they conquered.

Talvolte In the Maidu† Indian Creation Legend the head of a tortoise clan, and one of the survivors from the Deluge.

Tamanaque Indian Creation Legend
This Orinoco River tribe say that only
one man and one woman survived the
Flood and that from them sprang their
ancestors. They share this myth with
the Macusis†.

Tamesis In Celtic myth one of the 'lake,
river, and well goddesses', whose name
has become the Thames in English, and
the Tamise (a name for the Scheldt) in
French. She appears to have been displaced by Nodens† or Ludd†.

Tamil Myths The Tamils, one of the
Dravidian races, living in the south
of India, have lost the majority of
their myths to their Vedic conquerors.
Among their gods were Korraval†,
Mayon†, Murugan†, Seyon†, and
Silappadikaram†. They also worshipped
Varuna†.

Tammuz Very early Babylonian and Assyrian god; brother and lover of Belili†,
and later spouse of Ishtar†. He was a
spring-sowing god who was killed in the
autumn, presumably after the harvest.
Originally he was the ritual husband of
the harvest goddess, and gradually, with
the passing of the goddesses into the
background, he assumed greater importance. The autumn Tammuz festival,
which celebrated his death and resurrection, i.e. the nomination of the new
god, is referred to in Ezekiel viii. 14.
The fourth month of the year was
named after him, Du'uzu (June). The
story of the descent of Ishtar† to Hades,
to bring back Tammuz, is told under
that heading. In the Adapa† myth,
Tammuz intervened with Gishzida†.
Tammuz, who may to some extent be
equated with Hey Tau, and also Kingu†,
is a similar god to Osiris†. He was

sometimes given the title of Adonis†,
derived from Adon, which means Lord.
His Sumerian name was Dumuzi†.

Tamon One of the Japanese guardians
of the cardinal points. He was the guardian of the north. He was also known as
Bishamon†.

Tamtu In Babylonian myth the bitter
(sea) waters. A term similar to Tiamat†
or Tiawath†, the Hebrew Tohu†, and
Tchom†, the Nether Sea or Deluge. In
Egyptian myth there is a relationship to
Atmu† and Nu†. The deep watery abyss
Apsu† may also be another form of this.
Further details are given under
Babylonian† and Egyptian† Creation
Legends.

Tamu Culture hero of the Caribs who
was known as Kaboi† to the Karayas†,
Kamu† to the Arawaks†, and Zume† to
the Paraguayans†. He may also be the
Kame† of the Bakairi Caribs.

Tane Polynesian god of the forests and
light. In Hawaii he is known as Kane.

Tangaroa, or **Tangaloa** Former sky
and sun god of Mangaia. Elsewhere he
is Ta'aroa†.

Tanit(h) Alternative name for Rat-
Tanit, the mother of Harpokrates†, in
Egyptian myth.

Tano A river god in Togo and Ghana.

Taoism The religious philosophy of the
Chinese† thinker and mystic Lao-Tsze
appears to have been founded in the
sixth century before our era, some fifty
years prior to Confucianism†, and has
decided resemblances to the Ideas of

Plato. The fundamental work on the principles of Taoism attributed to the master himself is the Tao-Te-Ching, 'the Treatise of the Way and of Virtue'. The obscurity of this work suggests that it may be compiled from fragments saved at the time of the burning of the books. The other important work is contained in the writings of Kwang-Tsze, written some two hundred years after Lao-Tsze. Taoism is a system of moral teaching based on high ideals and at some later stage allied itself with the ancient cosmological doctrine of Dualism† known as the Yang† and the Yin†.

Taonoui In the Creation myth of the Society Islands she was the mother of the stars by Roua†. Her son was Fati†.

Tara, or **Taraka**. In Vedic mythology the wife of Brihaspati, carried off by Soma†, the moon, which led to a war between the gods and the Asuras†. Brahma† stopped the war and brought back Tara, but she gave birth to a child whom she said was the son of Soma, whom she called Budha.

Taran (**Taranis**) In Celtic myth a Gallic god of thunder.

Tarhun(t) An ancient Luwian and Hittite weather god, equated with Teshub†.

Tarnkappe In the Nibelungenlied† the cap of invisibility† which Siegfried† obtained from Andvari†, with the aid of which he assisted Gunnar† to win Brynhild†.

Tarquiup Inua In Eskimo mythology a moon spirit.

Taru Hattic weather god, equated with Tarhun(t)†.

Tarvos (**Trigaranus**) Early Celtic bull god about whom little is known.

Tashmetu In Babylonian myth the wife of Nabu†, god of wisdom; her name is interpreted as meaning 'Hearing' or 'Audience'.

Tashmishu In Anatolia brother and assistant of Teshub†, the weather god.

Tat Alternative spelling for Ded†, a symbol of Osiris† in Egyptian myth.

Tate The wind god of the Sioux Indians.

Tatenen One of the names of Ptah† in Egyptian mythology.

Tathlum In Celtic myth a magic stone, which was hurled by a catapult used by the Tuatha Dé Denann† at the Battle of Mag Tuireadh† for the killing of Balor†.

Tatumen Egyptian earth god, referred to in the Book of the Dead† as 'Creator of Man, Maker of the Gods of the South, and of the North, of the West and of the East'.

Taueret Egyptian goddess of fertility, domestic in interests, and presiding over childbirth, symbolized by a female hippopotamus and identified with Hathor†. She was also worshipped under the names of Opet† and Apet†.

Taus The Peacock Angel, a name given to Iblis† in pre-Islamic myth.

Taut In Egyptian myth a name given to the young Horus†.

Tauthe Appellation given by Damascius

in the Phoenician† Creation Legend to Tiamat† or Chaos†.

In the Babylonian† Creation Legend Damascius made Tauthe the mother of the gods, including Moymis† (or Mommu†), Lakhe† and Lakhus (or Lakhame† and Lakhmu), and Assorus† and Kissare† (or Anshar† and Kissar†).

Tawa The great sun spirit of the Pueblo Indians of North America.

Tawenduare Elder of two brothers, heroes of a Deluge story in the Tupi-Guarani Indian Creation Legend. The younger was named Arikute†. The brothers having quarrelled, Tawenduare stamped his foot so hard on the ground that water gushed forth in a flood and the two brothers and their families were only saved by taking refuge in high trees. In another version Tawenduare is the god of the day who daily conquers his brother Arikute, the god of the night, in their continually repeated combat. Another version of this story is given under Irin Mage† and Monan†.

Tawhaki One of the most famous Polynesian culture heroes. The cycle of his adventures deals with the early migrations of Polynesian tribes and forms part of the myth of nearly all the island groups. He was named after a god of lightning and was a descendant of Tawhiri†.

Tawhiri The Polynesian god of hurricanes and storms.

Tawiscara (**Taweskare**) In Huron Creation Legend twin brother of Tsentsa†, their mother, a virgin, having died in giving them birth. The virgin birth is a testimony as to their royal rank. After the Deluge he and his brother fought,

representing the opposition of good and evil.

Tawiskaron Another version of Tawiscara/Taweskare†, where the name Teharonhiawagon† is the equivalent of Tsentsa†.

Tcenes In the Kato† Indian Creation Legend he rescued the ancestor of the tribe, Nagaitco†, who as a child was clinging to the branch of a tree floating on the waters of the Deluge.

Tecciztecatl The Aztec moon god.

Tefnut Lioness-headed Egyptian rain goddess, twin and wife to Shu†, whom she assisted to raise the heavens, as personified by Nut†. One of the Heliopolis Company of Gods†, or Ennead†.

Tegld In Celtic myth he was the husband of Ceridwen†.

Teharonhiawagon *See* Tawiskaron†.

Tehom Name for the primeval Nether Sea or the Deluge. It is similar to Apsu†, Tiamat†, etc.

Tem Variant of Atmu† in Egyptian myth.

Temioua In the Creation Legend of the Uapes, a branch of the Tupi-Guarani† Indians, a girl of this name fled from her home to avoid an undesirable marriage and subsequently became the wife of a Yacami chief. She brought forth two eggs from which were hatched a boy, Pinon†, who became the constellation Orion, and his sister, who became the Pleiades.

Temmangu Japanese god of learning

and calligraphy. He was a Japanese equivalent of Confucius named Michizane born in AD 845, who was raised to divine rank after his death. He was also known as Tenjin†.

Tenen A very early creator god of Egypt, who at a later date became merged with Ptah† as Ptah Ten.

Tengus Malignant tree spirits of Japanese myth. They lived in the top branches of tall trees, but although they were hatched from eggs they still remained men.

Tenjin The Japanese god of learning and calligraphy.

Tepotatango In Polynesian myth the wife of Rangi†, one of the first rulers of Mangaia† after it had risen again from the depths of the sea where it had sunk with its ruler Rongo†. The other co-rulers of the new kingdom were Mokoiro† and Akatauire† with their respective wives Angarua† and Ruange†. The name Tepotatango means 'Bottom of Hades'.

Teoyaomiqui Aztec god of dead warriors, a military variant of Mictlantecuhtli†, the Aztec death god. He was also known as Huahuantli†, 'the Striped One'. He was the lord of the sixth hour of the day.

Tepeyollotl Aztec Puma god. The name means 'Heart of the Mountains'. He was the lord of the eighth hour of the night.

Terah Ancient Semitic name for the moon, equated with Terah, father of Abraham. It was also known as Eterah† and Jahir†.

Teshub Hittite god of upper Syria and Asia Minor, ruled over storms and rainfall, holding lightning in his hand. Similar to Adad† and Buriash†.

Teteoinnan Aztec mother of the gods, an alternative name for Tlazolteotl†.

Tethra Celtic sea god and lord of the other world.

Te Tumu *See* Kiho Tumu†.

Teutates A war god of the Gauls worshipped with human sacrifices. He was akin to Hesus†.

Teyrnon Twry Bliant In Celtic myth the ruler of that part of Wales lying between the Wye and the Usk, said to have been the best man in the world, who adopted the son of Rhiannon†, who had been kidnapped, giving the name of Gwri†, 'He of the Golden Hair'. He subsequently restored the child to its parents and it was named Pryderi†.

Tezcatlipoca 'Smoking Mirror', chief god of the Aztec pantheon and chief god of Texcoco. He has been identified with Itzli†, the stone knife god, and Itzacoliuhque† the curved obsidian knife god. He was the lord of the tenth hour of the day.

Thalna An Etruscan goddess of birth.

Thaukt (**Thokk**) In Nordic myth a giantess who after the death of Balder† was the only person who refused to weep for his passing, thereby preventing him from being raised from the dead, by saying: 'Thaukt will wall, with arid tears, Balder's bale fire. Let Hel hold what's hers.'

Theban Triad In Egyptian myth this triad consisted of Amon Ra†, Mutt†, and Khensu†.

Thekkr In Nordic myth a dwarf†. The name was also one of those given to Odin†.

Thesan The Etruscan goddess of the dawn, possibly also connected with childbirth.

Thialfi In Nordic myth he was the peasant's son, famous for his speed in running, who was the companion of Thor† on his encounter with Skrymir†, when he was defeated with ease by a runner who turned out to be a manifestation of thought.

Thiassi In Nordic myth a giant who with the aid of Loki† stole the golden apples of Iduna† upon which the Aesir† depended for health and strength. When it was discovered that Loki was responsible he was ordered to bring back Iduna and her apples. He accordingly borrowed Freyja's† feather cloak and succeeded in escaping through the air with Iduna and the apples although Thiassi chased Loki to the very doors of Asgard, where he was killed by the Aesir. Later a settlement was affected by his daughter Skadi† marrying Njord†. Alternative spellings Thjazi and Thiazi.

Thidrek Saga A version of the Nibelungenlied†, differing slightly from the Volsung Cycle† in that Siegfried† is adopted by the brother of Regin†, whom he later kills. He is betrothed to Brynhild†, but for reasons of policy marries Grimhild†. The rest of the story is as in the other versions.

Thien See Tien†.

Thokk See Thaukt†.

Thonapa Early Inca† culture hero similar to Quetzalcoatl† who later became identified with the son of the creator.

Thor In Nordic myth Thor was the son (or husband) of Fjörgynn†, or Jord†, or Hlodyn†, and the husband of Sif†. His father was said to be Odin† (though elsewhere he is the father of Odin). These domestic complications arose out of the endeavour to fit Thor, who was a culture hero and preceded the Aesir†, into the framework of a pantheon to which he did not belong. He is akin to Donar†, the thunder god of the Teutons, but it is by no means certain that they were the same. Thor, who was strong, brutal, with gross appetites, was the culture hero of a people on a far lower stage of civilization than the Aesir† or the Vanir† and was more akin to the giants, with whom he was perpetually at war. He was famous for his hammer and his belt of power, named Mjolnir and Megingjardir, for his chariot, and for his iron gauntlets, all of which formed part of his personal accoutrements. He was in essence the hero of the thrall and the churl as opposed to Odin†, the god of kings and earls, or fighting aristocracy. He had all the virtues of his class and all their vices. Bravery, strength, endurance were offset by stupidity, brutality, and bluster. The fact that he survived until the advent of Christianity is in all probability due to these very reasons and the consequent appeal which he had to the lower classes. Marriages, burials, and civil contracts were hallowed by the blacksmith's hammer of Thor. He was also known as Atli†. Thor's mansion was named Bilskinir. From him we get our Thursday. For stories of his activities *see* under Hymir†, Skrymir† and Thrym†.

Thoth One of the earliest Egyptian gods, represented as ibis-headed or as a dog-headed ape. He is reported to have invented numbers and arithmetic, geometry and astronomy, all of which were well known to the pre-dynastic Egyptians. For the story of his gamble with the moon for the intercalary days, *see* Osiris†. One of his manifestations was Aah-te-Huti†. He was associated with Khnemu†, Maat†, and Ptah† in the Creation. Alternative spellings are Djehuti† or Zehuti†. He was the arbiter between the gods, and had knowledge of the magic formulae needed by the dead to pass safely through the underworld. In the stories of the conflict between Osiris†, Isis†, and Horus† against Set†, it was Thoth on whose advice a satisfactory outcome always depended. Thoth, who was a moon god, dates back to the earliest times, and was of such influence that he had to be absorbed into the religion of Osiris and Ra†.

Thoume Kene Kimte Cacounche Creator god of the Natchez† Indian Creation Legend. He created first men, then tobacco, and then women.

Thraetona Early Persian culture hero who fought a great battle with Azhi Dahaka†. In later versions he is called Faridun†.

Thror In Nordic myth a dwarf† mentioned in the Eddas†. The name is also given to Odin†, thereby showing that he had some friendship with the dwarfs.

Thrudur In Nordic myth one of the

Valkyries†. The name Thudr, which is practically the same, is one of those given to Odin† in the Eddas†, and may involve some kind of relationship.

Thrym The Eddic Thryms-Kvida, or Lay of Thrym, also known as Hamarsheimt, 'the Homecoming of the Hammer', tells how Thrym the giant stole Mjolnir, the hammer of Thor†, and hid it underground. Loki† borrowed the feather cloak of Freyja† and visited Thrym, who told him that the hammer would only be returned if Freyja came to him as his bride. The news of this so infuriated Freyja that Brisingamen, her great necklace, fell to the ground. The Aesir† went into council and Heimdall† suggested disguising Thor and sending him in place of Freyja. Thor objected but was persuaded by Loki, who accompanied him as the bride's attendant. On arrival the supposed bride ate an ox and eight salmon, and drank three casks of mead. When the wedding was to be consecrated with the hammer – the traditional marriage rite – Thor seized it and murdered not only Thrym but all his womenfolk, including his aged sister, who had asked for a gift from the bride. If, as one may presume, the war between Thrym and Thor, of which the above is a version, resulted in the defeat of Thrym, it would explain why Thrymheim, his castle, was allotted to Skadi† as a residence.

Thu Chinese god of the earth and soil, also called She†.

Thunar The thunder god of the Anglo-Saxons, who may be equated to Thor† as being essentially a god of the people rather than one of the military aristocracy. The Teutonic equivalent was Donar†.

Tiahuanaco The vast area of cyclopean ruins, several square miles in area, at Tihuanaco, a few miles from the shores of Lake Titicaca, 15,000 feet above sea level, are those of a civilization which was already extinct when the first Incas arrived in South America. Although the ruins are now over thirteen miles from Lake Titicaca, the existence of wharfs and docks shows that at some remote period Tiahuanaco must have been a thriving port on a vast inland sea, some 350 miles from north to south, situated in the Andes. The mystery of this culture has baffled investigators for years. The great monolithic gateway of the temple of the sun is the largest example of its kind in the world. The rows of figures which decorate this gateway have been interpreted as consituting an ancient calendar. The god to whom this temple was built may have been Mancocoapact, or Viracochat. Temples also existed here to Copacatit and Ka-Ata-Killat.

When the Spaniards arrived in Peru they were told by the Incas that in the ancient days when there was no sun but only the moon and the stars, there lived a race of giants who built palaces and temples at Tiahuanaco. To them came a prophet who proclaimed the coming of the sun. The children of night, however, did not believe him and stoned him. Nevertheless, the sun rose and under its rays the godless race all perished and their bodies petrified into colossal blocks of stone. Another version says they were punished for having sacrificed to the moon goddess, Ka-Ata-Killa.

Tiamat A name given to the mass of bitter waters and the female principle in the seven Assyrian Tablets of the Creation, in the British Museum, as opposed to Apsut, applied to the sweet waters.

From the fertile depths of Tiamat sprang every living thing. The waters were confined in a vast bottomless mass. At a later stage Tiamat became the mother of Mommut by Apsut, the three forming a primeval trinity having no goodwill towards the higher and newer gods brought in by later generations in the development of religious thought.

Tiawath Variant of Tiamatt in the Babylonian myth.

Tieholtsodi A water monster in the mythology of the Navajo Indians.

Tien Chinese heaven god who had previously been a vegetation god, Shang-Tit.

Tig *See* Tiw and Tiwzt.

Ti-mu The Chinese earth mother, also known as Ti-ya.

Tin (Tinia) The Etruscan sky god. To the Etruscans he was the power who spoke in the thunder and descended in the lightning, and was always represented on monuments with a thunderbolt in his hand.

Tindalo A term used in Melanesiat to describe the spirit of any famous person who is being deified after his death.

Tinirau A Polynesian deity who had two manifestations, one divine and fishlike, the other human, with two faces and a dual personality.

Tirawa-Atius Alternate name of Atius-Tirawat, the chief deity of the Pawnee Indians. He figures in their Creation Legend.

Tir-nan-Beo In Celtic myth 'the Land of the Living', one of the distant lands to which the leaders of the Tuatha Dé Danann† fled after their defeat by the Milesians†. Other names were Tir-nan-Og†, 'the Land of Youth', Tir-Tairn-Gire', 'the Land of Promise', Mag-Mell†, and Hy-Brasil†.

Tir-nan-Og In Celtic myth 'the Land of Youth', one of the lands to which the leaders of the Tuatha Dé Danann† fled after their defeat by the Milesians†. The others included Tir-nan-Beo†, Mag-Mell†, and Hy-Brasil†.

Tistrya (Tishtrya) In Zoroastrian myth a name given to the star Sirius, an associate of Ahriman† in his battles against Ahura Mazda†.

Tiw The Old English form of Tyr† or Tiwaz†.

Tiwaz A sky god of Teutonic tribes who may be equated with the Nordic Tyr†.

Tlahuixcalpantecuhtli Aztec morning Venus god, 'Lord of the House of Dawn', equated with Quetzalcoatl†. He was the lord of the twelfth hour of the day.

Tlaloc The Aztec god of rain and moisture. One of the most important members of the Mexican pantheon. He was the husband of Chalchihuitlicue† and the father of the Tlalocs, the minor rain gods. His elder sister was Huixtocihuatl. He was the lord of the eighth hour of the day and the ninth hour of the night. God 'P'† may have been one of his children. In view of the importance of the rainy season to Aztec economy the place occupied by Tlaloc may be appreciated, but it is difficult to understand the necessity for the large numbers of children who were sacrificed to him every year, as the climate was not subjected to any great variations, unless these were in order to prevent a repetition of the Deluge or some kindred disaster associated with the early myths of this god.

Tlaltecuhtli Aztec earth monster god, 'the Lord of the Earth'. He was the lord of the second hour of the day.

Tlapallan A title occasionally given to Quetzalcoatl†, the Aztec culture hero.

Tlazolteotl Aztec earth mother goddess and goddess of dirt. She was the mother of Cinteotl. She is described in one of the codices as 'the Woman who sinned before the Deluge'. She was the lord of the fifth hour of the day and the seventh hour of the night. She was also known as Ixcuinan†, Teteoinnan†, Toci†.

Tlinkit Indian Creation Legend This west coast tribe of North America recount that after the Deluge all men and women and animals were turned into stones, with the presumable exception of the ancestors of the tribe.

Tloque Nahuaque Aztec creator god, lord of the close vicinity. Also known as Ometeotl†.

To'ar Priest of the sun god, husband and probable successor of Luminu'ut† in the myths of the Minehassa (Celebes†).

Toci (Toxi) 'Our Grandmother', a name given to Tlazolteotl†, the Aztec earth mother goddess.

Tohil Fire god of the Quichet Indians who is mentioned in their Creation Legend as told in the Popul Vuht. He was one of the gods who came into existence when the race left Tulan-Zuivat.

Tohu Primeval chaos monster of the Hebrews, whose name is perpetuated in the French expression *tohu-bohu*, meaning a hopeless muddle. It can be equated with Tamtut and Tiamatt.

Tonacacihuatl 'Lady of our Subsistence,' wife of Tonacatecuhtlit, the Aztec creator god. She was probably originally the goddess of mother earth and her husband may have been a later creation. She has been identified with Chicomecoatlt.

Tonacatecuhtli Aztec creator god, 'Lord of our Subsistence', husband of Tonacacihuatlt.

Tonantzin In Aztec myth a name meaning 'Our Mother', given sometimes to Cihuacoatlt.

Tonatiuh Aztec sun god. He was also known as Piltzintecuhtlit, meaning 'the Young Prince'. He was the lord of the fourth hour of the day.

Tornarsuk Chief god of the Eskimos, and ruler of the tornait or guardian spirits.

Toruguenket The moon, the principle of evil in the Creation Legend of the northern Tupi-Guaranit tribes. It is supposed that periodically the moon falls on the earth and destroys it and that it is the source of all baneful happenings such as floods and thunder-storms. Toruguenket appears to correspond to Jacyt.

Torushompek The sun, the principle of good in the myth of the northern Tupi-Guaranit tribes. He corresponds to Guaracyt.

Tou Mu In Chinese myth the bushel mother and goddess of the North Star. By her husband, the King of Chouyu, she had nine children, the Jen Huang of fabulous antiquity, the first human rulers of the world. She appears to be of Indian origin and to have been the same as Maritchit. She was worshipped by the Buddhists and the Taoists.

Treasures (*a*) Of the Aesir, (*b*) of Britain, (*c*) of the Tuatha, (*d*) other.

In European myth certain material objects are recorded as having formed part of the treasures of the Aesirt, of the British, of the Tuatha Dé Danannt, and of other races. The more important items among these may roughly be grouped as follows:

1. Swords: (*a*) Gungnirt, the sword of Odint; Höfudt, the sword of Heimdalt. (*b*) Dyrnwynt, the sword of Rhydderch Hael, or of Wrynach. (*c*) The sword of Nuda from Finiast, the lance of Lught from Goriast, the sword of Piscar.

2. Cauldrons: (*a*) Bodn, Odherirt (or Eldhrimirt) and Son, the magic cauldrons of the giantst. (*b*) The cauldron of Arawnt, Gwigawdt, Gwyddnot Longshank, that of Ceridwent, known as Ament, Ogyrvant, Tyrnog Diwrnacht, and the Grailt. (*c*) The cauldrons of Dagdat known as Undryt, of Brânt known as Lassar, of Manannant, of Midert, and that from Muriast, and the Magic Pool of the Boannt where Finnt caught the Salmon of Knowledge.

3. Chariots: (*a*) The chariot of Thort. (*b*) The chariot of Morgan

Mywnoawr†. (c) The chariot and horses† of Manannan.

4. Rings: (a) Draupnir†, the ring of Odin†, the arm-ring of Wayland Smith, the ring of Nanna†. (b) Luned – this should really belong to the garments of invisibility, details further on.

5. Hell-hounds: (a) Garm†, the moon dog. (b) The hell-hounds of Arwan. (c) Falinis, or the hound of Lugh†, the whelp of the King of Ioruaidhe, which turned water into wine – this property, which should belong to the cauldron of Dagda†, is in some stories given to the pigskin of King Tuis.

6. Horns: (a) Gjallar†, the horn of Heimdal†. (b) The drinking horn of Gwigawd, which gave whatever liquor was desired. The cup of Llwyr.

7. Ships: (a) Ellide, the ship of Thorsten. Naglfar†, the ship of Hrim; Skidbladnir†, the ship of Freyr† and Gerda†; Hringhorn†, the ship of Balder†. (c) Wavesweeper, the ship of Manannan†.

8. Stones: (a) The whetstone of Odin. (b) The whetstone of Tudwal Tudclud.

9. Thrones: (b) The Stone of Scone. (c) The Stone of Destiny from Falias†. (d) Alatuir†, the magic stone of Slavonic myth.

10. Fruits: (a) The apples of Iduna†. (d) The apples of the Hesperides, probably those of Iduna.

11. Tablets: (a) The Golden Tablets. (b) The stone of Gwyddon.

12. Garments of invisibility: (a) The Tarnkappe†, the ring of Fulla†. (b) The ring Luned; the tartan of Arthur†; the cloak of Caswallawn†.

13. Boars: (a) Saehrimnir, the boar which renewed itself after being eaten; Gullinbursti and Slidrugtanni, the boars of Freyr. (c) The pigskin of King Tuis which turned water into wine, the seven pigs of King Easal.

14. Other objects: (a) Mjolnir† and Megingjardir†, the hammer and the belt of Thor†; Brisingamen†, the necklace of Freyja†; Valhamr, the Feather Cloak† of Freyja. (b) The knife of Llawfrodded Farchawg, which would serve four and twenty men at meat at once; the halter of Clydno Eiddyn; the pan and platter of Rhegynydd Ysgolhaig; the chess-board of Gwenddolen, which played by itself; the garment of Padarn Beisrudd; the harp of Teirtu, which played by itself; the mantle of Tegau Eurvron for chaste women; the bottles of Gwyddolwyn the dwarf. (c) The cooking spits of the women of Fincara.

Treta In the Hindu† Creation Legend, the second of the four Yugas† of the current Mahayugas†, having a length of 3,600 divine years.

Triglav In Slavonic myth a three-headed god of Stettin and Brandenburg. His three heads represented heaven, earth, and the lower regions respectively, and the faces were veiled so that he might not see the sins of the world. He had a black horse, which was used to obtain omens. He is akin to Porevit†, Rugievit†, and Svantovit†.

Tripitaka The triple basket, the three collections of canonical works of the southern Buddhists written in the Pali language. These are divided into the Vinaya Pitaka, the Sutta Pitaka, and the Abhidhamma Pitaka. In the Sutta Pitaka is contained the Jataka five hundred and fifty birth stories of the Buddha, a collection of fables in the style of Aesop used in Buddhist instruction.

Trita A minor deity, usually connected with Indra†, who escaped from a well.

Trojanu In some parts of Russia the Emperor Trajan was made into a god under this name, and was to some extent equated with Peroun†.

Tsai Shen The Chinese god of wealth.

Tsao Chun The Chinese god of the kitchen.

Tsentsa *See* Tawiscara†.

Tsin King In Chinese myth the magic mirror of the rulers of Tsin which reflected the inward parts of those who looked upon it and revealed the seat of disease. From the description it would appear to have been some primitive kind of X-ray machine.

Tsui-goab Culture and rain god of the Hottentot tribes of South Africa.

Tsukiyomi Japanese moon god, brother of Amaterasu†.

Tsul 'Kalu Hunting God of the Cherokee† Indians who dwelt in the Blue Ridge Mountains of Virginia. The name means 'Slanting Eyes' and he may possibly have a resembled a deer.

Tuamutef In Egyptian myth an alternative spelling for Duamutef†, one of the four divine sons of Horus†.

Tuat The Egyptian nether world – also known as Amenti† – of which Osiris† became ruler after the defeat of Set†, was originally a place where there was neither water nor air and as dark as night, where it was not possible to gratify the cravings of affection. It was divided into twelve parts, which corresponded to the hours of the night. In shape it was rectangular, surrounded by water and intersected by streams, through which Ra† travelled nightly in his boat. It was the typical paradise of the desert dweller; its development from its first stage seems to imply that the original idea came from a non-desert country. The modern version of the name, Dwjt, is considered by some to be related to the name David. There is an oasis of that name in the Sahara. *See* Book of the Dead†.

Tuatha Dé Danann The folk of the god whose mother is Danu†. In Celtic myth these were a wave of migrants to Ireland following the Firbolgs† and the Fomors†. Being the latest arrivals they appropriated to themselves most of the qualifications of good, leaving to their predecessors the powers of evil. After a long succession of battles they defeated the Fomors at Mag Tuireadh (Magh Tuiredh) with immense slaughter on both sides. Eventually they themselves were defeated by the Milesians† and most of their leaders retired to the sea islands from which they had come.

Tuirenn In Celtic myth the father of Brian†, Iuchar†, and Iucharbar, the murderers of Cian†, the son of Dianchecht† and the father of Lugh†. As a penance for this crime they had to bring to the Tuatha Dé Danann† a series of objects most of which are listed under Treasures† of the Tuatha.

Tuisco A Teutonic culture hero who according to Tacitus was the father of Mannus, from whom sprang the three principal Germanic tribes.

Tulan-Zuiva In the Quichet Creation Legend as told in the Popul Vuht this place, known as 'the Seven Caves', was where the ancestors of the race started life after the extinction of the first race by fire and water and where they received their gods Avilix, Hacavitz, and Tohil. It resembles the Chicomoztoct of the Aztecs and maybe Xibalbat.

Tuleyone Indian Creation Legends This tribe of California Indians have two fire and deluge myths. In the first Sahtet, the evil spirit, set the world on fire and Ollet, the Coyotet, caused a great flood which put the fire out. The survivors were those who sought refuge on the Conocti Mountains. In the second version Wekwekt, the falcon, having stolen fire, carelessly dropped it on the world, which was set ablaze. Here again it was put out by Olle.

Tum Alternative spelling of Nefertumt or Atmut in Egyptian myth.

Tumu-I-Te-Are-Toka In the myth of Mangaiat a sea monster who was defeated by Ngarut. The same means 'the Great Shark'.

Tumu-ra'i-feuna In Polynesian mythology an octopus whose name means 'Foundation of earthly heaven'.

Tundun Culture hero of the Kurnei tribe of Australia. He was the self-styled son of Mungan-Nganat and became the ancestor of the tribe.

Tupan In one of the Tupi-Guaranit Creation Legends Tupan or Tupi was one of four brothers who alone survived the Deluge.

Tu-Papa, or **Tu-Neta** Youngest daughter of Papat, the great mother of the gods of Mangaiat. She married Ra, the sun god of Raiatea.

Tupi-Guarani Creation Legends This group of Brazilian tribes have a series of Creation Legends presumably arising from a common original, but which now differ considerably in detail. In one of these Monant, being vexed with mankind, determined to destroy the world by fire, which was extinguished by a great rainfall caused by Irin Maget. Another version of the story tells how the Deluge arose through a quarrel between Arikutet and Tawenduaret in which the latter stamped his foot so hard on the ground that a flood gushed forth, from which the brothers and their families only escaped by taking refuge in the tops of high trees. Yet another version, first reported in 1550, tells how Mairet endeavoured to destroy the world by a flood which which the three brothers Coemt, Hermittent, and Kriment escaped by climbing trees or by seeking refuge in caves. The southern tribes speak of four brothers instead of three, and name two of them as Tupant, or Tupi, and Guarani respectively.

Toruguenkett, the moon, figures largely as the power of evil which periodically falls on the earth and destroys it, and whose baleful influence is only slightly offset by Torushompekt, the sun, the principle of good. An alternative rendering makes Guaracyt the sun, Jacyt the moon, and Perudat the god of generation, the three creator gods. The Chaco Indians, a Guarani tribe, believe that a beetle constructed the universe and also a man and woman, the ancestors of the human race. When evil beings came from the hole in the ground scraped by the beetle, it protected the humans against them. This is presumably an account of a tribal war between people who had sought refuge in caves and those who had escaped on tree or mountains tops.

The Mundruku tribe have a myth that the god Rainit formed the world by placing it in the shape of a flat stone on the head of another god, and that the mountains were formed by Karut by blowing feathers about. The Uapes Indians tell that Temiouat was the mother of Pinont and his sister, the constellation Orion and the Pleiades respectively. They also have a purely male god named Juruparit. Others of the tribes believe the Southern Cross to be the footprint of an ostrich and the Pleiades to be a swarm of bees.

Tupimare The name given to the hilltop on which the ancestors of the Karayat and Ges Indians sought refuge from the flood which had been caused by Anatiwat, who sent fish to attack the hill and the people on it. One of the survivors was Kaboit. The story is given under Tupuyat and Ges Creation Legends.

Tupuya and Ges Indian Creation Legends The Karayat tribe of this group have a culture hero named Kaboit (known to the Arawakst as Kamut, to the Caribst as Tamut, to the Paraguayanst as Zumet, and to the Arovacst as Camut) who after the Deluge, when the ancestors of the tribe had sought refuge in a cavern, led them to the outer world, to which he was guided by hearing the call of a bird. In another version, Anatiwat having caused the flood, the Karayas fled to Tupimaret Mountain and were saved

thanks to Saracurat, the water hen, bringing earth to the hill-top as fast as the fish sent by Anatiwa nibbled it away. This story is shared with the Ges Indians. The Bakairi Caribs tell of their culture heroes, Keri and Kamet, who populated the world with animals after the disaster, having brought them in the hollow trunk of a tree, which may be taken to be a dug-out canoe. The name Kame is a rendering of Kamut.

Turan An Etruscan fertility goddess who corresponded to Venus.

Turms The Etruscan equivalent of Hermes who guided the souls of the departed to the underworld.

Tvashtri (Twashtri) In Vedic myth the artificer of the gods, the father of Saranyut and instructor of the Ribhust. He is a very ancient deity who probably came to India with the first Vedic invaders. He is akin to the various European artificers, and may therefore have been a dwarf. He should not be confused with Visvakarmat, the architect of the gods, who was his son-in-law.

Twanyrika In Australian myth the great spirit whose voice is heard in the bullroarer, similar to the Oro of Nigeria.

Twe A lake god in the mythology of Ghana.

Typhon In Egyptian myth another name for Sett in the nineteenth dynasty.

Tyr The most daring of the Nordic culture heroes, who is in some respects equivalent to Tiwazt. He lost his hand in the first fight with Fenrirt, but there is no record of his having been fitted with an artificial one like Nudat or

Ludd† in Celtic myth. At the time of Ragnarok he killed Garm†, the moon or hell hound, and died from his wounds. As was the case with Thor†, Tyr was a symbol of the viewpoint of the peasant and, as such, he was gradually pushed into the background by the more intellectual Odin†. Other details of the life of Tyr are under Aegir†.

Tyrnog Diwrnach A magic cauldron, one of the treasures† of Britain, which boiled meat for brave men only and not for cowards.

Tzental Indian Creation Legend Details of this are given under Maya† Creation Legends. The chief characters were Alaghom Naum†, Iztat Ix†, and Patol†.

Tzitzimime Minor Aztec† stellar god. The name means 'monsters descending from above', and probably refers to meteors.

U

Uadjit (Uatchit) Great crowned goddess of Lower Egypt, usually represented as a serpent, but occasionally as a vulture. Her Greek name was Bouto†. She was sometimes included in the Ennead†. Her sister Nekhebit† occupied a similar position in Upper Egypt.

Uapes Indians A subsidiary tribe of the Tupi-Guarani† Indians. Their culture heroes were Jurupari†, Pinon†, and Temioua†.

Ubar-Tutu Father of Utnapishti†, the Babylonian Noah.

Ubastet Alternative spelling for Bast†, the cat goddess of Egyptian myth.

Uccaihsravas In Vedic myth the wondrous horse, which was produced at the Churning of the Ocean in the Kurma† avatar.

Uert-Hekeu *See* Rat†.

Ueuecoyotl 'The Old' or 'Old Coyote' in the Aztec pantheon.

Uixtocihuatl Aztec salt goddess.

Uke-mochi Japanese food goddess who has tended to become merged with Inari†, the Japanese god of agriculture.

Ukwa In the Shilluk† Creation Legend the grandson of Kola†. Ukwa married

two Nile river priestesses and was the ancestor of the tribe.

Ule Culture hero and ancestor of the Anti† Indians. In their Creation Legend it is told how after all men had been destroyed by fire Titi† split open a tree from which came forth people, including a beautiful maiden who subsequently married Ule. From this couple sprang the tribe of Anti Indians. The word *ule* now means a tree in the Yurukare language.

Ullr (Ull) The stepson of Thor† and son of Sif†, a member of the Aesir† and a minor hero of Nordic myth.

Uma In Vedic myth perhaps the most attractive aspect of Parvati†, wife of Siva†. She is depicted as of great beauty, and as signifying the life of heavenly wisdom. She was worshipped as a representative of lofty abstract qualities. She was also known as Sati†, who sacrificed herself on the pyre to avenge her father's indignity, but this story is confused with one of Rudra† and his wife Ambika†.

Ummu-Khubur Another name for Melili†, wife of Benani†, and queen mother of the six thousand monsters raised by Tiamat† in her fight against Marduk†. For further details *see* Babylonian† Creation Legend.

Undry A name given to the cauldron of Dagda†, considered as one of the treasures† of the Tuatha Dé Danann†.

Uni Etruscan goddess equivalent to Hera or Juno.

Unneffer In Egyptian myth a title given to Osiris† (in the Book of the Dead), as the ruler of Ashet†, the place of spirits. The word Unneffer means 'the Good Being'.

Un(no) In Egyptian myth a name given to Osiris†.

Unt In Egyptian myth a name given to Isis†.

Untunktahe In Dakota† myth the water god, a great magician and seer who was constantly involved in struggles with Waukheon†, the thunder bird.

Upuaut In Egyptian myth a wolf god, brother of Anubis†, friend and companion of Osiris†. A cemetery god at Asyut or Siut (Lykopolis). Shares with Anubis the dominion of the Funeral Mountain, and is also known as the 'opener of the way', and also as Ophois†.

Uranus Alternative spelling for Ouranos† in the Phoenician† Creation Legend.

Urd The chief of the Nordic Norns† or fates. While in some stories she is said to have sat at the foot of Yggdrasill with her sisters Verdandi and Skuld†, in actual fact she appears to have been the titular leader of a college of sibyls at Asgard, or else she is a memory of a trinity of mother goddesses such as those worshipped by Frisian troops on Hadrian's Wall.

Urvasi A celestial nymph, one of the Apsarases† in Vedic mythology.

Usar-Hapi *See* Asar-Hap†.

Ushas In Vedic myth the goddess of the dawn, and the breath of life of the Vedas.

Usire *See* Asari†.

Utgard In Nordic myth the chief city of Jötunheim†, the land of the giants†.

Utgard-Loki, or **Magus of Utgard**, was the title of Skrymir† when he entertained Thor† and his companions.

Utnapishti Babylonian Noah, son of Ubar-Tutu†, who was warned by Anki, god of wisdom, of the intention of the gods to drown mankind, and to pull down his reed hut and make a boat or raft. He may be similar to Ziudsuddu†, the last of the ten Sumerian kings who reigned before the Flood.

Uto A name sometimes given to Uadjit† in Egyptian myth.

Utset Family name of the two sisters in the Sia† Indian Creation Legend who were the mothers of all mankind. The elder was the mother of all the Indians and the other, who was distinguished by being called Nowutset, was the mother of the rest of mankind. From the elder came the ancestors of the clan totems: eagle, coyote, bear, etc.

Uttu (Utu) Sumerian variant of Samas (Shamesh†), the sun god, one of the great gods to whom sacrifices were made by Ziudsuddu† or Ziudsuttu† to obviate the Deluge.

Uzume The Japanese goddess of jollity.

Uzza Name given to the star Venus by the Banu Ghatafan of Arabia, who worshipped her in the form of an acacia-tree. One of the three gods whom Mahomet would not recognize, the others being Allat† and Manat.

V

Vach In Vedic myth the goddess of speech, the mother of the Vedas. For some reason her personality has become merged with that of Sarasvati†, the wife of Brahma†.

Vadi (Wade) In Nordic myth a giant of Zealand, the island ploughed away by Gefjon†. He was the father of Völund†.

Vafthrudnir In Nordic myth one of the wisest of the giants. One day he was visited by Odin†, who had disguised himself under the name of Gangrad. The two agreed to test their wisdom for a forfeit and discuss all the various points on Nordic myth ranging from Bergelmir† to Ragnarok. Odin, however, won by asking 'What did Odin say in the ear of Balder† before he put him on the funeral pyre?' The story is told in the Vafthrudnismal Eddic poem.

Vaikuntha In Vedic myth the city of Vishnu†, situated on Mount Meru†.

Väinämöinen Culture hero of the Kalevala, the Finnish national epic. He was the son of Ilmatar, the virgin of the air, and was always depicted as a vigorous old man. He was pledged to Joukahainen†.

Vaivasvata (Vaivaswata) The son of Vaivasvat and, according to Hindu myth, the present Manu†, the seventh in order of succession. He is stated to have written a history of the Creation.

Vala A term for a sibyl or seeress common to most of the countries of northern Europe. In the Eddas† the term Völva† is used but without implying any alteration of function. In the south the word became Veela† and in the north-east it became Vila†.

Valhalla In Nordic myth the name given to the great hall of the palace of Gladsheim† in Asgard†. It had a ceiling covered with spears and five hundred and forty gates through each of which eight hundred men could march abreast. Allowing for pardonable exaggeration through the centuries, it seems that Valhalla was the 'Valaskjali', the house of Vali†, rather than the residence of Odin†. It was here the Einherjar† congregated.

Valhamr Name of Feather† Cloak of Freyja†.

Vali In Nordic myth the twin son of Odin† or Loki† by Siguna† or Rind†, one of the Aesir†. As Balder† and Hoder† were also twins, he had to be given Valaskjali or Valhalla, which may well have been his original residence transmuted at some later stage in the development of Nordic religion. His brother was Vidar†.

Valkyries In Nordic myth the Valkyries were priestesses of Freyja†, possibly dating back to the time when she was the supreme mother goddess of the Nordic race, or even providing a link with some Amazonian tribe of mounted women warriors. They are subordinate to the Norns† and, if the assumption is that the Norns were the chiefs of a college of sibyls, then the Valkyries may well have been their assistants, particularly as the Norn Skuld† always rode with them. The function accredited to them in popular myth, of bringing the souls of the slain to Odin†, seems to belong to the later stages of Scandinavian religion.

Valmiki The author of the epic poem Ramayana.

Vamana In Vedic myth the fifth or dwarf avatar of Vishnu†. He ousted Bali† from the upper and middle worlds. Vishnu† presented himself before Bali and solicited as much land as he could cover in three strides. When his request was granted he covered heaven and earth in two strides, but left Patala to Bali.

Vampires The idea that evil spirits take possession of the bodies of the dead in order to prey upon the living and exist by sucking the lifeblood of their victims is common in the Slav† world and the Balkans. It would appear to be related to some primitive ritual of blood drinking. Vampires in general behaviour are not unlike ghosts as conceived by the Greeks in Homeric times. The assumption that vampires remained immune from corruption appears to be of post-Christian origin. The remedies, such as piercing with a stake and burning, and the use of sprays of garlic, are frequently mentioned in European folklore and myth, and in the records of witch trials.

Van In Armenian myth a feathered monster or dragon.

Vanadevatas In Vedic myth Indian tree spirits, who took revenge on those who cut down their trees.

Vanadis In Nordic myth one of the names of Freyja† as a goddess of the Vanir† and also that of one of the members of the Asynjor†.

Vanemuine In the Hero† of Estonia, the national epic of that country, Vanemuine is the god of music, who departs from mankind because they did not appreciate his songs. He is the Väinämöinen of the Kalevala†.

Vanir In Nordic myth the Vanir were the culture heroes of a race which seems to have preceded the Aesir† in Scandinavia. A war between them was precipitated by the ill treatment of Gullveig†, a Vanir giantess or priestess. After the defeat of the Aesir, peace was made by both sides ritually spitting into Odherir, the magic cauldron of the giants (the story is told in the Conversations of Bragi), and by an exchange of hostages, Njord† going to the Aesir and Hoenir† to the Vanir. Later the two groups were fused into one. The Vanir would appear to have been a seafaring people, but probably of the same stock as the Aesir, as Freyr† and Freyja† were the children of Njord, whilst Frigg† came with the Aesir.

Vaoetere In Fijian myth the evil spirit of the ironwood trees was known by this name. Other relevant myths are given under Polynesia†.

Varaha In Vedic myth the boar, the

third avatar of Vishnu†, in which he dived to the bottom of the sea to deliver the world from the clutches of Hiranyaksha†. This appears to be another version of the battle with Haya-Griva† in the Matsya† avatar.

Vari-ma-te-takere In Polynesian and Indonesian myth the great mother of gods and men who lived in Avaiki, the land of the dead; the mother of Vatea†, who rules over the underworld, and grandmother of Tangaroa†, the sky god, and Rongo†, in the Mangaia Island Creation Legend.

Varuna In Vedic myth the god of the waters and of the west quarter of Mount Meru. He is a Poseidonian god who is usually depicted seated on a sea monster, known as Makara. In his aspect as a heaven god he is akin to Ahura Mazda†, the benign divinity of the Zoroastrian myths. He was gradually superseded by Indra†, although an annual festival of Varuna was held in Bombay until recently. He was an Aditya†. He was also a god of the Tamils.

Vasishtha In Vedic myth one of the seven great Rishis† and one of the Prajapatis†. He was the author of several hymns in the Rig-Veda, and was victor in a contest with Viswamitra†, a fellow Rishi. Vasishtha was the possessor of Nandi†, the Snow-white Bull of Siva†.

Vasudeva In Vedic myth patronymic of Krisna†. At the start of the Christian era Vasudeva, being a sun god, had partially supplanted Krisna, the dark sun, who then took the name Krisna Vasudeva. Actually, Vasudeva would appear to have been a sage of the Satvata or Vrisni clan, who was later identified as, or whose name was actually used by, the father of Krisna. Later the worship of a dark god for various reasons became unpopular, and to counteract this Vasudeva was actually referred to as Devadeva or god of gods. Subsequently the doctrine of rebirth was used to make Krisna Vasudeva, an avatar of Vishnu†, the Vedic sun god.

Vasuki In Vedic myth a ruler of the Nagas†, the serpent-worshipping people, akin to Sesha†.

Vasus In Vedic myth a group of eight divine attendants of Indra†. They are Apa (water), Dhruva (the Pole Star), Soma (moon), Dhara (*terra*, earth), Anala (fire), Anila (wind), Prabhasa (dawn), and Pratyusha (light).

Vatea (**Atea**) In the myth of Mangaia Island the husband of Papa† and the father of Tangaroa† and Rongo†. Although he liked Tangaroa, he allowed himself to be persuaded by his wife, Papa, to dispossess him in favour of Rongo.

Vayu Originally Vaya, or Vata, was the spirit of the wind, whose worship expired when the nature gods were superseded by Varuna†, Indra†, and others. He occasionally replaced Indra as a member of the triad with Agni† and Surya†. He was the father of Bhima† and Hanuman†, and later was considered as the father of the Maruts†.

Vedic Sacred Writings These are arranged in four main groups: the Vedas, the Upavedas, the Ved-Angas, and the Upangas.

The Vedas are subdivided into four:

the Rig, Yajur, Sama, and Artharva, consisting of hymns of praise, sacrificial texts, Soma† ceremonies, and magical spells respectively.

The Upavedas deal with the sciences of medicine, music, war, arts, and architecture.

The Ved-Angas deal with pronunciation, prosody and verse, grammar, phraseology, religious ceremonies, and astronomy.

The Upangas include the itihasas, puranas, yoga, mimansa, dharmasastras, and tantras, comprising epic poems, legendary histories, logic, philosophy, jurisprudence, and ritual.

From the point of view of study of the myth, the most important sections are the itihasas, which include the Ramayana† and the Mahabharata†; the puranas, in which most of the stories of the gods are to be found; the dharmasastras, or code of Manu†, containing accounts of the Creation and of the background of Brahmanical tradition. The tantras, which represent an attempt to bring Brahmanism down to a level which would endear it to the aboriginal races, are largely pornographic and are of little value.

Each subdivision of the Vedas is, in turn, divided into the following parts: Sanhita, comprising the Mantras and Ganas, or hymns and prayers; Brahmanas, describing the details of Vedic ceremonies; Jnana, or Upanishads, or philosophical part; and Aranyakas, 'belonging to the forest', intended for Brahmans in retreat. Closely connected with the Vedas are the Sutras and Parisishtas, abbreviated summaries for the use of students.

This vast mass of religious writings dates back to before the Hindus arrived in India, and probably to a period when they were living in a relatively cold climate. The Vedic hymns were probably put into their present form before 1000 BC but have naturally suffered certain modifications.

Other details are in Hindu† Creation Legends.

Veela In south-east Europe the Vala† or Völva†, the sibyl of the north, became the kindly sprite of the woods, such as Oossood†. This is a typical example of the degradation of the priestess sibyl into the semi-human dryad, under the influence of religious pressure. They loved to dance, and fairy rings are to this day called Vilinio Kollo in the Balkans. If disturbed while dancing – presumably part of their religious rites – they were hostile to men, but they could, nevertheless, be amiably disposed and help them. On occasions they married humans and bore children. Prince Marco† received great help from a Veela named Raviyoyla†. They were gifted with second sight and healing properties of flowers and herbs.

Vegtam The Edda† Vegtamskvida, the Lay of Vegtam the Wanderer, or sometimes known as Balder's Dream†, tells how Balder, having been tormented with dreams of death, the Aesir† assembled in council and empowered Frigg† to extract an oath from all things living that they would not harm Balder. Odin†, feeling that the precautions taken were insufficient, rode on his horse† Sleipnir† to visit Hel†, there to consult the famous Völva†, whom he causes to rise up from her grave, only to hear from her that Balder was doomed to fall by the hand of Hodur†. This seems to be even older than the Völuspa†, which quotes several lines from it.

Veja mate In Latvia the goddess of the winds, who controls the weather.

Veles A Czech variant of Volos†, the Serbian cattle god, who had been degraded to the rank of a demon, which position he still held as late as the fifteenth century.

Velu mate In Latvia the queen or mother of the dead.

Vendidad The first part of the Zend-Avesta†, the bible of the Zoroastrian religion, containing religious myth, laws, and the 'gathas'.

Verdandi In Nordic myth the Norn† of things present, who sat with her sisters Skuld† and Urd† at the foot of Yggdrasill. The Norns appear to have been a group of Völvas or sibyls, and the titles given to the three sisters may well have been hereditary.

Verethraghna In Zoroastrian myth god of war mentioned in the Zend Avesta†. He was one of the Yazatas†.

Vidar In Nordic myth the son of Odin† or Loki† by Siguna† or Rind†, brother of Vali†, known as 'the Silent One'. He was almost as strong as Thor† and was one of the Aesir†. After his father had been killed at Ragnarok by the wolf Fenrir† he avenged his death by tearing the wolf in half.

Vijaya In Vedic myth an aspect of Parvati†, wife of Siva†, as a goddess of battle. The name means 'the Victorious'.

Vila An eastern Slavonic† term for Vala† or Veela†. It was applied mainly to water sprites and probably originally meant the prophetic priestesses of the rivers and streams. It is well known to many by the song from *The Merry Widow*, 'Vilia, oh Vilia'.

Vili and **Ve** In Nordic mythology the sons of Bor† and brothers of Odin†. Together the three brothers created the earth from the remains of Ymir†, the giant they killed, and with his blood they made the sea.

Vilmeth and **Vidolf** The ancestors of all wizards and witches according to the Völuspa†.

Vinata In Vedic myth mother of Garuda†, wife of Kasyapa† and sister of the queen of the serpents, which makes her one of the Naga† family.

Vindhya-vasini In Vedic myth one of the terrible aspects of Parvati†, wife of Siva†. The name means 'the Dweller in the Vindhyas' and at her temple near Mirzapur it was said that the blood before her image was never allowed to cease from flowing.

Vira-Bhadra In Vedic myth a monster created by Siva† or Rudra† after his dispute with Daksha†, his father-in-law. This monster is said to have torn out the eyes of Bhaga†, to have knocked out the teeth of Pushan†, and to have cut off the head of Daksha.

Viracocha The hero of an Inca Creation Legend in which, together with Manco Capac† and Pachacamac†, he came from Pacari, 'the Cave of Refuge'. In an alternative version, Viracocha rose from the depths of Lake Titicaca near Tiahuanaco and created the human race by breathing the breath of life into some of the stone figures there. He was probably a relic of the pre-Inca culture at Tiahuanaco.

Viraj In Vedic myth the name given to a son of Satarupa† and of Brahma†, or possibly a son of Purusha†.

Visha In Vedic myth a poison produced at the Churning of the Ocean† in the Kurma† avatar. It was subsequently seized by the Nagas† and became the poison of the cobras.

Vishnu The rise of Vishnu to the position of supreme god of the Vedic pantheon appears to have followed the elevation of Krisna Vasudeva† to that position and the subsequent doctrinal enunciation that Krisna† was the eighth avatar of Vishnu. It is certain that this elevation of Vishnu was supported by the Brahmans to offset the popularity of Indra†, who was afterwards gradually superseded. These ten avatars† all appear to be pre-Vedic, and may be taken to represent geological or historical periods. The last five were renamed by the invaders, the others may have been too ancient to have been changed except by inclusion in the new religion. They are: 1, Matsya†, the fish; 2, Kurma†, the tortoise; 3, Varaha†, the boar; 4, Narasinha†, the man-lion; 5, Vamana†, the dwarf; 6, Parasu-Rama†, Rama with the axe; 7, Rama-Chandra†; 8, Krisna†; 9, Buddha†; 10, Kalki†.

Vishnu, the spirit of the sacrifice, is in some ways identical with the spirit of the Soma†. His first three avatars are different aspects of the same Deluge legend, the fourth and fifth are recollections of the conquest of India, and the sixth may concern the putting down of

the revolt on the part of the fighting forces, and the seventh deals with the attempted conquest of Ceylon. The eighth and ninth avatars arose for purely political reasons, while the tenth, which has not yet occurred, may be considered as prophecy.

Visperad The second part of the Zend Avesta†, the bible of the Zoroastrian religion, containing a collection of litanies.

Visvakarma For details *see* Vivasvat†.

Viswamitra In Vedic myth a Rishi† who was defeated in a literary contest by Vasishtha†.

Visweswara In Vedic myth a title meaning 'Lord of All', under which Siva† was worshipped at Benares.

Vivasvat In Vedic myth the sun. There exists considerable confusion between Vivasvat, Visvakarma†, and Tvashtri†. It would appear that Visvakarma, the Rishi†, was a priest of the sun who married the daughter of Tvashtri and became the father of Yama† and of the Asvins†. As an architect, Visvakarma built Amaravati and Lanka, cities of the gods, and designed Jagan-natha†.

Viviane (Vivien) *See* Merlin†.

Vlkodlaks Slavonic name for the werewolf, from *vlko* meaning wolf, and *dlaks* meaning hair. Popularly supposed to cause eclipses of the sun and moon, thereby showing a kinship with Fenrir†, the Nordic wolf. An alternative spelling is Vookodlaks.

Vogul Creation Legends (Northern

Urals) When survivors from the Deluge landed on the earth they found neither trees nor plants, and were threatened with death from starvation. Their culture hero Numitarom† succeeded, however, in growing crops and saving them from death.

Vohu Manah One of the seven Immortal Holy Ones, the attendants of Ahura Mazda†. Vohu Manah represented good thought.

Volos A cattle god worshipped by the Serbs. To the Czechs, however, Veles† was a demon. An alternative spelling was Volusu.

Volsung Cycle A series of some twenty Eddic poems covering the same ground as the Nibelungenlied†, but much closer to the original sources. The basis of the story is the theft of the treasure of the Nibelungen by the Aesir† in order to pay compensation for the murder of the brother of Fafnir†. The legacy of treason and murder and the curse of the Nibelungen devolved on Sigurd† (Siegfried†). There is considerable overlapping between the Thidrek Saga†, Volsung, Nibelungen, and to some extent, Beowulf† stories, as will be seen from the comparative of characters, as given under Nibelungenlied.

Voltumna Great god of the Etruscans at whose shrine state councils were held.

Völund The Nordic name for Wayland Smith†. The Völundar Kvida in the Poetic Edda tells the tragic story of his exploits. How he was the son of the giant Badi† and was apprenticed first to Mimir† and later to two dwarfs with

whom he quarrelled and slew. He then served with King Nithud†, who later had him hamstrung. With the aid of his brother Egil† he built a flying machine and flew home, leaving behind him the heartbroken Bodvild†, the king's daughter, whom he had seduced. Völund, who is called 'the Wise Elf', is a smith artificer of the type of Goibniu† and, as such, linked with the dwarfs who provided the technical background for the Nordics, the Teutons, and the Celts.

Volundar Kvida In Nordic myth one of the heroic stories of the Poetic Edda†. Its main characters were Badi†, Bodvild†, Egil†, Mimir†, Nithud†, and Völund†.

Völuspa The title of the Völva's† prophecy in the Edda†, in which is told the story of Ragnarok†. The text seems to be a continuation of the interview of Odin† with the sibyl described in the Vegtams-Kvida†. The device of putting a relation of past facts in the mouth of a prophet as a forecasting of future events is very common in myth, and may generally be disregarded. Although the Völuspa is younger than the Lay of Vegtam, the text itself seems to have undergone less modification and it may be taken as the story of the end of the Aesir† which was handed down by survivors to future generations. The shorter version of the Völuspa was found in the Flatey Book†, while a copy of the main text was found in the Book of Hauk†, another fourteenth-century manuscript, besides being repeated in the Prose Edda.

Volusu In Slavonic myth alternative spelling of Volos†, the Serbian cattle god.

Völva In Nordic myth the sibyl of the Völuspat, the Völva's prophecy, and she also appears to have been the one consulted by Odint in the story of Vegtamt. It is of interest to note that in spite of their predominantly masculine outlook, the Nordic races continued to venerate the women seers of the previous occupants of the area until well after the arrival of Christianity. The term Völva may have been a similar one to the Slavonic Valat, Veelat, and Vilat. The Völva of the Völuspat was named Gullveigt.

Voodoo Worship Details of this are given under Bocort, Mamaloit, and Paparloit.

Vookodlaks In Slavonic myth an alternative form of Vlkodlakst.

Vör or **Vara** Nordic goddess of contracts and guardian of marriage.

Votan Central American god in the Popul Vuh Quiche Creation Legend who may be assimilated with Tepeyollotlt, the Aztec god.

Vrihaspati (**Brihaspati**) In Vedic myth the preceptor of the gods, and the son of Angirast, the Rishit.

Vritra The dragon or demon of drought, slain by Indrat, for which deed he acquired the title of Vritrahant. In actual fact the whole story is borrowed from the earlier Zend-Avestat, wherein the god of war, Verethraghnat, slew Verethrat. Even this earlier version is doubtful and may have been invented to account for the title. In India, Vritra was a spider-like being, also known as Ahit, the son of Danut, the serpent god. He was one of the Asurast, and was probably a serpent-worshipping king. In his battle with Indra he appears to have cut off the water supplies of the invading Hindus, a story which accounts for his being the demon of drought. The statement that he was a Brahman may be dismissed. In some respects the story of Vritra resembles that of Seshat.

Vrtraghna In Vedic myth a title given to Indrat.

Vue A term used in Melanesiat to describe the race which built the megalithic structures scattered all over the Pacific Islands. These persons were potent as givers of life, being full of Manat.

Vukub-Caquix A giant of the Quiche Creation Legend as told in the Popul Vuh. His name meant 'Seven times the colour of fire' and he had two sons, known as 'Earth Heaper' and 'Earthquake', by his wife Chimalmatt. He was eventually destroyed by Hunapút with the aid of Xbalanquét.

Vukubcame Co-ruler of Xibalbat with Huncamet, as told in the Quichet Creation Legend in the Popul Vuht.

Vukub-Hunapu In the Quichet Creation Legend as told in the Popul Vuht the brother of Hunhunapút and with him was murdered by the rulers of Xibalbat, Huncamet and Vukubcamet. Later his death was avenged by his nephews.

W

Wachitt The mother of Wade†.

Wade The father of Wayland†.

Waitiri Grandmother of Tawhaki† and priestess of a thunder goddess.

Wallum Olum The Creation Legend of the Lenape† Indians. In it is told how after the Deluge they dwelt with the manly turtle beings – presumably some tribe of seafarers – and that Talli†, their culture hero, led them over the frozen lands to the Snake Land, which they conquered.

Washo Indian Creation Legend The myth of this California tribe tells of a great seismic upheaval which causes the mountains to catch fire, the flames rising so high that the stars melted and fell to earth. This was followed by a deluge, and some of the men who tried to escape from it by building a high tower were changed into stones.

Watch Merti In Egyptian myth a name given to Isis† and Nephtys† in the Book of the Dead†. The term may also refer to Mert†, the goddesses of the north and south inundations.

Waukheon In Dakota† myth the thunder bird who was constantly involved in struggles with Untunktahe†, the water god.

Wayland (or **Weyland**) **Smith** Name by which Völund† or Wieland† is usually known in the English-speaking world. Perhaps the last of the makers of fairy or magic swords, in which capacity he is still remembered in Britain. Wayland was the son of Wade, who had a magic boat, and the grandson of a sea-witch called Wachilt. This may possibly indicate that the tradition of sword-making had been brought from overseas, possibly from the Mediterranean at some early stage in the classical period.

We *See* Vili and Ve.

Wekwek The falcon of the Tuleyone† Indian Creation Legend who stole fire and when pursued dropped it, thereby setting the world in flames, which were put out by Olle†, the Coyote†, who sent a great rain which flooded the earth.

Wenceslas In Slavonic myth the King of Bohemia, who sleeps under a mountain, together with his knights. Another version of this story calls him the Knight Stoymir†. Other references are given under Sleeping Princess†.

Wennofer Alternative rendering of Unneffer (for Osiris) in Egyptian myth.

Wen Tsch'ang (**Wen-chhang**) Chinese Taoist god of literature identified with a constellation near the Great Bear. As he descended to earth and became incarnate this may be one of the usual instances of a great philosopher being deified after his death.

Werewolf The werewolf of the Teutons and Slavs† is a faint memory of the ritual dances and sacrifices of wolf totem clans such as the Neuri mentioned by Herodotus. The possibility that manifestations of frenzy like those of the authentic mental disease lycanthropy might have been brought on by cold and exposure also exists. The belief in lycanthropy persisted in mountainous districts of central and eastern Europe until at least 1939.

Weyland Smith *See* **Wayland Smith**

Whaitiri A cannibal chieftainess who descended from the sky in Maori mythology.

Whakarere-Anu In Polynesian myth 'Space of Extreme Cold', one of the Multitude of Space†.

Whakatoro-Anu In Polynesian myth 'Cold Space Creeping On', one of the Multitude of Space†.

Where-Ao In Polynesian myth primal god, ancestor of Tawhaki†.

White Magic This is now taken to mean any ritual practice carried out for the benefit of others, as opposed to black magic†, meaning any ritual carried out for personal gain or lust. An important point of difference is that white magic is devoid of any sexual motive. Earlier, however, it meant any practice that was officially approved of, as opposed to those which were disapproved of – for example, the persecution of witches by

people who were using similar spells and rites for their own purposes. Originally it meant ritual intended to produce or maintain health or fertility.

Wichita Indian Creation Legend After the Deluge had subsided the culture heroine of this tribe discovered some ears of corn and planted them, thanks to which the ancestors of the tribe survived.

Wieland The High German form of Völund†.

Wili *See* Vili† and Ve.

Wimpe In Algonkian† myth a powerful sorcerer who was defeated by Gluskap† . The story goes that Wimpe in a contest grew until he overtopped the pine forest, but Gluskap grew even taller and managed to kill him.

Wind A name given to Kolpia† in the Phoenician Creation Legend† of Philo Byblos.

Winefred A variant of Unneffer† in Egyptian myth.

Wintun Indian Creation Legend The myth of this California tribe relates that Katkochila† sent a great fire to burn up the earth to show his displeasure at the theft of his magic flute. Later, however, there was a great flood and the fire was put out.

Wip In Egyptian myth a variant of Anubis†.

Wisagatcak A trickster character in the mythology of the Eastern Cree Indians of North America.

Wisaka In the Sac† and Fox Indian Creation Legend he was the ancestor of the
tribe. He incurred the displeasure of two
powerful Manitous who tried to burn
the land and then to drown it with a
deluge. He sought refuge in a high tree
on a mountain top, and when the waters
were on the point of covering it he was
rescued by a canoe.

Woden, Wotan In West Germanic languages the Nordic culture hero Odin†
was known as Woden. The fact that the
Eddic stories are much fuller than anything which West Germanic myth has
so far produced supports the assumption
that Odin was the earlier form, and that
their preservation was due to Christianity breaking down the Germanic
myths before they were reduced to
writing. The High German form is
Wotan.

Wolkenthrut One of the Valkyries†
whose name meant 'cloud-power'.

Woto Twin brother of Moelo† in the
mythology of the Bushongo people.

Wyirrawarre In Australian myth a
name for heaven or the sky in the myth
of the Narrinyeri tribe. It was to this
that their culture hero, Nurrundere†,
ascended.

X

Xbalanqué (Ixbalanqué) In the Quiche Creation Legend as told in the Popul Vuh he and his brother Hunapú avenged the murder by Huncame and Vokubcame, sovereigns of Xibalba, of their father Hunhunapú and their uncle Vukub-Hunapú.

Xelhua Hero of an Aztec† Creation Legend who escaped the Deluge by going to the top of the mountain of Tlaloc†, the water god. He was a giant† and was credited with the construction of the step pyramid at Cholula.

Xhosa Myths This African tribe have a supreme being, Quamta†. They also have stories of Sasabonsum† and Srahman†, the forest-dwellers. Huntin†, the African tree spirit, is associated with the Xhosa.

Xibalba In the Creation Legend of the Quiche† Indians as told in the Popul Vuh† Xibalba was an underground world inhabited by Huncame† and Vukubcame†, who challenged Hunhunapú† and Vukub-Hunapú† to a game of ball. However, the invitation was a trap in that they first had to cross a river of blood, and then, on arriving at the palace they were deceived by dummy figures of wood; when they were invited to sit, the seat turned out to be a red-hot stone; afterwards they were sacrificed and buried. The head of Hunhunapú was suspended from a gourd-tree and a princess, Xquiq†, stopped to look at it, when the head spat into her palm and told her that she would become a mother. Later it was her children Hunapú† and Xbalanqué† who finally defeated the rulers of Xibalba. In actual fact Xibalba does not seem to have been an abode of the dead, but rather a series of underground dwellings where ceremonies were held for the initiation of kings, as is the case with the majority of these stories of the harrowing of Hades by great rulers. At a later stage in history the Mayan† empire was known as the empire of Xibalba. It resembles Chicomoztoc† of the Aztecs and Tulan-Zuiva†. Camazotz†, the bat god, was an important figure in these stories.

Xilonen Aztec goddess, the young maize mother; she appears to have originated among the Huichol tribes.

Xipé Totec One of the old gods of the Aztecs depicted as a being in a human skin and known as 'Our Lord the Flayed One'. He may be compared with the Mayan God 'F'†.

Xisuthros Tenth pre-diluvial King of Babylon; according to Berosus, he was the hero of the Deluge legend, and was the son of Opartes. May also be Utanapishti, the Babylonian Noah. He may be equated with El-Khadir†, Hasis-Atra†, and Ziudsuddu†. For further details *see* Babylonian† Creation Legend.

Xiuhtecuhtli Ancient Aztec fire god and lord of the year. He was also sometimes known as Huehueteotl†, 'the Old God'. He was the lord of the first hour of the day and the first hour of the night.

Xmucane and Xpiyacoc Mother and father gods linked with Gucumatz† in the Quiche† Creation Legend as told in the Popul Vuh†. After making the animals they made the first human beings, who were destroyed in a great natural disaster. They resemble Ometecuhli† and Omeciuatl†, the Aztec mother and father gods. Their mythological son was Hunhunapú†.

Xochipilli Aztec god of pleasure. The name means 'Flower Prince'. He was also known as Macuilxochitl†. He was the lord of the seventh hour of the day.

Xochiquetzal Aztec goddess of flowers and craftsmen, wife of Cinteotl†. The name means 'Flower Feather'. In one instance the name Macuilxochiquetzalli, meaning 'Five Times Flower Feather', is given to Chalchihuitlicue†. Mother of Quetzalcoatl† by Mixcoatl†. She was considered as being the first woman and as such the companion of Piltzintecuhtli†, the young prince. At some later stage she became the patron goddess of prostitutes.

Xolotl Early culture hero of the Aztecs who occupied the territory of Tenayuca. At some period he became the mythological twin of Quetzalcoatl†.

Xquiq In the Quiche† Creation Legend as told in the Popul Vuh† she was a princess of Xibalba† who, having seen the gourd-tree on which hung the head of Hunhunapú, became the mother of his two children, Hunapú and Xbalanque†. Seeking refuge from the rulers of Xibalba she went to Xmucane†, who looked after her until the children were born.

Y

Yabune Early Japanese house god who is mentioned in an old ritual.

Yaghuth Pre-Jewish Arabian god, cognate with the Uz and the Jeush of Genesis. Is regarded as a personification of time.

Yahweh Alternative form of Jehovah, the god of the Old Testament.

Yama In Chinese mythology the king of the Seventh Hell, and the Buddhist king of the dead.

Yama and Yami In early Vedic myth Yama and Yami were a hero king and his sister, or wife, rulers of a Valhalla of the Aryans, where the valiant would for ever enjoy the delights of a carnal paradise. Later, however, with the ousting of the early gods by Brahman importations, Yama gradually became grim and harsh, finishing as the guardian of the hell of the Hindus. Yama was an Aditya†. In Chinese myth he was known as Yen-Wang†. Yama and Yami were the children of Saranyu†. Yama corresponds to the Zoroastrian Yima†.

Yamilka A story from the Arabian Nights relating, *inter alia* how the family of a serpent king were killed by the falling of a star from heaven. It is an early disaster myth which has survived by being incorporated in Arab folklore. There is also a marked similarity to the Gilgamesh† story and the story of the Shipwrecked Sailor†. *See also* Serpent Myths†.

Yamm Babylonian sea god killed by Baal† with the aid of two clubs fashioned by Kathar-Wa Hasis, called 'Driver' and 'Expeller'. With the first he was struck on the body and driven from his throne; with the second he was struck on the head and driven from the seat of his authority. This may have been the ritual for deposing a god.

Yana Indian Creation Legend This Indian tribe of the west coast of North America have a myth which tells how a man in need of fire saw a mountain emitting sparks. With four companions he went to steal some fire from the mountain but on the return journey Coyote†, who was carrying the fire, dropped it and everything in the world was burned up.

Yang The Yang and the Yin† are the names given by the Chinese to the opposing forces in a cosmological system of Dualism† which is said to have been invented by Fu-Hsi in the third millennium BC and to have been elaborated in the Yih-King† about 1122 BC. While these dates are uncertain it may be said that by the time of the foundation of Confucianism† or Taoism† these doctrines were so old that their origin had almost been forgotten. The symbol of the Yang, the male element, is an undivided line (———) and that of the Yin, the female principle, a broken or divided line (——— ———). The combinations of these in pairs denote the heavenly bodies or the seasons, while the trigrams denote the elements or the forces of nature. With the degeneration of Taoism into poly-demonism the Yang has developed into the 'Shen', the gods of the earth and the air, while the Yin has become the 'Kwei', demons to be feared and propitiated. The Japanese equivalents are the In† and the Yo†.

Yangwu The sun crow of Chinese myth which may be equated with the Yatagarasu†, the sacred bird of the Japanese sun goddess Amaterasu†.

Yao A mythical Chinese emperor who, together with the heavenly archer Shen Yi†, conquered the winds.

Yarih Moon god of Ugarit, and lover of Nikkal†; he sent Hirihbi†, King of Sumer, to ask Baal† for her hand, offering 1,000 shekels of silver, even 10,000 shekels of gold, saying: 'I shall send gems of lapis lazuli, I shall make her fields into vineyards, and the field of her love into orchards.' This offer was accepted, thus fulfilling the prophecy of El† that Nikkal would be the mother of a wonderful son.

Yasna The third part of the Zend-Avesta†, the bible of the Zoroastrian religion, containing liturgical works.

Yatagarasu The eight-hand crow, the sacred bird of Amaterasu†, the Japanese sun goddess. It may be identified with the Yangwu† of Chinese myth.

Yatis In Vedic myth a group of holy

men who were slain by Indra† and cast to the jackals. This story may indicate the failure of an early attempt by the Brahmans to put down the worship of Indra. The name is that of a present sect of the Jains. In the Zoroastrian† myth they were sorcerers.

Yazata In Zoroastrianism, a guardian spirit of the sun, moon or stars as well as a personification of abstract ideas such as truth or peace.

Ydalir The zodiacal† house of Ullr†.

Yehl *See* Yetl†.

Yemaja River and lake goddess of the Yoruba† people. She was the daughter of the earth goddess Odudua† and the sister and wife of Aganju†. The child of this marriage was Orunjan†, god of the midday sun.

Yen-lo *See* Yen Wang†.

Yen-Wang (**Yen-lo**) In Chinese myth the name given to Yama†, the ruler of the Hindu other world. To the Chinese, however, his power only extends to the lower spheres of existence, he has no power over those who by their own striving after purity and goodness pass from the realm of life and death directly to that of incarnate thought.

Yeti For centuries there have been legends of strange man-like beasts to be seen in the snow-covered mountains of Tibet. The Tibetan name for the snowman is 'Yeti,' while the females have been called 'Ladni.'

The first reports on the snowmen came from Beton, the surveyor of Alexander the Great's Expedition to India, who stated: 'Beyond the other Scythian man-eaters in a certain valley of Mount Imaus (the Himalayas) there is a region called Abarimon where live wild people with their feet turned round behind their legs, they are extraordinarily swift, and roam everywhere with the wild beasts. They are unable to breathe in an unfamiliar atmosphere and could not be taken captive to the neighbouring chiefs or to Alexander.' The source of this is Pliny the Elder. The odd point is that the Tibetans of today believe that the snowmen have their feet pointing backwards, a fact which enables them to climb mountains speedily.

Yetl (Yehl) In the Athapascan Creation Legend it was a great raven with eyes of fire and wings whose noise was the thunder who descended to the flooded world and dragged the earth up to the surface. He appears to have been the chief of a raven totem clan.

Yggdrasil The world tree in Nordic myth. It was also the gallows on which Odin† had hung for nine days in order to acquire wisdom. The elaboration in the Edda† of the memories of a sacred grove seems somewhat disproportionate and would in all probability be dissipated if there were access to earlier texts. The harts who were said to gnaw its shoots were named Dain†, Davalin†, Durathror, and Duneyr, all of whom appear to have been dwarfs†, possibly the guardians of the grove. The squirrel Ratatösk†, which ran up and down the tree to breed discord between the eagle at the top and the dragon at the foot, may well have been a messenger between the guardians of the grove and its sacred fountain. The assumption that the powers of evil are beneath the roots of Yggdrasil is expressed in the Grimnis-Mal, where it says, 'Yggdrasil's ash, more hardship bears, more serpents lie, under Yggdrasil's ash, than simpletons think of; Goinn and Moinn, the sons of Grafvitnir, Grabak and Grafjollud, Ofnir and Svafnir.' As both Goin and Moin are shown in the lists of dwarfs†, it seems probable that the other names mentioned are also of dwarfs. It is an interesting speculation whether Yggdrasil is in any way related to the Hy-Brasil of the Tuatha Dé Danann†.

Yi See Shen Yi†.

Yiacatecuhtli 'The Lord who Guides' the Aztec god of travelling merchants.

Yih-King The first of the nine authoritative works on Confucianism†. The name means 'Book of Changes'. The author was a certain Wen Fang, the founder of the Chou dynasty, who reigned about 1122 B C. The work explains all the phenomena of cosmology, nature, and human existence by diagrams made up of straight lines arranged horizontally. These were said to have been invented by Fu Hsi in the third millennium B C. Of the explanatory essays, half were written by Wen Fang, and the remainder by his son Chou. The original signification of these sixty-four diagrams must have been esoteric and magical and they are associated with the origin of the Yang† (the undivided line or male principle) and the Yin† (the divided line or female principle). The appendices include the ideas of Confucius himself on these subjects. The following work is the Shu-King†.

Yima In the Zoroastrian Creation Legend, Yima was warned of the Flood by Ahura Mazda† and told to build a Var, a cave or enclosure, in the Persian mountains in which representatives of all classes of things living should take refuge until the Flood was over. When the disaster had passed Yima sent the bird Karshipta to carry news of his safety to any survivors. The story that the treasure of Yima is still hidden in a cave remains a part of modern Persian tradition. Yima was invited to carry out a religious reform similar to that of Zarathustra, but refused to do so. Yima corresponds to the Vedic Yama†.

Yin The female principle of Chinese Dualism† as opposed to Yang†, the male principle.

Ymir In Nordic myth a giant who was father of the Hrimthursar, the Frost giants or Jotun†. He was also known as Orgelmir. He was killed by Odin† with the aid of his two brothers, Wili† and We†, and his body served to build the world, while his blood caused a deluge which drowned all the Frost giants except Bergelmir† and his wife, who escaped in a ship. In Ragnarok, however, another version refers to the Frost giants sailing away in the ship Naglfar, steered by Hrim, who may have been Ymir himself. Other details are given in Audhumla†.

Ynglingasaga, Ynglingatal Names respectively of a prose recension by Snorri Sturluson and a (lost) panegyric by Thjodolf of Kvina in verse on the family called 'the Children of Yngvi' who became kings first of Uppsala in Sweden, then of Vestfold in Norway, and finally of all Norway. The mythological interest in the story is (1) the equation of Yngvi with Freyr†, son of Njord†. (Com-

pared with Odin†, Freyr was not a fashionable ancestor in historical times: only one English royal family – the East Anglian – traced their descent from him, the rest from Odin); (2) the possible identity of the Ynglingar with Tacitus, *Germania*, ii; (3) the highly rationalized account of Odin's adventures in 'Asia' = Asgard†.

Yo In the mythology of the Bambara people of West Africa Yo created two male elements, air and fire, and two female elements, earth and water.

Yo In Japanese myth the Chinese Dualistic principles Yang† and Yin†, male and female respectively, became In† and Yo. Details will be found under Koji-Ki†.

Yokut Indian Creation Legend In the myth of this south Californian tribe it is told how in the beginning there was an island in the primeval ocean on which lived Eagle and Coyote†, who created men and women to populate the earth. As there was no food for them they sent the dove to bring seeds for sowing.

Yomi The other world of Japanese myth. It is presumably that realm which was ruled over by Emma-O†.

Yoruba Creation Legend The myths of this West African tribe centre mainly around the personality of Shango†, their first king, a leader of great ferocity, who lived in a palace of brass, where he kept 10,000 horses. It would appear that all their gods were tribal leaders at some stage preceding their arrival in West Africa and any other religion they may have had involving abstract gods has long since dropped out of use. Further details are given under Aganju†, Amirini†, Eda Male†, Gwalu†, Ibe Dji†, Magba†, Obatalla†, Odudua†, Ogun†, Oko†, Olokun†, Olorun†, Orishako†, Orunjan†, Ose-Shango†, Oshalla†, Oya†, Shango†, Shankpanna†, and Yemaja†.

Yu-chhiang Chinese god of the ocean wind.

Yuga In Hindu Creation Legend† we are living in the fourth Yuga (or age) of the present Mahayuga† (or epoch). The four Yugas are named Krita†, 4,800 divine years in length; Treta†, 3,600 divine years in length; Dwapara†, 2,400 divine years in length; and Kali, 1,200 divine years in length. Each divine year is 360 human years in length. If this latter exaggeration of the Brahmans is omitted, this would give a period of some 12,000 years since the Vedic races came into existence, which accords very well with the origin of the Hindu calendar in 11,500 BC.

Yuh-Hwang-Shangte (Yu-huang Shang-di) Saviour of the world and lord of creation in Chinese Taoist myth, sometimes known simply as Yu-di.

Yule A Nordid festival held on 14th January, when sacrifices were made to the Aesir†; it may have been the day of their annual meeting. The date was put back nine days to correspond to Old Christmas Day by order of Haakon the Good about 956.

Yum Kaax 'The Lord of the Harvest', a Maya agricultural deity who may be God 'E'†.

Z

Zabel of the Sea Phoenician marine beast encountered by Khoser† in his fight against Baal†. This may be a memory of the battle between the sea and land religions for the domination of the coasts of Phoenicia.

Zahhak *See* Zuhak†.

Zamna Alternative name of Itzamná†, the Maya moon god. He was also known as Kabul.

Zarathustra By about six hundred years B C the Zoroastrian religion appeared to have reached its nadir, and had it not been for the work of Zarathustra, who reorganized it, it would doubtless have vanished. His writings have come to us in the Zend-Avesta†, which endeavoured to lay down a standard text for the stories forming the basis of the doctrine. He appears to have been a religious leader of the type of Moses, bringing the people back to their fatih. In 520 B C Darius substituted the new monotheistic religion of Zarathustra for the polytheism then existing. In 485 B C an attempt to suppress the new religion was put down by Xerxes. In 404 B C the old religion was incorporated in the new one.

Zarpanit Babylonian goddess, wife of Marduk†, possibly a form of Aruru†. She was also known as Sarpanitu†.

Zarya In Slavonic† myth a beautiful lake or river priestess† of the healing waters who lived on the island of Bouyan† near Alatuir†, the magic stone.

Zcernoboch An alternative spelling for Czarnobog†.

Zehuti Alternative spelling for Thoth† in Egyptian myth.

Zend-Avesta The Zend-Avesta, the bible of the Zoroastrian religion, originally consisted of twenty-one books, of which one whole book and a few fragments have come down to us. The work is divided into three parts, the Vendidad†, containing religious myth, laws, and the 'gathas'; the Visperad†, a collection of litanies; and the Yasna†, another liturgical work. Details of the myths are given under Zoroastrian† Creation Legend. The book itself appears to have been made up some time subsequently to the seventh century B C. The name Zend-Avesta is given to the Pahlavi translation of the original, on which most modern research is based.

Zerpanitum Alternative spelling of Zarpanit† in Babylonian myth.

Zervan (Zurvan) Akarana In the Zoroastrian religion eternal time or destiny, and the father of Ahura Mazda† (Hormazu†) and Ahriman†. Later, when

Mithraism had spread to Europe, he became the chief power. The later Persian Akra may be related to Akarana.

Zeus Demaros His inclusion as a child of Ouranos† and Gea† in the Phoenician† Creation Legend of Philo Byblos may be due to a mistranslation of the name of some local divinity, such as El†.

Zigarun In Babylonian myth an early name for Apsu†, meaning 'the mother that has begotten Heaven and Earth'.

Zin A water spirit in the mythology of the Songhay.

Zin-kibaru Another version of Zin†.

Zio, Ziu, Ziumen, or **Ziu-Wari** Old High German or Swabian names for Tiwaz†. While it is possible that Ziu and Zeus may spring from the same Indo-Germanic root word, it seems highly improbable that there was any resemblance between the religious concepts implied by the two names.

Zipacná The eldest son of Vukub-Caquix†.

Ziudsuddu, or **Ziudsuttu** The last of the ten Sumerian kings who reigned before the Flood. Ziudsuddu is named as a survivor in both the Sumerian and the Akkadian flood legends, and is recorded as having sacrificed an ox and a sheep to Uttu†, the sun god, whose representative he would appear to have been. His Sumerian name was Ziusudra.

Zoa In Songhay mythology an ancestor of the people, a sage, and their protector.

Zocho One of the Japanese guardians of the cardinal points. He was the guardian of the south.

Zodiacal Houses In Nordic myth certain of the houses of the Aesir† and the Asynjor† have been identified as signs of the Zodiac. Gladsheim†, the house of Odin†, has been identified as the circumpolar stars which do not at present constitute a sign of the Zodiac. A list of equivalents is given below:

Skadi†, Thrym†-heim (Taurus); Vali† and Vidar†, Valaskjali (Valhalla†) Breidablik (Gemini); Heimdall†, Himinbjorg (Cancer); Freyja†, Folkvangr†, Sessrumnir (Leo); Forseti†, Glitnir (Virgo); Njord†, Noatun (Libra, Scorpio); Ullr†, Ydalir (Sagittarius); Freyr†, Alfheim† (Capricorn, Aquarius); Saga†, Sokkvabekk (Pisces).

Zoroaster Whether Zoroaster is another rendering of Zarathustra†, or whether he was the actual founder of the religion known under his name, is not clear. It is, however, reasonably certain that the religious doctrines of Zoroaster were definitely in existence for a considerable period prior to 600 B C, when Zarathustra is said to have put the Zend-Avesta† into writing. Further details are given under Zoroastrian† Creation Legends.

Zoroastrian Creation Legends The Creation Legends of the Zoroastrians are divided into stages. In the beginning there was Anahita†, the mother goddess, whose influence was so strong that even the Avesta† had to recognize it. Then we have the shadowy background of Zervan Akarana†, the father of Ahura Mazda†, the power of good, and of Anra Mainyu† (or Ahriman†), the leader of the powers of evil. The stories of the battles between Anra Mainyu and Ahura Mazda and their attendant hosts of angels or demons are similar to the Vedic stories of the fights between Indra† and the demons. They obviously refer to the struggles of the Indo-Germanic races for a foothold in the Middle East.

Ahura Mazda stated that the world would last for 12,000 years, a figure which recalls the 12,000 divine years of Brahma†, one thousandth part of a Kalpa†. One may, therefore, conclude that the figures were drawn from a common source, but that the Vedic estimates were carried many stages further. This period was divided into four stages of 3,000 years each, and Ahriman was unable to bring his counter activities to work until the first stage was ended. For the next three stages every good work of Ahura Mazda was matched by some evil one of Ahriman, and the battle will go on until the millennium, when Ahriman is defeated.

The creation of living things took place from the limbs and body of the World Cow, and not a giant as in most stories. Finally, a man, Gayomart†, was created, only to be killed by the force of evil. After his death his twin children, Mashia† and Mashiane, were born (in some stories, as a shrub or tree), and from them humanity descended.

At the time of the Deluge, Yima†, the patriarch, was warned of the disaster, and told to build a Var, or cave of refuge, in the hills, to which he and representatives of all living things would retreat until it was over. Later, however, Yima was defeated in battle by Azhi Dhaka†, the king of a serpent-worshipping people. This disaster legend is of interest as it shows that the cave motif is not confined to the Americas alone.

The worship of the sacred fire, which the Indo-Germans brought with them from their northern habitat, was carried to extreme limits under later Zoroastrianism. The guardians of the flame had to see that it was never defiled by the light of day, or by direct contact with human beings. In the same manner the fear of defilement of the sacred elements of earth, fire, and water led to the custom of disposing of the dead by placing the body at the top of a tower, similar to the towers of silence of the modern Parsees. Here the body was subjected to a process of weathering, if it escaped being devoured by carrion eaters. Meanwhile the soul hovered around the body for three days, and on the fourth was escorted by Sraosha† to the Chinvat Peretu† Bridge over the abyss. Here it was judged by Mithra† and Rashnu† and, after immediate penance for evil deeds, proceeded across the bridge. This, however, is broad and pleasant for the good, but narrow and impassable for the wicked, who fall into the clutches of the demons waiting beneath.

This view of the future life represents a compromise between the Egyptian Hall of Judgment and the relative indifference as to good or evil of the Vedas†.

The Zoroastrian conception of Dualism†, with its balanced groups of good and evil powers, persists until today in various parts of the Middle East.

Zotzilaha Chimalman (Zotz) Bat god of the Mayas who is probably the same as Camazotz† mentioned in the Popul Vuh of the Quiche Creation Legend. The fear of bats manifested in the myths of the Central American races may be linked with the time when they were residing in caves such as those mentioned in the Aztec and Quiche Creation Legends and Nina Stahu, the Cave of Refuge of the Black-foot Indians.

Zu Assyrian storm god symbolized in the form of a bird. A tablet in the British Museum says that Zu once stole the Tablets of Creation from Enlil† and took them to a mountain top, where he hid them. Adad† was chosen as champion of the gods but refused to fight for them. The rest of the tablet is missing, but in the legend of Etana† it is said that Shamash† eventually secured their return with the aid of a net in which Zu was ensnared. Zu's role in this resembles that of Haya-Griva in the Vedic myths. He may be equated with Garuda†.

Zuhak (Zahhak) In Zoroastrian myth the enemy of Jamshid†, the King of Persia, whom he slew by cutting him in half.

Zulummar *See* Enlil†.

Zume Culture hero of the Paraguayan† Indians known as Kaboi† to the Karayas†, Kamu† to the Arawaks†, and Tamu† to the Caribs. He originated from the Place of Sunrise and to some extent resembles Quetzalcoatl†. He may also be the Kame† of the Bakairi† Caribs.

Zuñi Indian Creation Legend The myths of this tribe, which they share with the other Pueblo Indians, tell how at the time of the Deluge mankind sought refuge in deep caves. As the waters receded Awonawilona†, their principal deity, caused the sun to play on the mists spreading over the waters, which dissipated, leaving behind aggregations of green scum which eventually, with the drying up of the flood, became the earth and the sky. After this Poshaiyankaya†, the founder of the tribe, made his way from the caves and found that with the vanishing of the Flood the world was a flat expanse of slippery mud which the sun father dried up, allowing mankind to live. At some time during the Deluge a boy and a girl were sacrificed and thrown into the water. Afterwards two rocks were known as Father and Mother in their memory.

Zurvan In Zoroastrian myth the personification of Time, the ultimate source of good and evil, and the father of Ahriman† and Ohrmazd†.

Bibliography

General

Böttcher, H.M. *Gott hat viele Namen*. Munich, 1962.

Campbell, J. *The Masks of God* (4 vols: *Primitive Mythology, Oriental Mythology, Occidental Mythology & Creative Mythology*). New York & London, 1959–68.

Dumézil, G. *Les dieux des Indo-Européens*. Paris, 1952.

Getty, A. *The Gods of Northern Buddhism*. Tokyo, 1962 (3rd ed.).

Grimal, P. *Larousse World Mythology*. London, 1965.

Herbig, R. *Götter und Dämonen der Etrusker*. Heidelberg, 1948.

James, E.O. *The Concept of Deity*. London, 1950.

Jamme, A. *Le panthéon sud-arabe préislamique d'après les sources épigraphiques*. Louvain, 1947.

Jokel, R. *Götter und Dämonen, Mythen der Völker*, Darmstadt, 1953.

Langton, E. *Essentials of Demonology*. London, 1949.

Lurker, M. *Dictionary of Gods and Goddesses, Devils and Demons*. London 1987.

MacCulloch, J.A. & Gray, L.H. *The Mythology of all Races* (13 vols.). New York, 1922.

Petersdorf, E. *Dämenologie* (2 vols.). Munich, 1956–7.

Pfiffig, A.J. *Religio Etrusca*. Graz, 1975.

Plancy, C. de & Simon, J.A. *Dictionary of Demonology*. London, 1965.

Radke, G. *Die Götter Altitaliens*. Münster, 1979 (2nd ed.).

Robbins, R.H. *The Encyclopedia of Witchcraft and Demonology*. New York, 1959.

Trigg, E.B. *Gipsy Demons and Divinities*. London, 1976.

Tritton, A.D. 'Spirits and Demons in Arabia' *Journal of the Royal Asiatic Society*, London, 1934.

Wipf, K.A. *Religion und Götter der Altkanarier*. Hallein, 1983.

Wölfel, D.J. *Die Gottesnamen der Kanarier und der Berber*. Vienna, 1949.

Africa

Abrahamsson, H. *The Origin of Death*. London, 1952.

Arnott, K. *African Myths and Legends Retold*. London, 1962.

Baumann, H. 'Afrikanische Wild- und Buschgeister' *Zeitschrift für Ethnologie* 70/1938.

Bonins, W.F. *Die Götter Schwarzafrikas*. Graz, 1979.

Cardinall, A.W. *Tales told in Togoland*. London, 1931.

Forde, D. (Ed.). *African Worlds*. London, 1954.

Fuja, A. *Fourteen Hundred Cowries*. London, 1962.

Grianle, M. *Conversations with Ogotomméli*. London, 1956.

Herskowitz, M.J. 'African Gods and Catholic Saints in New World Negro Belief' *American Anthropologist* 39/1937.

—— *Dahomey*. New York, 1938.

Idowu, E.B. *Olodumare, God in Yoruba Belief.* London, 1962.

Itayemi, P. & Gurrey, P. *Folk Tales and Fables.* Harmondsworth, 1953.

Kenyatta, J. *Facing Mount Kenya.* London, 1953.

Krige, E.J. & D.D. *The Realm of a Rain-Queen.* London, 1943.

Kuper, H. *An African Aristocracy. Rank among the Swazi.* London, 1947.

Lienhardt, G. *Divinity and Experience. The Religion of the Dinka.* London, 1961.

Little, K.L. *The Mende of Sierra Leone.* London, 1951.

Parrinder, E.G. *African Mythology.* London, 1967.

—— *African Traditional Religion.* London, 1962.

—— *West African Religions.* London, 1949.

—— *Witchcraft, European and African.* London, 1963.

Rattray, R.S. *Ashanti.* London, 1923.

—— *Religion and Art in Ashanti.* London, 1927.

Rouch, J. *La Religion et la Magie Songhay.* Paris, 1960.

Schapera, I. *The Khoisan Peoples of South Africa.* London, 1930.

Schebesta, P. *Les Pygmées du Congo Belge.* Brussels, 1952.

Smith, E.W. (Ed.). *African Ideas of God.* London, 1961.

Smith, E.W. & Dale, A.M. *The Ila-speaking Peoples of Northern Rhodesia.* London, 1920.

Smith, E.W. & Parrinder, E.G. (Eds.). *African Ideas of God.* London, 1967.

Tempels, P. *Bantu Philosophy.* Paris, 1959.

Verger, P. *Dieux d'Afrique.* Paris, 1954.

Wagner, G. *The Bantu of North Kavirondo.* London, 1949.

Werner, A. *Myths and Legends of the Bantu.* London, 1933.

Zwernemann, J. *Die Bedeutung von Himmels-und Erdgott in westafrikanischen Religionen.* Mainz, 1954.

China

Birch, C. *Chinese Myths and Fantasies.* London, 1962.

Brewitt-Taylor, C.H. *Romance of the Three Kingdoms* (2 vols.). Shanghai, 1925.

Chang, Kwang-chih. *The Archaeology of Ancient China.* New Haven, 1963.

Cheng Te-Kun. *Archaeology in China: prehistoric China.* Cambridge, 1961.

Christie, A. *Chinese Mythology,* London, 1968.

Duyvendank, J.J.L. *China's Discovery of Africa.* London, 1949.

Eberhard, W. *Folktales of China.* London, 1965.

—— *Lokalkulturen im alten China.* Leiden, 1943.

—— *Typen chinesischer Volksmarchen.* Helsinki, 1937.

Fitzgerald, C.P. *China, a Short Cultural History.* London, 1935.

Granet, M. *Danses et Légendes de la Chine ancienne.* Paris, 1926.

—— *Etudes sociologiques sur la Chine.* Paris, 1953.

—— (trans. Innes, K.E. & Brailsford, M.R.) *Chinese Civilisation* London, 1930.

—— (trans. Edwards, E.D.) *Festivals and Songs of Ancient China,* London, 1932.

Hentze, C. & Kim, C. 'Göttergestalten in der älteren chinesischen Schrift' *Studien zur früchinesischen Kulturgeschichte,* 2/1943.

Karlgren, B. 'Legends and Cults in Ancient China' *Bulletin of the Museum of Far Eastern Antiquities*, 18/1946.
Maspero, H. *Mélanges posthumes sur les religions et l'histoire de la Chine* (3 vols.). Paris, 1950.
Münke, W. *Die Klassische chinesische Mythologie*. Stuttgart, 1976.
Needham, J. *Science and Civilisation in China*. Cambridge, 1956.
Shih, J. 'The Notion of God in the Ancient Chinese Religion' *Numen*, 16/1969.
Watson, W. *Early Civilisation in China*, London, 1966.
Werner, E.T.C. *Myths and Legends of China*. London, 1922.

Egypt

Ames, D. (trans.). *Egyptian Mythology*. London, 1965.
Daumas, F. *Les dieux de l'Egypte*. Paris, 1970 (2nd ed.).
Hart, G. *A Dictionary of Egyptian Gods and Goddesses*. London, 1986.
Hornung, E. *Der Eine und die Vielen. Ägyptische Gottesvorstellungen*. Darmstadt, 1971.
Kees, H. *Der Götterglaube im Alten Ägypten*. Berlin, 1977 (3rd ed.).
Lurker, M. *Gods and Symbols of Ancient Egypt*. London, 1980.
Stadelmann, R. *Syrisch-palästinensische Gottheiten in Ägypten*. Leiden, 1967.
See also:
MacCulloch, J.A. & Gray, L.H. *The Mythology of all Races*. New York, 1922.

Europe

THE CELTS

Benoit, F. *Art et dieux de la Gaule*. Paris, 1969.
Cross, T.P. *Ancient Irish Tales*. London, 1937.
Dillon, M. *Early Irish Literature*. Chicago, 1948.
Duval, P.M. *Les dieux de la Gaule*. Paris, 1937.
Filip, J. *Celtic Civilization and its Heritage*. Prague, 1960.
Hatt, J.-J. 'Les dieux gaulois en Alsace' *Revue archéologique de l'Est et du Centre* 22/1971.
Henry, F. *Irish Art in the Early Christian Period to A.D. 800*. London, 1965.
Le Roux, F. *Les Druides*. Paris, 1961.
MacCana, P. *Celtic Mythology*. London, 1970.
MacCulloch, J.A. *Celtic Mythology*. Boston, 1918.
—— *The Religion of the Ancient Celts*. Edinburgh, 1911.
Murphy, G. *Saga and Myth in Ancient Ireland*. Dublin, 1955.
O'Rahilly, T.F. *Early Irish History and Mythology*. Dublin, 1946.
Parry, T. *A History of Welsh Literature*. Oxford, 1955.
Powell, T.G.E. *The Celts*. London, 1961.
Rees, A. & B. *Celtic Heritage*. London, 1961.
Ross, A. *Pagan Celtic Britain*. London 1967.

Sjöstedt, M.L. *Gods and Heroes of the Celts*. London, 1949.
Thévenot, E. *Divinités et sanctuaires de la Gaule*. Paris, 1968. .
Vries, J. de. *Keltische Religion*. Stuttgart, 1961.

THE GERMANS

Dérolez, R.L.M. *Götter und Mythen der Germanen*. Einsiedeln, 1963.
Dumézil, G. *Mythes et dieux des Germains*. Paris, 1939.
Gutenbrunner, S. *Die germanischen Götternamen der antiken Inschriften*. Halle, 1936.
Jung, E. *Germanische Götter und Helden in christlicher Zeit*. Munich & Berlin, 1939.
Leyen, F. von der. *Die Götter der Germanen*. Munich, 1938.
Schneider, H. *Die Götter der Germanen*. Tübingen, 1938.
Vries, J. de. *Altergermanische Religionsgeschichte*. Berlin, 1956 (2nd ed.).

SCANDINAVIA

Brønsted, J. *The Vikings*. Harmondsworth, 1960.
Davidson, H.R.E. *Gods and Myths of Northern Europe*. Harmondsworth, 1964.
—— *Pagan Scandinavia*. London, 1967.
—— *Scandinavian Mythology*. London, 1969.
Gelling, P. & Davidson, H.R.E. *The Chariot of the Sun*, London, 1969.
Grønbech, V. *The Culture of the Teutons*. London, 1926.
Jones, G.A. *A History of the Vikings*. Oxford, 1968.
Lid, N. *Scandinavian Heathen Cult Places*. Stockholm, 1957–8.
Oxenstierna, Count E. *The Norsemen*. London, 1966.
Simpson, J. *Everyday Life in the Viking Age*. London, 1966.
Stenburger, M. *Sweden*. London, 1962.
Turville Petre, E.O.G. *Myths and Religion of the North*. London, 1964.

India

Archer, W.G. *The Loves of Krishna*. London, 1957.
Barnett, L.D. *Hindu Gods and Heroes*. London, 1923.
Basham, A.L. *The Wonder that was India*. London, 1954.
Dowson, J. *Classical Dictionary of Hindu Mythology*. London, 1961.
Dubois, J.A. *Hindu Manners, Customs and Ceremonies*. Oxford, 1906.
Elmore, W.T. *Dravidian Gods in Modern Hinduism*. Madras, 1925.
Elwin, V. *The Myths of Middle India*. London, 1949.
—— *The Tribal Myths of Orissa*. London, 1954.
Garratt, G.T. *The Legacy of India*. Oxford, 1937.
Gray, J.E.B. *Indian Folk-Tales and Legends*, London, 1961.
Humphreys, C. *Buddhism*. Harmondsworth, 1951.
Ions, V. *Indian Mythology*. London, 1967.

Jaini, J. *Outlines of Jainism*. Cambridge, 1940.
Keilhauer, A. & P. *Die Bildsprache des Hinduismus*. Cologne, 1983.
Marshall, Sir J. *Mohenjo Daro and the Indus Civilisation* (3 vols.). London, 1931.
Morretta, A. *Gli Dei dell'India*. Rome, 1966.
Riencourt, A. de. *The Soul of India*. London, 1961.
Sahai, B. *Iconography of Minor Hindu and Buddhist Deities*. New Delhi, 1975.
Smith, V.A. *The Oxford History of India*. Oxford, 1958.
Stevenson, S. *The Heart of Jainism*. London, 1915.
Weber, M. *The Religion of India*. London, 1958.
Woodward, F.L. *Some Sayings of the Buddha*. London, 1938.
Zaehner, R.C. *Hinduism*. London, 1962.

Japan

Anesaki, M. *Japanese Mythology* (Vol. 8 of *The Mythology of all Races*, New York, 1922).
Aston, W.G. (trans.) *Nihongi*. London, 1956.
Bosworth, A.R. *The Lovely World of Richi-San*. London, 1960.
Davis, F.H. *Myths and Legends of Japan*. London, 1913.
Garis, F. de (for Yamaguchi, H.S.K.). *We Japanese*. Yokohama, 1934/5.
Dorson, R.M. *Folk Legends of Japan*. Rutland, Vermont, and Tokyo, 1962.
Eliséev, S. *Asiatic Mythology: The Mythology of Japan*. London, 1932.
Hearn, L. *Glimpses of Unfamiliar Japan*. Boston, 1894.
—— *Japan: An Attempt at Interpretation*. New York, 1920.
—— *Kokoro*. Boston, 1896.
—— *Kwaidan*. Boston, 1904.
—— *Out of the East*. Boston, 1895.
—— *The Romance of the Milky Way*. Boston, 1905.
—— *Shadowings*. Boston, 1925.
Joly, H.L. *Legend in Japanese Art*. London, 1908.
Kennedy, M. *A Short History of Japan*. New York, 1964.
Latourette, K.S. *The History of Japan*. New York, 1953.
Lum, P. *Fabulous Beasts*. London, 1952.
McAlpine, H. & W. *Japanese Tales and Legends*. London, 1958.
Ozaki, Y.T. *The Japanese Fairy Book*. London, 1903.
Redesdale, Lord. *Tales of Old Japan*. London, 1908.
Seki, K. (Ed.) *Folktales of Japan* (trans. Adams, R.J.). London, 1963.
Smith, R.G. *Ancient Tales and Folklore of Japan*. London, 1908.
Storry, R. *A History of Modern Japan*. Harmondsworth, 1967 (rev. ed.).
Webster, R.G. *Japan: From the Old to the New*. London, 1905.

Mexico and Central America

Anders, F. *Das Pantheon der Maya*. Graz, 1963.
Asturias, M.A. *Hombres de Maiz*. Buenos Aires, 1957.

Burland, C.A. *Art and Life in Ancient Mexico*. London, 1947.

—— *The Gods of Mexico*. London, 1967.

—— *Magic Books of Mexico*. Harmondsworth, 1953.

Bushnell, G.H.S. *Ancient Arts of the Americas*. London, 1965.

Caso, A. *The Aztecs, People of the Sun*. Oklahoma, 1958.

Castellanos, R. *The Nine Guardians*. London, 1959.

Coe, M.D. *The Maya*. London, 1966.

—— *Mexico*. London, 1962.

Collis, M. *Cortes and Montezuma*. London, 1954.

Cordan, W. *Götter und Göttertiere der Maya. Resultate des Merida-Systems*. Berne/Munich, 1963.

Diaz, B. (trans. Cohen, J.M.). *The Conquest of New Spain*. Harmondsworth, 1963.

Goetz, D. & Morley, S.G. *Popol Vuh* (trans. from Spanish of Adrian Recinos). London, 1951.

Hagen, V.W. von. *The Ancient Sun Kingdoms*. London, 1962.

Morley, S.G. *The Ancient Maya*. London, 1946.

Nicholson, I. *Firefly in the Night*. London, 1959.

—— *Mexican and Central American Mythology*. London, 1967.

—— *The X in Mexico*. London, 1965.

Parkes, H.B. *The History of Mexico*. London, 1962.

Peterson, F. *Ancient Mexico*. London, 1959.

Séjourné, L. *Burning Water*. London, 1957.

—— *El Universo de Quetzalcoatl*. Mexico City, 1962.

Soustelle, J. (trans. O'Brian, P.). *Daily Life of the Aztecs*. London, 1961.

—— *L'univers des Aztèques*. Paris, 1979.

Spranz, B. *Göttergestalten in den mexicanischen Bilderhandschriften*. Wiesbaden, 1964.

Thompson, J.E. *The Rise and Fall of Maya Civilisation*. Oklahoma, 1956.

Vaillant, G.C. *The Aztecs of Mexico*. Harmondsworth, 1952.

Wuthenau, A. von. *Pre-columbian Terracottas*. London, 1970.

See also:

Grimal, P. *Larousse World Mythology*. London, 1965.

MacCulloch, J.A. & Gray, L.H. *The Mythology of all Races* (13 vols.). New York, 1922.

The Near East

GENERAL

Albrektson, B. *History and the Gods*. Lund, 1967.

Beek, M.A. *Atlas of Mesopotamia*. London, 1962.

Gray, J. *Near Eastern Mythology*. London, 1969.

Grollenberg, L. *Atlas of the Bible*. London, 1957.

Winton Thomas, D. (Ed.) *Documents from Old Testament Times*, London, 1958.

MESOPOTAMIA

Contenau, G. *Everyday Life in Babylon and Assyria*. London, 1954.

Bottéro, J. 'Les divinités sémitiques en Mésopotamie ancienne' *Studi Semitici* 1. Rome, 1958.

Buren, E.D. van. 'Symbols of the Gods in Mesopotamian Art' *Analecta Orientalia* 23/1945.

Campbell, R.C. *The Devils and Evil Spirits of Babylonia*. 1903/4.

Deimel, A. *Pantheon Babylonicum*. Rome, 1914.

Falkenstein, A. van Dijk J. *Sumerische Götterlieder*. Heidelberg, 1959–60.

Frank, C. 'Lamastu, Pazuzu und andere Dämonen' *Mitteilungen der Altorientalischen Gesellschaft*, 1941.

Frank, K. *Bilder und Symbole babylonisch-assyrischer Götter*. Leipzig, 1906, repr. 1968.

Frankfort, H. *Kinship and the Gods*. Cambridge, 1948.

Hooke, S.H. *Babylonian and Assyrian Religion*. London, 1953.

—— *The Labyrinth* (Ed.). London, 1935.

—— *Myth, Ritual and Kinship*. London, 1958.

Langdon, St. 'Babylonian and Hebrew Demonology' *Journal of the Royal Asiatic Society*, 1934.

Laroche, E. *Recherches sur les noms des dieux hittites*. Paris, 1947.

Pritchard, J.B. (Ed.). *Ancient Near Eastern Texts relating to the Old Testament*. Princeton, 1954.

Roberts, J.J.M. *The Earliest Semitic Pantheon*. Baltimore & London, 1972.

Saggs, H.W.F. *The Greatness that was Babylon*. London, 1962.

Tallqvist, K. 'Akkadische Götterepitheta' *Studia Orientalia*. Helsinki, 1938.

CANAAN

Contenau, G. *La civilisation phénicienne*. Paris, 1949.

Cork, S.A. *The Religion of Ancient Palestine in the Light of Archaeology*. London, 1930.

Dahood, M.J. 'Ancient Semitic Deities in Syria and Palestine' *Studi Semitici* 1. Rome, 1958.

Driver, G.R. *Canaanite Myths and Legends*. London, 1956.

Gray, J. *The Canaanites*. London, 1964

—— *The Legacy of Canaan*. Leiden, 1965 (2nd ed.).

Schaeffer, C.F.A. *The Cuneiform Texts of Ras Shamra-Ugarit*. London, 1939.

Stadelmann, R. *Syrisch-palästinensische Gottheiten in Ägypten*. Leiden, 1967.

ISRAEL

Albright, W.F. *Archaeology and the Religion of Israel*. London, 1953 (3rd ed.).

Bright, J. *A History of Israel*. London, 1960.

Johnson, A.R. *Sacral Kinship in Ancient Israel*. Univ. of Wales, 1967 (2nd ed.).

Kampel, H. *Die Dämonen in Alten Testament*. Augsburg, 1930.

Patai, R. *The Hebrew Goddess*. New York, 1967.

Schrade, H. *Der verborgene Gott. Gottesbild und Gottesvorstellung in Israel und in alten Orient*. Stuttgart, 1949.

North American Indian

Burland, C.A. *North American Indian Mythology*. London, 1965.

Carpenter, E. *Eskimo*. London & Toronto, 1959.

Catlin, G. *Life among the Indians*. London & Edinburgh, 1874.

Clark, E.E. *Indian Legends of the Pacific North-West*. Cambridge, 1958.

Coccola, R. de. *Ayòrama*. London & Toronto, 1955.

Collier, J. *The Indians of the Americas*. New York, 1947.

Grinnell, G.B. *The Cheyenne Indians, their History and Ways of Life* (2 vols.). New York, 1962.

Judson, K.B. *Myths and Legends of Alaska*. Chicago, 1911.

La Farge, O. *A Pictorial History of the American Indians*. London, 1962.

Macmillan, C. *Glooskap's Country*. London, 1956.

Martin, P.S. *Indians before Columbus*. Chicago, 1947.

Palmer, W.R. *Why the North Star stands still*. London, 1957.

Simmons, L.W. (Ed.). *Sun Chief: The Autobiography of a Hopi Indian*. Yale, 1942.

Spence, L. *Myths and Legends of the North-American Indians*. London, 1914.

Thalbitzer, W. 'Die kultischen Gottheit der Eskimos' *Archiv für Religionswissenschaft*, 1928.

See also:

MacCulloch, J.A. & Gray, L.H. *North American Mythology* in *The Mythology of all Races* (13 vols.). New York, 1922.

Oceanic: Polynesia, Micronesia, Melanesia and Australia

GENERAL

Buhler, A. et al. *The Art of the South Seas*. London, 1962.

Dixon, R.B. *Mythology of Oceania* (Vol. 9 of *The Mythology of all Races*, New York, 1922).

Guiart, J. *The Arts of the South Pacific*. London, 1963.

Poignant, R. *Oceanic Mythology*. London, 1967.

POLYNESIA

Beckwith, M. *Hawaiian Mythology*. Yale, 1940.

Grey, Sir G. *Polynesian Mythology*. London & Christchurch, 1965.

Metraux, A. *Easter Island*. London, 1957.

Nevermann, H. *Götter der Südsee. Die Religion der Polynesier.* Stuttgart 1947.
Suggs, R.C. *Island Civilisations of Polynesia.* London, 1960.
See also:
The bulletins of the Bernice P. Bishop Museum in Honolulu.

MICRONESIA

Burrows, E.G. *A Flower in my Ear.* Seattle, 1963.
Grimble, Sir A. *A Pattern of Islands.* London, 1952.
Lessa, W.A. 'Tales from Ulithi Atoll' *Folklore Studies* 13, University of California, 1961.

MELANESIA

Burridge, K.D.L. *Mambu.* London, 1960.
Codrington, R. *The Melanesians.* Oxford, 1891.
Drabbe, P. 'Folktales from Netherlands New Guinea' *Oceania* vols. 18–20, Sydney, 1947–50.
Humphreys, C.B. *The Southern New Hebrides.* Cambridge, 1926.
Landtman, G. *Folktales of the Kiwai Papuans.* Helsinki, 1917.
Powdermaker, H. *Life in Lesu.* London, 1933.
Wheeler, G.C. *Mono Alu Folklore.* London, 1926.

AUSTRALIA

Berndt, R.M. *Djanggawul.* London, 1952.
—— *Kunapipi.* Melbourne, 1951.
Berndt, C.H. & R.M. *The World of the First Australians.* Sydney, 1965.
Berndt, R.M. (Ed.). *Australian Aboriginal Art.* Sydney, New York, London & Toronto, 1964.
Howitt, A.H. *The Native Tribes of South-eastern Australia.* London, 1904.
McConnel, U. *Myths of the Munkan.* Cambridge, 1957.
Stanner, W.E.H. 'On Aboriginal Religion' *Oceania* 11, Sydney, 1963.
Strehlow, T.G.H. *Aranda Traditions.* Melbourne, 1947.

Persia

Arberry, A.J. *Legacy of Persia.* London, 1963.
Benveniste, E. *The Persian Religion According to the Chief Greek Texts.* Paris, 1929.
Cameron, C.G. *History of Early Iran.* Chicago, 1936.
Campbell, L.A. *Mithraic Iconography and Ideology.* Leiden, 1968.
Carnoy, A.J. *Iranian Mythology* (Vol. 6 of *The Mythology of all Races*, New York 1922).

Christensen, A. *Essai sur la démonologie iranienne*. Copenhagen, 1941.
Cumont, F. *The Mysteries of Mithra*. New York, 1956.
Dhalla, N. *History of Zoroastrianism*. New York, 1928.
Duchesne-Guillemin, J. *Symbols and Values in Zoroastrianism*. New York, 1966.
—— *La religion de l'Iran ancien*, Paris, 1962.
Frye, R.N. *The Heritage of Persia*. London, 1962.
Ghirshman, R. *Iran*. London, 1961.
—— *Iran, Parthians and Sasanians*. London, 1962.
Gray, L.H. *The Foundations of the Iranian Religions*. Bombay, 1925.
Hinnells, J.R. *Persian Mythology*. London, 1973.
Jackson, A.V.W. *Zoroaster, the Prophet of Ancient Iran*. New York, 1965.
Levy, R. *The Epic of the Kings, Shah-nama*. London, 1967.
Masani, R.P. *The Religion of the Good Life*. London, 1954.
Modi, J.J. *The Religious Ceremonies and Customs of the Parsees*. Bombay, 1937.
—— *A Catechism of the Zoroastrian Religion*. Bombay, 1962.
Mole, M. *Culte, Mythe et cosmologie dans l'Iran ancien*. Paris, 1962.
—— *La légende de Zoroastre selon les textes Péhlevis*. Paris, 1967.
Nyberg, H.S. *Die Religionen des alten Iran*. Osnabrück, 1966.
Oesterley, W. *Persian Angelology and Demonology*. London, 1936.
Pavry, J.D.C. *The Zoroastrian Doctrine of a Future Life*. New York, 1965.
Thieme, P. *Mitra and Aryaman*. New Haven, 1958.
Varenne, J. *Zarathushtra et la tradition mazdéenne*. Paris, 1966.
Vermaseren, M.J. *Mithras, The Secret God*. London, 1963.
Widengren, G. *Die Religionen Irans*. Stuttgart, 1965.
Zaehner, R.C. *The Dawn and Twilight of Zoroastrianism*. London, 1961.

South America

Baudin, L. *A Socialist Empire: The Incas of Peru*. New Jersey, 1961.
Baumann, H. *Gold and Gods of Peru*. London, 1963.
Bellamy, H.S. & Allen, P. *The Calendar of Tiahuanaco*. London, 1956.
Bushnell, G.H.S. *The Ancient People of the Andes*. Harmondsworth, 1949.
—— *The Arts of the Ancient Americas*, London, 1965.
—— *Peru*. London, 1956.
Flornoy, B. *Inca Adventure*. London, 1956.
—— *The World of the Inca*. New York, 1957.
Guppy, N. *Wai-Wai: Through the Forests North of the Amazon*. New York, 1958.
Hagen, V.W. von. *The Ancient Sun Kingdoms*. London, 1962.
—— *The Desert Kingdoms of Peru*. London, 1965.
Kirkpatrick, A. *The Spanish Conquistadores*. London, 1946.
Leicht, H. *Pre-Inca Art and Culture*. London, 1960.
Mason, J.A. *The Ancient Civilisations of Peru*. Harmondsworth, 1957.
Osborne, H. *South American Mythology*, London, 1968.
Owens, R.J. *Peru*. London, 1963.
Prescott, W.H. *History of the Conquest of Peru*. London, 1963.

Salas, M.P. *A Cultural History of South America*. Los Angeles, 1965.

Steward, J.H. & Faron, L.C. *Native Peoples of South America*. New York, 1959.

Tschiffeley, A.S. *Coricancha*. London, 1949.

Zerries, O. *Wild- und Buschgeister in Südamerika*. Wiesbaden, 1954.

See also:

MacCulloch, J.A. & Gray, L.H. *The Mythology of all Races* (13 vols.). New York, 1922.